Fly Safe, Fly Smart

The Insider's Guide to a Hassle-Free Flight

by Sascha Segan

Previously published as
Frommer's What the Airlines Never Tell You

Hungry Minds™

Best-Selling Books • Digital Downloads • e-Books • Answer N
e-Newsletters • Branded Web Sites • e-Learning

New York, NY • Cleveland, OH • Indianapolis, IN

ABOUT THE AUTHOR

New York-based author **Sascha Segan** has lived on three continents and worked for *Expedia Travels* magazine, ABCNEWS.com, *The Guardian* in the U.K., and the *Sunday Times* in South Africa.

HUNGRY MINDS, INC.

909 Third Avenue
New York, NY 10022

Copyright © 2002 Hungry Minds, Inc.

ISBN 0-7645-6613-X
ISSN 1524-1491

Editor: Kelly Regan
Production Editor: Donna Wright
Photo Editor: Richard Fox
Production by Hungry Minds Indianapolis Production Services

Special Sales

For general information on Hungry Minds' products and services please contact our Customer Care department: within the U.S. at 800-762-2974, outside the U.S. at 317-572-3993 or fax 317-572-4002. For sales inquiries and reseller information, including discounts, bulk sales, customized editions, and premium sales, please contact our Customer Care department at 800-434-3422.

Manufactured in the United States of America

5   4   3

CONTENTS

ACKNOWLEDGMENTS

Special thanks to Stacy Lu, Rosemary Ellis, and especially Matt Hannafin, without whom I would never have written this book. The words in this book owe much to Kelly Regan, editor extraordinaire; Maureen Clarke, who wrote the first edition (many fragments of which survive in these pages); and publisher Mike Spring. And my every day owes much to Leontine Greenberg, who keeps me creating.

An Invitation to the Reader

In researching this book, we discovered many useful tips and helpful resources — websites, hot lines, books, and more. We're sure you'll find others. Please tell us about them, so we can share the information with your fellow travelers in upcoming editions. If you were disappointed with a recommendation, we'd love to know that, too. Please write to:

Frommer's Fly Safe, Fly Smart, 2nd Edition
Hungry Minds, Inc.
909 Third Ave.
New York, NY 10022

An Additional Note

Please be advised that travel information is subject to change at any time — and this is especially true of prices. We therefore suggest that you write or call ahead for confirmation when making your plans. The authors, editors, and publisher cannot be held responsible for the experiences of readers while traveling. Your safety is important to us, however, so we encourage you to stay alert and be aware of your surroundings. Keep a close eye on cameras, purses, and wallets, all favorite targets of thieves and pickpockets.

FROMMERS.COM

Now that you have the guidebook to a great trip, visit our website at **www.frommers.com** for travel information on nearly 2,500 destinations. With features updated regularly, we give you instant access to the most current trip-planning information available. At Frommers.com, you'll also find the best prices on airfares, accommodations, and car rentals — and you can even book travel online through our travel-booking partners. At Frommers.com, you'll also find the following:

- Daily Newsletter highlighting the best travel deals
- Hot Spot of the Month/Vacation Sweepstakes & Travel Photo Contest
- More than 200 Travel Message Boards
- Outspoken Newsletters and Feature Articles on travel bargains, vacation ideas, tips and resources, and more!

INTRODUCTION

The terrorist attacks of September 11, 2001, sounded a tragic wake-up call to the U.S. airline industry. For too many years, airlines had placed bigger profits ahead of better safety and security. The hijackings left people questioning the airlines' commitment to their passengers. And in the immediate aftermath, travelers stayed home in droves.

What's the upside? For one thing, Americans are now traveling again, after an understandable period of doubt and concern. And response to the crisis has been swift. The airlines, along with the Federal Aviation Administration, have scrambled to implement stronger security measures. By the time you read this, some of the resulting chaos and inconsistency should be smoothed over. A new federal office, the Transportation Security Administration, has assumed responsibility for airline security. And underpaid, untrained security screeners — at one time paid less than fast-food employees — are becoming federal employees with greater benefits and law-enforcement supervision (which should mean better training and fewer errors). The federal government has also required that all baggage be scanned for bombs by the end of 2002, an action security experts first demanded after the explosion of Pan Am flight 103 over Lockerbie, Scotland — *14 years ago.*

Without question, the travel slump hit U.S. airlines hard, resulting in a $10-billion government bailout — courtesy of your tax dollars. Yet, even as they bleed money, the major carriers don't seem to have a clue about how to please consumers. Instead, they cut meal service, cling to a Byzantine fare structure, and make weak pledges with non–legally binding "customer service commitments." It's no wonder that in a 2001 University of Michigan survey, fliers said they enjoyed their airline experiences about as much as filing their taxes.

But take a closer look, and the good news emerges. In recent years the biggest boon to travel consumers has been the explosion of information on the Internet — from seating charts to last-minute deals to the popularity of ultra–low fare ticket services such as Priceline. The average flier has reaped enormous financial rewards by doing independent research, forcing many travel agents to fill a niche role as skilled negotiators for more complex trips. And the reduction in flights after September 11 had the positive effect of easing delays caused by air-traffic gridlock — a problem that had ballooned to absurd levels in 1999 and 2000.

The resurgence of the alternative "budget" airlines is yet another sign of hope. Even with the sharp drop in passengers following the 9/11 attacks, Southwest, JetBlue, and Frontier all turned a profit in 2001. Southwest in particular has emerged as a major U.S. carrier, bucking the traditional airline business model to provide cheap, cheerful service that delivers on its (admittedly modest) promises. Efficient, affordable, and safe, these carriers may be an example of what American leisure travelers really crave: honesty, quality, and lower, less-restrictive fares.

So what's a traveler to do in this time of flux? Fly, for one thing. But fly smart and get good value for your money — on secure carriers, in comfortable seats, for the lowest price.

That's where this book comes in. As mentioned, security *is* improving. But in the immediate future, air travel may continue to be a hassle for everyone. In response, we've compiled a wealth of insider advice to help you fly in safety and comfort.

In this book, you'll learn (among other things):

- The situation with security — and what you can, and should, bring onto a plane

- What airlines do and don't owe you when things go wrong (or when they go bankrupt)

- The best and worst seats on a plane for comfort and safety

- How to deal with fears of terrorism, "economy class syndrome," and jet lag

- How to get thousands of frequent-flier miles without ever setting foot on a plane

- How to use the Internet to find the lowest airfares

- Who to complain to if you feel you've been mistreated or racially profiled

Arm yourself with this knowledge, and you'll be ready to take back the skies.

1

A Whole New World: Safety in the Air & on the Ground

On September 11, 2001, Americans suddenly began paying attention to airport and airline security.

What they found was a horror — a mess of missed warnings, failing practices, and incompetent employees at every level of the process that eventually allowed 19 suicidal terrorists to board 4 flights on the same day.

The good news is that the U.S. is trying to learn from its mistakes. Things *are* getting better. At press time, however, improvements were still being rolled out. And the growing pains of the American airport security system have frustrated and confused some travelers.

1 Security at the Airport: Past, Present & Future

A LOOK AT THE PAST: THE WARNING SIGNS

It's not like no one saw the disasters of 2001 coming. According to a report released in June 2000 by the congressional

General Accounting Office, U.S. airport security had been a shambles for years. In 1987, security screeners allowed 20% of dangerous objects to pass through checkpoints, and their performance only declined with time, according to GAO official Gerald Dillingham in September 2001.

In May 2000, undercover federal agents used fake law enforcement badges (printed on home ink-jet printers or bought at costume shops) to penetrate the secure areas of two major U.S. airports. One agent was carrying a suitcase that could have contained a bomb.

What's the source of the problem? You've heard the media reports. Security experts are unanimous: You get what you pay for. Until February 2002, the airlines were responsible for airport security. They subcontracted security operations to the lowest bidders, who in turn hired underpaid, undertrained, dissatisfied workers to make sure America's skies were safe. These employees received a mere 12 hours of training in how to do their jobs — as compared with the amount of training French screeners (60 hr.) and Belgian screeners (at least 56 hr.) receive.

In one (typical) airport, security screeners were paid a starting salary of $6.25 an hour — compare that with the $7 an hour earned by employees at one of the airport's fast food restaurants. (Screeners in Belgium are paid $14 per hr.) No wonder, then, that between May 1998 and April 1999, turnover among security screeners averaged 126% at the nation's 19 largest airports. One airport had an annual turnover rate of 416%, according to the GAO.

As for Argenbright Security, one of the major contractors hired to do the job: In October 2000, Argenbright was convicted in a Philadelphia federal court of Federal Aviation Administration (FAA) violations that included hiring convicted felons as security screeners. They were fined more than $1.5 million. One year later, the Department of Transportation (DOT) found that Argenbright still employed 20 convicted felons and 37 people with outstanding arrest warrants.

On September 11, 2001, Argenbright ran the screening operations at 46 of the nation's busiest airports.

The FAA — which aviation insiders call the "tombstone agency" because of its reluctance to take action until someone gets killed — was required by a 1996 law to establish a program to certify security screeners. As of September 11, 2001, they still had not established one.

THE STATE OF FLYING TODAY

Since 9/11, several serious moves have been made to improve airport security. But it has been a gradual rollout, and if you're reading this before fall 2002, many of the measures will not yet be in full effect.

What you see today are armed National Guardsmen in the airports, reinforced cockpit doors on aircraft, tougher regulations on carrying ID, stricter baggage regulations, and random checks of both passengers and bags for dangerous items.

A new federal agency, the Transportation Security Administration (TSA), has assumed responsibility for airport security, with plans to hire better-trained, higher-paid screeners. Behind the scenes, bags are matched to boarding passes to make sure every bag is linked to a passenger on a direct flight (this will soon be standard for connecting flights as well). The scanning of checked luggage for explosives, now done on a random basis, will be standard by the end of 2002.

Because this is a transitional period, you won't yet see consistency among airports. As mentioned, you won't see all checked bags being scanned for explosives, which Britain and Germany have been doing for years. And you'll be paying extra: There's a new $2.50 federal "security tax" in place on every one-way flight (that's $5 round-trip).

The "interim" regime now in place has been roundly criticized. Between November 3 and November 12, 2001, federal teams found 90 instances at 58 airports where security personnel had either missed dangerous items that passed through X-ray machines or neglected to randomly check passengers boarding their aircraft.

FAA SECURITY VIOLATIONS FOR THE 15 BUSIEST AIRPORTS, 1991–2000

AIRPORT	NUMBER OF VIOLATIONS	SIZE (RANK AMONG THE NATION'S BUSIEST AIRPORTS)
Los Angeles	8,182	3
Dallas	5,889	4
Phoenix	4,738	9
New York–JFK	3,738	13
San Francisco	3,730	5
Denver	2,602	6
Houston	2,546	14
Atlanta	2,484	1
Detroit	2,217	7
Miami	2,154	10
Chicago–O'Hare	2,054	2
Las Vegas	1,807	11
St. Louis	1,693	15
Minneapolis	1,528	12
Newark	730	8

Source: CNN report "Flight Risk." Size rankings are judged by number of passengers enplaned in 1999.

And the new procedures are more inconvenient for travelers. Never mind the long lines. In the last 2 months of 2001, according to the *New York Times,* airport terminals were evacuated 30 times (because of suspicious packages or errors made by security staff) and passengers on 434 planes were taken off their flights to be re-screened.

WHAT'S TO COME?

The most sweeping change to airport security will happen when all screeners become federal employees in November 2002 — their salaries will increase (significantly) to $35,000 a year, and they'll receive benefits worthy of a job somebody cares about. (At press time, Congress was not planning to require high school diplomas for screeners, though they did intend to require that screeners be U.S. citizens. According to the *New York Times,* the citizenship requirement alone would throw out 80% of the screeners at San Francisco International Airport.)

The screeners at major airports will be supervised by highly paid security directors, who will report to the new Transportation Security Administration (TSA), which in turn reports to national Homeland Security Director Tom Ridge. New screeners are being phased in at the rate of 25 airports a week, and the process should be completed by November 2002.

The new regime should bring much-needed consistency to security procedures. Higher-quality screeners are expected to make fewer errors, meaning airports should be evacuated less often. And as already mentioned, by the end of 2002, all checked bags will be matched to passenger boarding passes for both direct and connecting flights. In addition, all airports with regular commercial service will be required to screen all luggage for explosives, using a combination of hand inspection, machine scans, and bomb-sniffing dogs. (The TSA hopes to have 300 dogs snooping at 80 airports by the end of 2002.)

2 WHAT TO EXPECT AT THE AIRPORT

IN THE CURRENT CONFUSED SECURITY CLIMATE, YOU can't arrive at the airport too early. Security lines are completely unpredictable. In Tucson in December 2001, I whizzed through security in 5 minutes; in San Francisco that same month, I waited more than an hour. Airlines now publish on their websites extensive lists of suggested arrival times based on the size and complexity of each airport they serve. If you need one rule of thumb, arrive 90 minutes early for domestic flights, and 2 to 3 hours early for international flights. The worst that can happen is you'll have to read a book or magazine while you wait.

If you're worried about missing your flight, tell an airline representative; they will often move you to the front of the line. A case could be made for arriving late and asking to be bumped to the front — but airlines are under no obligation to help you out, so you could miss your flight.

Whatever your strategy, it's critical that you make the airlines' boarding gate deadline — each airline sets one, and if you're late, you may find that your seat has been given away. Find out the deadline for your flight when you book your ticket.

After some chaos in late 2001, parking and curbside check-in are back to normal at most airports. (It is, however, up to each individual airport whether curbside check-in is allowed, and some have chosen to abolish it altogether.) If your airport allows curbside check-in, it's a great way to avoid long ticket lines. But don't leave your car unattended in an airport terminal's drop-off lane, or it will certainly be towed or removed.

When you get to the airport, get your "government-issued photo ID" — passport, driver's license, or state-issued non-driver's ID — ready. Several people will ask for it. (Minors under 18 don't need photo IDs, but the adult checking in with them must provide one.)

Keep an eye out for suspicious or unattended packages. If you see them, tell an airport employee.

FROM THE CHECKPOINT TO THE GATE

With two exceptions, only passengers with proof of their tickets can go through the security checkpoints to the gate. You'll need a boarding pass, an e-ticket receipt, a printed-out confirmation page from the airline's website, an e-mail from the airline, a travel agent's paper itinerary, or a paper ticket. The exceptions are escorts for travelers with disabilities and parents accompanying minors; they'll be permitted to go through security after talking to an airline representative.

Keep in mind that you may be in line (both in the ticket line and the security line) for quite a while. Stop at the bathroom before beginning the ordeal; and buy books and magazines before getting in line. If you're traveling with

It's All Relative in an Imperfect World

The inconsistencies in today's airport security procedures are enough to drive a frequent flier crazy. Flying out of New York's JFK airport near the end of 2001, I checked the FAA's list of prohibited items and found out that nail clippers were allowed in carry-on luggage. Yet my nail clipper was confiscated at the security checkpoint and thrown into a huge drawer (full of nail clippers, I might add).

Some airports scan your shoes. Some don't. Some make you take off your belt. Some don't. At press time, even the FAA admitted that security procedures were wildly inconsistent. Pack your sharp toiletries, and anything else you don't want confiscated, in checked baggage – and be prepared for anything. For the latest official security news, go to the TSA's website at www.tsa.gov.

---

children, make sure you have games and food to keep them happy while you wait.

If you don't have the fortitude to stand for long periods of time, request a wheelchair when making your reservation. When you get to the airport, find an airline representative; your wheelchair will be delivered to you and you can proceed through security in the chair.

"Assistive devices" for passengers with disabilities, including wheelchairs and canes that unfold into seats (but probably *not* actual folding lawn chairs), are protected by the airlines' contracts of carriage, and can be brought on freely. (Your wheelchair will be stowed as cargo on the plane; folding cane-seats can usually fit in the overhead compartment.) It's best to bring a doctor's note mentioning your frailty or bad back, just in case airline employees get testy.

If you're not frail — just lazy — Samsonite (www. samsonite.com for a store near you) sells a $9.99 cushioned seat that attaches to their hard-sided carry-on luggage so you can take a rest while on the line. (For more helpful post-9/11

No Laughing Matter

Although it may seem like humor is the only way to survive the airport experience, don't joke around. I can't stress this enough. Any mention of guns, bombs, or terrorism, even as an obvious joke, is an easy way to get yourself dragged aside, and perhaps even arrested.

---

travel items, see "Post–September 11 Suitcases & How They Work for You," in chapter 4.)

Before you pass through security, remove all change, keys, and other metal items from your pockets and put them in your carry-on. Take your laptop out of its case. Prepare to remove your coat, and possibly your shoes; both may have to go through the X-ray machine.

To keep lines moving, avoid wearing anything that might activate the metal detectors — large belt buckles, clunky metal jewelry, or steel-toed boots, for example. Even some underwire bras have been known to set off metal detectors. If you have piercings or metallic replacement body parts, inform the screener before you step into the machine, and prepare to be patient. Representative John Dingell (D-Mich.) had to drop his trousers at a security checkpoint in late 2001 to show off the pin in his hip, which kept setting off metal detectors.

At press time, the FAA specifically banned these items from carry-on luggage:

- Cutting instruments of any size, shape, or material.

- Corkscrews.

- Metal scissors.

- Metal nail files.

- Straight razors.

- Knitting needles.

- Baseball bats, golf clubs, and pool cues.

- Mace and pepper spray.

- Any hand or power tools.

- Ski poles and hockey sticks.

- Toy weapons.

- Fireworks.

- Weapons and ammunition of any kind.

- Fuel, paint, lighter fluid, "strike-anywhere" matches.

- Drain cleaners and solvents.

- Pressurized canisters, like oxygen tanks and aerosol cans.

- Dry ice, gasoline-powered tools, wet-cell batteries, camping equipment with fuel, radioactive materials (except limited quantities), poisons, and infectious substances.

These items, however, are permitted:

- Nail clippers. (But see box on p. 7 for problems with these.)

- Safety razors.

- Syringes (with an original pharmacy prescription label).

- Tweezers.

- Eyelash curlers.

- Canes.

- Umbrellas.

- Cameras and film. In fact, you should always take film in carry-on baggage, as the machines used to screen checked luggage may damage film.

For more information about baggage requirements, see chapter 4.

As you reach the security checkpoint, you'll probably see uniformed National Guard troops with guns guarding the airport. These officers are mostly a psychological tactic; anti-terrorism experts agree their presence would do little to deter determined terrorists. "You might as well put a wooden top in there. There's no real value, except to make the public feel warm and fuzzy," said Jeremy Spindlove, author of *Terrorism Today: The Past, The Players, The Future* (Prentice Hall, 1999).

If you're selected to be taken aside for a hand search, FAA guidelines say that if you request, the search must be done by a screener of your gender (if one is available) or in a private place.

You may be selected to have your luggage examined both at the checkpoint and at the gate. Cooperate; the security officer will unpack your carry-on bag and you'll help the officer re-pack. If a security officer tries to separate you from your luggage while your $4,000 laptop remains on the conveyor belt, politely but firmly demand to have your bags accompany you.

When you board the plane, have your photo ID ready — you'll need to show it with your boarding pass.

WHAT ARE THEY LOOKING FOR?

Security personnel are looking for more than just suspicious items. They're looking for suspicious people. Among the things that arouse suspicion:

- **Nervousness at the security questions.** Airport security expert John Currie says those silly security questions ("Did you pack your bag yourself?") are more of a lie detector test than anything else. Security personnel are looking for people who might look like they're lying when they invariably answer yes.

- **A lack of specific purpose.** Some people look like business travelers; some look like leisure travelers. Anyone who can't be easily put into a box will get a second looking-at.

- **Flying long distances with little luggage.**

- **Flying with a one-way ticket.**

- **Tickets purchased with cash or on the day of departure.**

- **Ethnicity.** Unfortunately, because the terrorists of September 2001 were from the Middle East, anyone who looks even vaguely "Middle Eastern" to an ignorant observer — and that includes South Asians, Latinos, or even Caucasians with tans — may get stopped. If you feel like you have been racially profiled — a practice that is illegal — consult chapter 10 for information on how and where to register a complaint.

3 Safety on the Plane

AIR TRAVEL IS THE SAFEST MODE OF TRANSPORT. BUT things can still go wrong in the air — from onboard fires to terrorist acts.

Since September 11, airlines and the government have taken steps to make terrorist attacks less likely to succeed. The U.S. airline fleet is now equipped with reinforced cockpit doors, much more difficult to break down than the old ones. And the government has expanded the mysterious air marshals program, which puts pairs of armed undercover agents on select commercial flights every day.

AIR MARSHALS

Secretive, undercover crack shots, federal air marshals are our last official line of defense against terrorism on airplanes.

The current program puts at least two undercover agents with James Bond–like "licenses to kill" aboard random passenger flights each day. It began in 1985 after the hijacking of TWA Flight 847 from Athens to Beirut. Trained on simulated aircraft to make every shot count, air marshals know that if they miss their mark, they could do the terrorists' jobs for them.

Formerly managed by the FAA, the air marshals program is now being managed by the new Transportation Security Administration (TSA).

The details of the air marshal program are kept top secret (keep an eye out for pairs of well-built young people on flights). The government won't say which flights marshals are on, but they are more likely to be on flights into and out of Reagan National Airport in Washington, DC, than any other single point. Pilots and flight crew know when marshals are on board their flights, and air marshals can be on domestic or international flights of any U.S. carrier.

The Sky Marshals program, predecessor of the air marshal system, had more than 2,000 marshals flying each day in the early 1970s, but the number had dwindled to 32 by mid-2001, according to an October 2001 speech given by Transportation Secretary Norman Mineta to the National Association of Counties.

The government won't reveal precisely how many air marshals are in circulation, but the FAA says there are more now than there were before September 11, and the number grows daily. "In the aftermath of the terrorist attacks . . . the agency has received funding to greatly expand the Federal Air Marshal program," the FAA said in a September 2001 press release.

Still, nobody claims that air marshals will be on all — or even most — of the tens of thousands of commercial flights that travel the country every day. They're a deterrent, just like stationing National Guard troops in the airports. In comparison, Israeli airline El Al puts air marshals on every flight, but they schedule fewer than 200 flights per day. Australia, the Philippines, and several European countries (notably Austria, France, and Germany) also have limited air marshal programs.

OTHER MEASURES

Airlines are also debating arming their pilots. At press time, United was the only one to propose doing so — the company will arm its pilots in the cockpit with Tazer "stun guns" to take care of miscreants.

Pilots still must leave the cockpit to use restrooms. This puts the U.S. behind the world's airline security leader, Israel's El Al, which keeps pilots in sealed-off cockpits with kitchen and bathroom facilities (and, as already mentioned, puts air marshals on every plane).

Recent events indicate that passengers are assuming responsibility for air safety as well. In late 2001, news reports abounded of fliers who subdued fellow travelers who displayed crazed, angry, or threatening behavior.

On September 15, 2001 — shortly after U.S. airports reopened for business — an unnamed pilot on United Airlines Flight 564 gave these instructions to passengers, according to an Internet e-mail and the Associated Press:

"If someone or several people stand up and say they are hijacking this plane, I want you all to stand up together. Then take whatever you have available to you and throw it at them. Throw it at their faces and heads so they will have to raise their hands to protect themselves. The very best protection you have against knives are the pillows and blankets. Whoever is close to these people should then try to get a blanket over their head — then they won't be able to see. Once that is done, get them down and keep them there. Do not let them up. I will then land the plane at the closest place and we *will* take care of them. After all, there are usually only a few of them and we are 200-plus strong! We will not allow them to take over this plane."

✐ HIJACKINGS: COULD THEY HAPPEN AGAIN?

The September 11 hijackers didn't just rely on poor security. They also relied on pilots and passengers believing in an earlier philosophy of hijacking. Before 2001, the only fatal hijacking of a U.S. plane on U.S. soil was the result of a vendetta by a disgruntled ex-employee – not an act of foreign terrorism. Hijackers primarily used planes as bargaining chips to get demands fulfilled – and if they got what they wanted, nobody was hurt.

Now passengers are aware of the possibility of suicidal hijackers – and they're willing to take action to stop them. "If there's somebody charging the cockpit, they'll be apprehended by one, five, or ten people aboard. The days of passive passengers are gone," said Dr. Harvey Kushner, author of *Terrorism in America* (Charles C. Thomas Publishing, 1998).

That adds a layer of security against hijacking that wasn't there before, Kushner said. It might not deter fools or madmen from trying to take over a plane, but it very well might prevent a September 11–type tragedy from ever happening again.

FIRE, FLOOD & BAD LANDINGS

Unfortunately, terrorism isn't the only worry for air travelers. The threat of a plane crash does exist, though the actual occurrence of such a crash is extremely rare. Mile for mile, planes are still the safest way to travel — much safer than cars, and few people think twice before hitting the road.

During the year ending September 2001 (and taking into account the 9/11 attacks), 0.05 people died on U.S. air carriers per 100 million paid passenger miles. (Viewed another way, an average of one person per two *billion* passenger miles died — and that's about the distance from

Earth to Uranus.) However, on America's highways in 1999 (the most recent year for which data is available), 1.6 passengers and drivers were killed per 100 million vehicle miles. Here's another perspective check. According to the Centers for Disease Control, every year approximately one out of every 7,500 deaths in the U.S. is caused by someone drowning *in his bathtub.*

So the chance you'll need any of this information is slim. Life is dangerous. And as life activities go, flying is a pretty safe one. (For more information on the safety of planes versus other modes of transportation, see chapter 5.)

The majority of airplane crashes happen during takeoff and landing. Your best safeguards in these situations are your seat belt and your ability to make a fast escape before fumes incapacitate you — which can happen in as little as 90 seconds. Preparedness could end up saving your life.

Tips for Staying Safe in the Air

Some things you can do to keep you safer in the air:

- **Keep your seat belt fastened snugly around the hips** — not the waist — even after the captain turns off the FASTEN SEAT BELT sign. According to the FAA, the most common flying injuries result from turbulence that occurs suddenly and throws passengers from their seats. If your flight suddenly hits turbulence, your seat belt will keep you safe.

- **Sit near an exit.** Most plane crash fatalities result from smoke inhalation. The faster you can escape in the event of a disaster, the safer you'll be.

- **Don't drink and fly.** Alcohol will affect you more rapidly at high altitudes and make it more difficult to escape quickly in the event of an emergency.

- **Don't smoke in the restrooms.** This can cause a fire even if the plane is in perfect working order.

- **Don't store heavy or pointed objects in the overhead bins.** These can become projectiles in a crash or even during severe turbulence.

- **Wear flat shoes on the plane.** You'll be able to evacuate the aircraft more quickly, in case of an emergency, and you won't risk puncturing the emergency slide.

- **Wear natural fabrics when you fly.** Synthetics can melt and adhere to the skin in a fire. (You'll also be more comfortable in natural fabrics — they breathe better and will adjust more readily to shifting cabin temperatures.)

- **Listen carefully to the flight attendant's safety briefing and read the safety card in your seat pocket.** You'll learn where emergency exits are and how to open them. You will also learn how to operate any other emergency equipment on the aircraft, such as oxygen masks and flotation devices. After you've digested the safety information, mentally rehearse your escape while the plane is still on the ground.

- **Count the seats to two of the nearest exits before you take off.** If the cabin begins to darken with smoke, you won't have to rely on sight to make your escape. If one of the doors is blocked or overcrowded, you'll be ready to escape through another.

- **Choose to fly only in aircraft with more than 20 seats.** These airplane models are held to the strictest federal safety regulations.

- **Fly nonstop when you can.** The fewer takeoffs and landings per flight, the lower the accident risk.

When Accidents Do Happen: What You Can Do

According to the National Transportation Safety Board, 60% of passengers involved in plane crashes end up surviving. Between 1978 and 1995, there were 164 accidents with at least one passenger fatality. In 37 cases, more than 90% of all passengers survived. While it's obviously best not to dwell on the prospect of an emergency situation, it's wise to give it some consideration — to the same extent that you would rehearse a fire drill in school or in the workplace.

- If the flight crew instructs you to adopt a brace position, make sure your seat belt is low and tight across your hips. Bend from the waist and bring your chest as close to your knees as you can. Your head should touch the seat in front of you. Place your hands on top of your head, one on top of the other, and protect your face with your forearms. Pull your feet back slightly behind your knees.

- The minute you detect smoke, cover your nose and mouth with a cloth, preferably a damp one. If you know where the smoke or fire is coming from, move away as quickly as possible. Listen carefully for directions from the flight crew, as they may know more than you do about the source of the smoke or fire.

- As you evacuate the cabin, stay as low to the cabin floor as possible. Do not attempt to salvage any of your possessions.

- Check for fire outside the emergency exit door before you open it. If you find a fire, use another exit. This is why it's important to mentally rehearse your evacuation, while you're still on the ground, using more than one nearby emergency exit.

- If you're wearing high heels, take them off before you evacuate on the emergency slide. They can puncture the slide and jeopardize you and passengers behind you.

- Once outside the plane, move away as quickly as possible. Help those who need assistance if you can, but never step back inside or return to a burning aircraft.

Magellan's (☎ **800/962-4943;** www.magellans.com)
sells an emergency escape hood that protects your eyes and
lungs from heat, smoke, and soot for up to 20 minutes.
Evac-U8 ($69, two for $125) will make you look like a
Martian when you slip its Teflon-coated hood over your
head, but it could save your life as it protects your face from
up to 800°F temperatures.

Dr. Harvey Kushner, author of *Terrorism in America,*
says a flashlight, a bottle of water, and a handkerchief (to
hold over your nose and mouth) may come in handy during
onboard emergencies.

4 FLYING A SAFE AIRLINE

IF YOU'RE FLYING A MAJOR U.S. AIRLINE, YOU'RE FLYING
one of the world's safest.

When crashes occur in the U.S., they're mostly isolated
events. And when a plane goes down, FAA and National
Transportation Safety Board officials swarm over it, analyzing the cause and locking in rules to prevent the same thing
from ever happening again.

Many consumers would be thrilled to see the FAA rate
individual airlines for safety, but the government has refused
to do so. FAA officials argue that it's nearly impossible to
predict when a plane is going to crash because all of the
major carriers need to meet rigorous safety regulations in
order to operate at all. They argue that past crashes don't
help predict the cause of future accidents either, because
figuratively speaking, lightning seldom strikes twice in the
same place. As mentioned, crash causes are quickly detected
and corrected to prevent a similar accident from happening
again. Experts say that even an analysis of minor safety
infringements or snafus does not necessarily help predict
major ones. Some experts even argue that if an airline
catches those minor flaws, it's the sign of a good inspection
program that will prevent the major problems from devel-
oping. Furthermore, some of the information used to rate

U.S. Airlines: Are They Targets?

Is American Airlines a particular terrorist target? Dr. Harvey Kushner, author of *Terrorism in America*, thinks so – and he says it's no fault of American's. "You have the name of the country on the side [of the plane]," which incites the wrath of anyone who hates the USA, he said.

As a result, according to the research firm Skytrax, Europeans are voting with their feet. In a survey of 2,884 European business travelers conducted during October and November of 2001, 64% of the travelers who had used U.S. airlines in the past said they would switch to airlines based in other countries because of terrorism fears.

---

the airlines would have to come from the airline itself, and safety inspectors may be inclined to doctor data.

The FAA does publish safety data on its website (www. faa.gov), which includes the National Transportation Safety Board's Incident/Accident Database, organized by carrier. The FAA warns, however, that the definition of an aviation accident is very broad. If a flight attendant breaks his leg in the aisle, this qualifies as an accident — as does a CFIT, or "controlled flight into terrain," when a normally functioning plane that has passed inspection crashes, usually due to a flight-crew error. So the raw data can be misleading. It's nearly impossible for the general public to extrapolate any type of safety ranking from the statistics on the FAA site.

SO WHAT DOES THIS MEAN
FOR YOU, THE PASSENGER?

Mary Schiavo, former inspector general of the U.S. Department of Transportation, published a whistle-blowing expose called *Flying Blind, Flying Safe* (Avon: New York, 1997). Her tenure in the FAA convinced her that airline and FAA employees were cutting corners on safety and placing the flying public at greater risk than necessary. Some of Schiavo's recommendations:

1. Do not fly on foreign carriers that fail FAA checks or receive only conditional approval (see "Finding a Safe International Airline," below).

2. Do not fly on planes built in the former Soviet Union or on airlines operating from China. The crash rate is extremely high and may not even include the total number of accidents, since it's nearly impossible to obtain accurate data.

3. If you're flying to Africa or Latin America, use a U.S. airline.

4. Purchase your ticket with a charge card in the United States, even if you're flying on a foreign aircraft. You will have far more legal protection as a passenger in case something goes wrong.

5. Avoid commuter airlines and "prop" planes if possible. They are far more vulnerable in bad weather, and they are more affected by turbulence created in the wake of larger jets.

6. When you choose a carrier, pay attention to its overall performance. Overall performance does not necessarily correlate with the safety of an airline. But common sense suggests that if a carrier is consistently late, if it loses or mishandles a relatively high amount of baggage per passenger, and if it receives a proportionately large number of complaints, chances are it's cutting corners on safety standards as well. (See data relating to on-time arrival ratings in chapter 2, "Ticketing Pitfalls"; incidents of lost or mishandled luggage per carrier in chapter 4, "Lost in Space"; and number of complaints lodged per passenger in chapter 10, "The Squeaky Wheel.")

PASSENGER AIRLINES GROUNDED
BY THE FAA, 1998–2001

AIRLINE	REASON FOR GROUNDING
Pro Air (9/00)	Grounded by the FAA for poor maintenance procedures and unairworthy planes
Kiwi Airlines (3/99)	Grounded by the FAA for poor maintenance procedures and unairworthy planes

FINDING A SAFE INTERNATIONAL AIRLINE

Foreign airlines don't have to abide by U.S. standards. But the FAA checks whether other countries' air-safety systems meet the standards set by the International Civil Aviation Organization (ICAO), a U.N. division based in Montreal. The FAA has failed certain countries based on reports issued by the ICAO, so you may want to avoid airlines in those countries.

Not all nations are members of ICAO, however, and not all ICAO members are rated by the FAA. Myanmar, which has a notoriously bad state-run airline, doesn't show up; neither does China Airlines of Taiwan, which has experienced an unusually high number of accidents for a state-run carrier in a developed country. Also, the FAA doesn't list the world's most fatal airline, Cuba's Cubana de Aviacion.

Statistics indicate that Canada, Australia, Hong Kong, and Japan have some of the safest major air carriers outside the United States. None of the airlines based in those countries has had a fatal crash in the past 15 years, and all pass ICAO standards.

No Western European carriers rank in the most dangerous third of airsafe.com's list of 89 major air carriers (airsafe.com ranks airlines in order of estimated fatal event rate since 1970 — this takes into account the percentage of passengers killed per crash and the number of crashes). Aer Lingus, Finnair, and Icelandair have never had a fatal crash, and only SWISS/Crossair, Air France, and SAS have had

AIRLINES GIVEN FAILING GRADES BY ICAO*

COUNTRY	PRIMARY CARRIER
Bangladesh	Biman
Belize	Maya Airways
Cote D' Ivoire	Air Afrique
Dominican Republic	Air Santo Domingo
Ecuador	Saeta
El Salvador	TACA
Gambia	Gambia International
Greece	Olympic Airways
Guatemala	Aviateca
Haiti	No international carrier
Honduras	TACA
Kiribati	Air Kiribati
Nauru	Air Nauru
Nicaragua	Nicaraguense de Aviacion
Organization of Eastern Caribbean States (OECS) covers: Anguilla, Antigua & Barbuda, Dominica, Grenada, Montserrat, St. Lucia, St. Vincent and The Grenadines, St. Kitts and Nevis	Liat
Panama	COPA
Paraguay	TAM Paraguay
Suriname	Suriname Airways
Swaziland	Royal Swazi/Airlink Swaziland
Trinidad & Tobago	BWIA
Turks & Caicos	Lynx Air
Uruguay	Pluna
Venezuela	Avensa
Former Zaire	No international carrier
Zimbabwe	Air Zimbabwe

* Note: The failing grades given by the ICAO apply to all airlines based in that country. "Primary Carrier" indicates which airline in that country receives the most international passenger traffic.

Source: ICAO report, December 2001

fatal crashes since 1996. (SWISS/Crossair has had three.) Security experts John Currie and Jeremy Spindlove said, when interviewed in January 2002, that after the Israelis,

European carriers and airports have the most experience with terrorism and the best airport security.

In a January 2002 interview, John Currie picked British Airways, KLM, Lufthansa, and Aer Lingus as his favorite international carriers for safety. (As this book went to press, however, Aer Lingus was having financial problems.) Several countries in the Caribbean fail ICAO standards, but that hasn't seemed to affect the safety records of their major airlines, which (except for Cubana and various Dominican airlines, all banned from flying to the U.S. for safety reasons) haven't had a fatal crash in 15 years.

As for airlines in the rest of the world, Mary Schiavo says, in her 1997 book *Flying Blind, Flying Safe,* that Cathay Pacific and Dragonair are the safest airlines in northern Asia. Statistics bear out her claim — neither has had a fatal crash since 1972.

All of the terrorism and security experts interviewed for this book who offered opinions warned against flying on sub-Saharan African airlines; Schiavo's 1997 book calls

NON-U.S. AIRLINES WITH NO FATAL CRASHES, EVER

COUNTRY	AIRLINE
Australia	Qantas
Austria	Austrian Airlines
Finland	Finnair
Honduras	TACA
Iceland	Icelandair
Ireland	Aer Lingus
Jamaica	Air Jamaica
Japan	Japan Air System
Taiwan	EVA Air
Tunisia	Tunis Air
UAE	Emirates
UK	Virgin Atlantic
West Indies	BWIA

Source: airsafe.com, February 2002. Note: airsafe.com lists Air China as having no crashes, but expert Mary Schiavo says airline safety data from China is untrustworthy.

Nigeria the least safe place on Earth to fly. Airlines in South and Central America, meanwhile, are rife with fatalities, with 12 fatal accidents by major carriers since 1996 and 9 countries that fail ICAO standards.

If, like Dustin Hoffman in *Rain Man,* you insist on flying an airline that's never had a crash, know that you'll be leaving some very safe airlines out of the running. Even British Airways, statistically one of the safest fleets in the air, has crashed in its history. See the table above for a list of non-U.S. airlines that have never had a fatal crash.

2

TICKETING PITFALLS: KNOW YOUR RIGHTS BEFORE THE FLIGHT

With air tickets, you're not guaranteed to get what you paid for.

You paid hundreds of dollars to go from point A to point B at a certain time. But your flight might be delayed by an hour, or a day. The airline may have sold two tickets for the same seat. Or the airline may go bankrupt in the middle of your trip, leaving you with a worthless piece of paper instead of a ticket.

You're not completely helpless. If you know the rules and your rights, you'll be able to save a lot of time and hassle when you're on your way.

1 WHAT THE AIRLINES PROMISE YOU

BELIEVE IT OR NOT, YOU DO HAVE RIGHTS AS AN AIR traveler. Those rights are listed in your airline's legally binding **contract of carriage,** supplemented by the non-binding **customer service commitments** that all airlines put into place in late 1999, after much federal pressure.

Each airline's contract of carriage and customer service commitment are posted on its website, though some are very hard to find. For a much easier explanation of the rules, go to OneTravel.com (www.onetravel.com) and click on "Rules of the Air" on the left-hand side. Online travel agency One-Travel has boiled down the contracts of carriage into plain (plane?) English, which you can print out and take to the airport.

(For flights on non-U.S. carriers, different regulations apply, and the contract is referred to as the "tariff rules." Foreign carriers usually keep a copy of the tariff rules at city and airport ticket offices.)

The contracts of carriage and customer service commitments cover issues including:

- what the airline will do if your flight is delayed or canceled or if you're involuntarily bumped;

- what the airline will do if your plane gets stuck on the tarmac;

- your rights regarding lost, damaged, or delayed luggage;

- your right to hold a reservation for 24 hours without paying.

Unfortunately, the rights provided in these contracts are always less than travelers deserve, and the customer service commitments often are not fulfilled, according to a February 2001 report by the Department of Transportation's inspector general.

While "the airlines were making progress," the report found that "the airlines' commitment does not directly address the most deep-seated, underlying cause of customer dissatisfaction — flight delays and cancellations, and what the airlines plan to do about them."

DON'T MESS WITH A FORCE MAJEURE

When a "force majeure" event – such as a war or natural disaster – occurs while you're traveling , there's no guarantee that you'll actually get where you're going.

I should know. At 9am Eastern time on **September 11, 2001**, I was on a plane traveling from **Glasgow to New York**, with a scheduled stop in Reykjavik, Iceland. Upon landing in Reykjavik, I was informed by a cheerful Icelandair employee that "America is closed," and that I'd get further information when I got to my hotel.

I stayed in Iceland for 2½ days; 1 night's hotel was paid for by the airline, and the 2nd night was at a 50% discount. The Hotel Loftleidir in Reykjavik was set up as a center for displaced Americans, and Icelandair's second-in-command updated us in person every few hours on the status of American air space – and on the status of New York City.

The moment the U.S. reopened its airspace, stranded Americans were hustled to the airport and put on planes to North America. But too late! The FAA closed the airspace while we were over Greenland, and we were forced to land at Mirabel Airport, north of Montreal, Canada. Icelandair then rustled up buses to drive American passengers across the border. I declined the 8 hour, midnight bus ride, went downtown, had a steak sandwich, crashed at a friend's house, and took Amtrak home the next day.

Icelandair wasn't required to do any of the things it did for me and the other passengers on September 11 – it wasn't even legally required to get me to my destination. U.S. airlines, by the way, are only required to offer partial refunds in "force majeure" situations. But Icelandair decided to help us out anyway.

Although the airlines all promise timely information about delays and cancellations, the OIG report found timely, gate-area announcements about delay status were only made 66% of the time, and that the announcements provided adequate information only 57% of the time. For 21% of delayed flights, the flights were listed on airport video screens as on time when they were actually more than 20 minutes late.

And although the airlines promise to tend to passengers' needs during extended delays on the tarmac, their ideas of an "extended" delay can vary from 45 minutes to 3 hours, according to the report.

"We think it is unlikely that a passenger's definition of an extended on-aircraft delay will vary depending upon which air carrier they are flying," the report noted.

According to the Aviation Consumer Action Project, a consumer watchdog group founded by Ralph Nader in 1971, buying an airline ticket is a lot like buying a car or a TV. Their advice? Ask a lot of questions, shop around, and make sure you're familiar and satisfied with the fine print.

2 CROWDS IN THE SKY: THE BUSINESS OF BUMPING

ACCORDING TO THE AIR TRANSPORT ASSOCIATION, 10% to 15% of ticketed airline passengers in the United States — many of them business travelers with expensive, refundable tickets — don't show up at the airport on the day of departure. Consequently, airlines have developed the habit of **overbooking**, or selling more tickets than they have available seats.

As you may know from first-hand experience, when too many people show up for a flight, airlines ask for volunteers to take a later flight in exchange for a free ticket or flight coupon that can be worth as much as $500 or more.

As airlines cut flight schedules throughout 2001, there were fewer "voluntary bumpings" in the first 9 months of 2001 than in 2000. But 698,997 people still chose to take free tickets in exchange for a bit of a wait. You could be one of them.

VOLUNTARY BUMPINGS

For the traveler with some spare time, voluntary bumping can be a great way to get free tickets.

It works like this: book a ticket on a full flight. Tell the gate agent that you're willing to "go DV," or "denied voluntary." If the flight is overbooked, you'll be put on a later flight and you'll scoop up a free coupon redeemable for a future ticket purchase (plus hotel accommodation and possibly meals if you have to wait overnight).

But DV can be a "D"-saster if you're traveling on the holidays, when the airline may not be able to find another available seat to put you in. So ask these questions first:

- **When is the next flight on which you can get a *confirmed seat?*** The Department of Transportation recommends that you ask for a confirmed seat before you give up your original. Don't end up on standby.

- **What strings are attached to your free ticket?** How long is it valid? Where can you travel and when? Are holidays included? Can you reserve a seat, or must you fly standby?

- **Will the airline take care of you until the next flight out?** For long waits you may be entitled to phone calls, meals, taxis, even a hotel room.

- **Are there other volunteers?** Find out how many volunteers the carrier needs. If it's clear that you're the only one and the airline needs more, don't take the first offer. Wait until the gate agent ups the ante, then use your advantage to bargain for extra perks like hotel stays, phone calls, and meals.

While the government regulates the minimum the airline must pay you if you're involuntarily bumped, there isn't a fixed minimum or maximum if you offer up your seat. (The airlines are at least supposed to give everyone bumped off the same flight the same amount, but the DOT inspector general's report found two unnamed airlines weren't playing along, and anecdotal evidence backs up that finding.) The amount you receive will depend on how desperately the carrier needs your seat, how effectively you bargain, and the gate agent's receptiveness to your demands.

INVOLUNTARY BUMPINGS

In the absence of good Samaritans, the situation gets a little hairier. The airline requires certain passengers to travel on a later flight, in a practice known as **"involuntary bumping."**

Typically, passengers who booked or checked in last are the first to get the shaft. You're also an easy target if you arrived at the airport without a seat reservation — so be sure to check in early if this is the case. If your reservation requires reconfirmation, don't skip this crucial step; your timely passage may be hanging on a simple phone call.

It's wise to take a morning flight if you're booking last-minute travel during a major holiday. If you are bumped, you'll have greater opportunity to fly later that day.

MONEY-BACK GUARANTEES: WHAT ARE YOU OWED?

If you do get bumped, the airline owes you cash as long as you meet two requirements. You must have a confirmed reservation, and you must have met the check-in deadline.

Check-in times vary according to both the carrier and the airport, so be sure to ask for specifics when you book. On domestic flights, the check-in deadline is 1 to 2 hours before departure; on international trips, it's 90 minutes to 3 hours before takeoff. If you are holding a non-refundable ticket and you miss the airline's boarding gate deadline — usually between 10 and 30 minutes before takeoff — the airline has the right to void your ticket, with no money back. But most airlines have an informal "flat tire exception" that lets you stand by for another flight if you miss your plane by 2 hours or less.

The Department of Transportation says that if the airline can get you where you're going within 1 hour of your scheduled arrival, it owes you nothing. Comfort yourself by thinking that even if you'd made it onto the plane, it could very well have been delayed that long.

If the carrier can put you on a plane that arrives between 1 and 2 hours after your scheduled arrival, it must compensate you for the cost of your one-way fare, up to $200. If you arrive more than 2 hours late (4 hr. late for international travel), you are entitled to twice the value of your one-way ticket, up to $400. If these amounts seem low, it's because they haven't been changed since 1978. In large part because of these low limits, passengers involuntarily bumped often get less compensation than DV passengers from the same flight.

If the delay ends up, say, costing you a job or causing some other type of irreparable damage, you can turn down the airline's offers and demand more money from the complaint department. Remember, however, that once you've accepted an offer of money, you won't be able to go back and renegotiate for more. (See chapter 10, "The Squeaky Wheel.")

Once you've agreed to the airline's compensation, the airline must issue your free ticket, cash, or check immediately. If it doesn't, forget the deal and ask them to refund your original ticket on the spot.

Note: The Department of Transportation does not mandate compensation for bumped passengers on small plane flights (under 60 passengers) or travelers whose flights were rerouted onto a smaller aircraft for safety or operations reasons. (However, if you were booked on a large aircraft and were then "downsized" to a smaller plane that could not fit all of the passengers on your original flight, those passengers bumped would be compensated.) If you refuse the airline's offer to place you in another section of the aircraft at no extra charge, they owe you no compensation. Also, the DOT requires no compensation if you are bumped from charter

AIRLINES' BOARDING GATE DEADLINES
(Before Departure)

CARRIER	DOMESTIC (IN MINUTES)	INTERNATIONAL
Alaska	20	30
America West	30	60
American	30	30
Continental	15	30
Delta	20	45
Northwest	30	60
Southwest	10	N/A
United	20	30
US Airways	10	30

AIRLINES' SUGGESTED CHECK-IN TIMES
(Before Departure)

CARRIER	DOMESTIC (IN HOURS)	INTERNATIONAL
Alaska	Varies	Varies
America West	Varies	Varies
American	2	2
Continental	Varies	Varies
Delta	2	2
Northwest	1.25	2
Southwest	Varies	N/A
United	1.5	2
US Airways	1	1.5

Note: Airline check-in times were in flux at press time, and may change as airport security procedures are altered. If a column says "Varies," ask your airline about conditions at your specific airport.

flights, international flights returning to the United States, or flights from one foreign city to another (the DOT considers the latter two situations outside their jurisdiction).

The Department of Transportation requires that airlines provide bumped passengers with a written explanation of overbooking and involuntary bumping — including a summary of who gets bumped and who doesn't. Be sure to ask for this written explanation and read the fine print carefully to be sure you're getting your due.

In general, the busiest flight times are between 7:30 and 9:30am and 5:30 to 7:30pm, especially during the week. The sky is especially crowded on Monday mornings, and Friday and Sunday evenings. Air traffic and flights also tend to be congested during major holidays and the few days before and after. Take extra care to check in early if you're flying at these times.

WHEN AN AIRLINE GOES BANKRUPT: THE ULTIMATE BUMP

The hideous travel market of late 2001 claimed the livelihoods of several major airlines: Ansett, Australia's second-largest carrier; Canada 3000, that nation's second-largest airline; Midway; MetroJet, US Airways' low-cost subsidiary; Swissair (resurrected as SWISS, now a division of Crossair); and Sabena.

The market has improved somewhat, but bankruptcy (or "carrier default") is still a very real risk. In early 2002,

THE BUMP RAP: WHO BUMPED MOST IN JANUARY TO SEPTEMBER 2001
(Denied Boardings)

AIRLINE	VOLUN-TARY	INVOLUN-TARY	PASSEN-GERS	INVOLUNTARY BUMPS PER 10,000 PASSEN-GERS
US Airways	65,589	1,357	43,258,363	0.31
American	103,966	1,937	55,466,583	0.35
America West	40,010	604	15,622,332	0.39
Northwest	58,054	1,557	38,495,416	0.4
Delta	135,690	4,544	69,750,219	0.65
Continental	54,383	2,599	29,749,486	0.87
United	120,191	5,499	54,721,034	1.00
Alaska	25,922	1,567	10,624,014	1.47
Southwest	63,289	9,215	56,439,110	1.63

Source: U.S. Department of Transportation.

Note: Does not include canceled, delayed, or diverted flights.

Denied Boarding Overseas

The bumping policies of international carriers, especially in small or underdeveloped countries, are unpredictable. If you must take an international flight into the United States, or fly an international carrier between foreign cities, be sure you understand the airline's bumping policy before you book your ticket.

---

rumors were circling around Aer Lingus and United, as analysts wondered if they'd be able to make it out of their financial slumps. America West had to get additional financial help (in the form of loan guarantees) from the U.S. government in December 2001.

If your airline goes bankrupt in mid-trip, you may be utterly screwed. If you're lucky, another airline will agree to honor your ticket home. If not, you'll have to buy another ticket on the spot, often at extremely inflated prices. Travel insurance is your best way around this rare, but costly eventuality.

You can protect yourself against airline bankruptcies. Follow these rules:

- **Book conservatively.** Read the news and pick airlines with relatively solid financial standing.

- **Buy travel insurance.** But make sure your insurance specifically covers carrier default for the airline on which you'll be flying — many insurers have been cutting back on coverage. For more on travel insurance, see chapter 6, "Life Preservers."

- **Use a credit card.** A federal law, the Fair Credit Billing Act, means you'll be able to get money back for your original ticket if an airline goes under. Submit the ticket, itinerary, or receipt to your credit card company within 60 days of the bankruptcy, explaining that the airline went out of business before you could use the ticket. The credit card issuer is required to refund your fare.

WHERE ARE AMERICANS FLYING?
(To New York, Apparently)
The 20 Most Traveled City Pairs in the United States during
the First Quarter of 2001

FROM	TO	PASSENGERS/DAY
Ft. Lauderdale, FL	New York, NY	9384
New York, NY	Orlando, FL	7224
Los Angeles, CA	New York, NY	6006
Chicago IL	New York, NY	5920
Boston, MA	New York, NY	5863
Atlanta, GA	New York, NY	5675
Dallas, TX	Houston, TX	5503
New York, NY	West Palm Beach, FL	5112
New York, NY	Washington, DC	5047
Las Vegas, NV	Los Angeles, CA	5024
Los Angeles, CA	Oakland, CA	4328
New York, NY	SAN Francisco, CA	4008
Las Vegas, NV	New York, NY	3864
Miami, FL	New York, NY	3853
New York, NY	TAMPA, FL	3670
Chicago, IL	Los Angeles, CA	3371
Chicago, IL	Las Vegas, NV	3352
Chicago, IL	Minneapolis, MN	3243
Chicago, IL	Detroit, MI	3239
Los Angeles, CA	Phoenix, AZ	3214

Source: USDOT

- **Get paper tickets.** If another airline agrees to honor
  the bankrupt airline's tickets, it'll be easier to make the
  switch if you have a paper ticket instead of an e-ticket.

3 Dealing with Delays, Cancellations & Lost Tickets

ONE GOOD RESULT OF THE AIRLINES' SLASHING
schedules in late 2001 was a dramatic drop in the number of

Stuck at the Airport?

During a long, weather-related delay, there may be no room at the local inns. If you have to sleep in an airport because of a delay, ask airport employees if you can get a cot or access to the first-class lounges (see "Lounging Around," later in this chapter).

For worst-case scenarios, see **www.sleepinginairports.net**, Canadian Donna McSherry's comprehensive guide to napping in terminals. Her picks for the best U.S. airports to catch some Z's: Pittsburgh and Portland (Ore.). The worst? Boston and Detroit.

---

delayed and canceled flights. But cancellations do happen, and it's good to know your rights.

RULE 240

Each airline's contract of carriage has a rule, colloquially (but not legally) known as "rule 240" which explains what an airline owes you if your flight is delayed or canceled. **Rule 240 is your legal right** and you should demand what it allows. The major airlines' rule 240 contracts are quite similar; they go something like this:

IF a flight is delayed or canceled . . .

. . . and the delay is NOT due to weather, labor disputes, terrorism, or certain other "force majeure" events:

- the airline MUST confirm you on their next flight to your destination on which space is available, at no extra cost.

- If that flight is not acceptable to you, the airline must confirm you on another airline's flight, at no extra cost.

- If none of these options are acceptable, the airline must refund your ticket, even if it's "non-refundable," with no penalty.

- If a flight is diverted to an unscheduled point and the layover is expected to exceed 4 hours between 10pm and 6am, the airline must provide you with hotel accommodations.

    BUT if the flight is delayed at your origination or destination point, or diverted to an airport within the same metro area as your destination, the airline is not required to do so.

    BUT the non-binding customer service commitment may say the airline will provide accommodations if there's a delay caused by events within its control.

Notice that rule 240 almost never requires an airline to pay for meals, phone calls, or other incidental expenses incurred because of a delay. Airlines will often do so as a show of good faith — especially if you're an elite frequent flier or traveling on a costly business ticket. Be nice, be sympathetic, and ask. Remember the gate agents are as harassed as you are, but it is their job to help you.

In general, low-fare airlines' rule 240 contracts (including that of Southwest, which calls their version "rule 85") are not up to snuff. Most don't give you passage on another airline if requested — AirTran is one exception to that rule. And most give you no rights to amenities in case of delays, with Midwest Express the exception in that situation. MWE will offer you a meal voucher and a phone call if delays stretch to 4 hours or more. Spirit's contract doesn't even promise a refund for a canceled flight, which is a major problem. Most low-fare airlines may *choose* to put you on another airline's flight if they feel they can't get you home in time — but that's entirely up to their whim and discretion.

WHAT YOU SHOULD DO

If your flight is delayed or canceled, *Consumer Reports Travel Letter* advises that first you find out why — that will determine what the airline owes you. Then call your travel agent or the airline and immediately book yourself on the next available flight. Finally, go to the gate for your new flight and get your ticket converted.

If it looks like you'll be stuck overnight, airlines will at least try to find you accommodation (though they're not required to do so). At the very least, ask about "distressed passenger rates" at nearby hotels. As always, elite status and a good rapport with gate agents can pay off big-time here.

If you don't get anywhere with the airline, try calling the **American Society of Travel Agents' (ASTA)** 24-hour toll-free referral line (☎ **800/965-2782**). They can recommend a travel agent in the area where you're waylaid who may be able to tell you which local hotels offer distressed passenger rates.

If you're unsure of an airline's policy regarding cancellations and delays, inquire when you book your ticket. You probably know this already, but it's also wise to fly the day before an engagement that may make or break your bank account, career, or reputation.

MISSED CONNECTIONS

Should a delay cause you to miss a connecting flight on a different airline, the airline is not required to pay you a dime for your hardship. If you have to make a connecting flight, it's wise to allow yourself anywhere from 45 to 90 minutes to make your connection — depending on the size of the airport, the history of delays for that particular flight, and the amount of baggage you checked.

According to the Aviation Consumer Action Project, the airlines allow anywhere between 20 and 90 minutes turnaround time between segmented flights. Every minute spent on the ground costs a carrier money, so they keep profits high by scheduling quick turnarounds.

If your flight leaves late and you're concerned about missing a connection, ask an attendant if the airline would be willing to arrange for special transportation to your connecting gate. Peruse the in-flight magazine to familiarize yourself with the layout of the airport you're going to have to navigate at breakneck speeds in order to catch your next plane. Remember that these magazines are meant to be taken home, so don't be shy about taking it with you — or at least tearing out the airport map.

SO WHAT DOES "ON TIME" REALLY MEAN?

When you book a flight, get in the habit of asking the reservationist what the **on-time arrival performance** is for the flight you're planning to take. On a reservationist's database, each flight is assigned a number between zero and nine. If a flight rates a six, this means it arrives on time 60% to 69% of the time. If it's especially important that your flight be prompt, look for one that rates at least an eight.

Note: Keep in mind that a flight is considered "on time" if it lands within 15 minutes of its scheduled arrival. Also know that it's common industry practice for an airline to pad its flight times to improve its promptness rating. If a flight takes 45 minutes, for instance, some carriers will say it takes up to 90 minutes — and then come out looking "on time" when it arrives 70 minutes after departure.

MAJOR AIRLINE PROMPTNESS RATINGS
(On-time Arrivals for 2001)

AIRLINE	PERCENTAGE OF ON-TIME ARRIVALS
Southwest	81.7
Continental	80.7
Northwest	79.7
US Airways	78.2
Delta	78.0
American	75.9
America West	74.8
United	73.5
Alaska	69.0

Source: Department of Transportation.

Note: A flight is considered on time if it arrives within 15 minutes of schedule.

STUCK ON THE TARMAC

So you got on your plane, and now it's sitting there, not taking off. Other than dig out a good book, what can you do?

Airlines' customer service commitments outline weak promises about what can happen. But their promises are little better than suggestions, and loaded with weasel-words like "may" instead of "will." In general, they promise that during an extended delay they'll make "every reasonable effort" to provide food, water, restrooms, and medical treatment for passengers stuck on the tarmac for an "extended" time.

But the airlines leave the decision to return to the gate up to the flight crew, not the passengers, according to the Department of Transportation inspector general's report. And the type of food and when it will be provided is left up to the flight crew and the local catering staff.

There's little you can do, but you can do a little. Pack your own food, water, and reading material just in case. If you're stuck on the tarmac beyond your airline's "extended" deadline, don't take it out on the flight crew. They're as frustrated as you are. Do speak up, politely, and ask about the

DEADLINES FOR STUCK-ON-THE-TARMAC DELAYS

AIRLINE	"EXTENDED" PERIOD
Alaska	90 minutes
American	3 hours
ATA	1 hour
America West	1 hour
Continental	2 hours
Delta	45 minutes
Hawaiian	1 hour
Midwest Express	2 hours
Northwest	1–3 hours
Southwest	Not specified
United	90 minutes
US Airways	Not specified

Source: DOT OIG report AV-2001-020

provisions that their bosses promised you during long delays. And later, write a letter to the airline specifying the length of the delay, mentioning the airline's self-imposed deadline, explaining in detail that they fell short of their commitment, and asking for a refund or travel voucher.

LOST TICKETS

If you lose your paper ticket, you'll be in a much better position to replace it if you **wrote down the ticket number when you first received it in the mail.** The airline will be able to process your refund more quickly if you make time for this little bit of documentation. At the same time, it's wise to make sure the name and other information on the ticket is accurate as well.

The most common fee for replacing a lost ticket is $75, but depending on the airline and the rules for your specific fare, the cost may run higher than $100. While some airlines will replace your ticket as soon as you fill out the application and pay the fee, others may reimburse you later — sometimes as long as 2 to 6 months later — and require you to buy a new ticket for immediate travel at the going rate for that time period. If you're replacing the ticket on the day of departure, for instance, you may end up paying over three times the amount you paid for an advance-purchase fare. If you tend to lose things, get an e-ticket.

THE ABCs OF E-TICKETS

All U.S. airlines now offer "e-tickets," a fancy way of saying you're flying with no ticket at all. The proof of your flight is in the airlines' computers. This means no worries about losing a ticket, but a potential hassle if your airline goes bankrupt.

E-tickets are much cheaper than plain paper tickets for airlines — there's no printing cost and no mailing cost. So the airlines promote them with extra frequent-flier miles and innovative ways of checking in. Most major airlines allow e-ticket customers with hand baggage to check in at electronic kiosks at the airport, bypassing ticket lines. Northwest,

Alaska, and Delta even allow passengers to check in over the Internet, by logging on to the airline's website the day of departure. Passengers print out their boarding passes on their home printers and zoom to the gate. (If your printer breaks mid-boarding-pass, your ticket's safe but you need to go to the ticket counter at the airport to get it.)

Airlines and travel agents love e-tickets so much that many have started charging fees of between $5 and $12.50 for paper tickets. E-tickets are great for forgetful travelers, travelers taking a reliable route on a reliable airline, or travelers who need to change their tickets (as there's no paper ticket that must be exchanged).

Stay away from e-tickets on airlines that might have a strike or airlines with financial trouble; if the airline goes under, you want paper proof that the airline owes you money. And if the airline temporarily shuts down, other airlines will accept paper tickets more quickly than e-tickets.

But don't worry about using e-tickets on a route likely to be delayed. It used to be that holders of paper tickets could jog over to another airline's counter and get their ticket endorsed onto the second airline while e-ticket holders had to wait at their original airline's desk. Now, most discount tickets require that they be converted by the original airline before being used on a second airline, so e-ticket and paper ticket holders are in the same boat.

If you go the e-ticket route, make sure to print out the online receipt and bring it with you to the airport. You'll need it to get past security.

"HOT" TICKETS

If you're not careful about choosing a reputable travel agent or consolidator, you could find yourself with a ticket that was stolen from someone else. While this happens rarely, it is possible, and you probably won't find out about it until you check in on the day of your flight. Only your airline representative will know for sure, and will most likely confiscate the hot property and force you to buy another if you want to fly that day — which means you could end up paying the full last-minute fare.

Should you find yourself a victim of ticket fraud, you do have legal recourse — though you still will probably have to lay out money for a new ticket.

The easiest way to get your money back is to go through your credit card company. (You did buy the ticket with a credit card, *right?*) The Fair Credit Billing Act protects you from purchasing a service that doesn't exist.

To cover the price of the new ticket you'll have to buy, turn to the airline and the Department of Transportation. While the airline is under no obligation to understand your plight, it's still a good idea to write to its customer affairs office immediately and explain what happened. Try as best you can to document the fact that you had no idea you were purchasing illegitimate tickets, and request a refund or voucher for future travel. (See chapter 10 for the customer relations numbers of the major carriers.)

At the same time, write to the **Department of Transportation (DOT),** Aviation Consumer Protection Division, U.S. Department of Transportation, C-75, 400 7th St. SW, Room 4107, Washington, DC 20590 (☎ **202/366-2220**). Ask them to intervene on your behalf in requesting a refund. Be sure to mention prominently in your letter to the airline that you're approaching the DOT for help. In fact, send the airline a copy of the DOT letter and send a copy of the airline letter to the DOT. (For other tips on how to complain effectively, see chapter 10.)

4 LOUNGING AROUND: TAKING ADVANTAGE OF THE AIRPORT LOUNGE

A BRACING COCKTAIL IN A COMFY CHAIR, A NEWS-paper, a few snacks, some Web surfing, and a lot of relaxation . . . at the *airport?* Welcome to the airport lounge. Hidden behind discreetly marked doors in most large airports around the world, airline-affiliated lounges can make layovers and multi-hour delays a pleasant experience.

Airlines grant free admission to their airport lounges for passengers with first- and business-class tickets (Alaska and United also provide free lounge admission to their elite frequent fliers). If you don't fall into one of these categories, you can often buy an entry pass at the door. This can get costly ($40 to $50 per person per day), so if you get bumped or your flight is delayed, compare the price of a lounge pass with the price of the local airport hotel (and factor in the convenience of staying inside the terminal, where you can rush to catch a flight in minutes, if necessary.)

Frequent fliers should consider the **Priority Pass** travel club (☎ **800/352-2863;** www.prioritypass.com), which grants access to more than 300 airport lounges worldwide. Priority Pass has member lounges at 46 U.S. airports and many more elsewhere in the world; 37 of the world's 40 busiest airports are on the list, including 19 of the 20 busiest U.S. airports (St. Louis is excluded). Coverage at European airports is quite good: five lounges in France, eight in Germany, 15 in Great Britain, and five in Italy. An annual membership costs $295, or $99 plus $24 per lounge visit. Each guest, even a child, costs $24 per visit.

If you mostly fly with one airline, fly to the same destinations frequently, or usually travel with a companion, joining an individual airline's club may prove to be a better deal than Priority Pass. Each major U.S. airline has roughly 40 lounges at hub airports and other major destinations; often, partner airlines have reciprocity agreements so their members can gain admission to more clubs. (For more on airline partnerships, see "Allied Forces," later in this chapter.) Club memberships can be costly (from $375 to $450 annually), but some airlines offer discounted memberships if you've accumulated a lot of frequent flier miles. And club members can bring one or two guests and any number of children for free. You can buy memberships in advance or at the club door. Smaller airlines charge less for membership but have fewer clubs. America West's $300 annual fee is a good deal, because members also get access to Northwest clubs.

Two credit cards give their members limited lounge privileges as well. The American Express Platinum Card (cost: $300 per yr.) provides access to 42 Continental, Northwest, and other airport lounges, with a decent selection of major U.S. airports. (Las Vegas and Phoenix, however, are not on the list.) But coverage in the rest of the world is scant; London Gatwick and Frankfurt are the only European airports included. Your spouse and children under 21, or up to two companions, are admitted free with each member.

Diners Club (cost: $80 per yr.) provides free admission to 54 airport lounges around the world — though the only U.S. lounges in the plan are Miami and Newark. Many of the lounges are Diners Club–run; some are managed by the airports, and some by individual airlines. It's a peculiar list; many international transfer points (Amsterdam, London, Brussels, Tokyo, and Frankfurt, for example) are part of the program, but other big hubs (Hong Kong and Bangkok, to name two) are missing. Also, some participating lounges are found in smaller German and Japanese cities (Hanover? Matsuyama?) that aren't popular travel destinations. Charges for member-accompanied guests vary from lounge to lounge.

5   THE HUB HULLABALOO

BEFORE THE AIRLINE INDUSTRY WAS DEREGULATED in 1978, commercial planes traveled according to the point-to-point system — from departure city to destination in pretty much a straight line, making stops along the way like a Greyhound bus. Planes usually left the ground 60% to 64% full. After deregulation, however, airlines established the **hub-and-spoke system** in order to operate fuller planes — and thereby secure greater profits.

HOW THE HUB SYSTEM WORKS

Rather than transport passengers directly from small airports to their destination cities or from large airports to smaller towns, "feeder planes" now deliver passengers first to the hub city, where certain carriers may control as much as 80% of the business. From there, the carrier dispatches travelers to their destinations.

If you're traveling from a small city to a large one, you will most likely travel to the hub in a small jet and then to your destination in a much larger plane, along with passengers who came in from umpteen other places. For example, a typical flight from Chicago to New York gets its passengers from about 10 feeder planes. Rather than send 10 different half-empty flights (from 10 different points of origin) all to New York, the airline consolidates the flights at its Chicago hub. Conversely, if you're flying from a large city to a smaller one, you will most likely travel to the hub in a large, full jet and from there be dispatched to your small city on a smaller plane. This consolidation has allowed airlines to expand service dramatically, and move into many smaller markets.

Southwest is the only major airline to buck the hub trend. The low-fare carrier focuses on short-haul, point-to-point routes that can financially support frequent flights, rather than try to serve every small community in a region, said Kevin Michalenko, Southwest's manager of pricing. (Southwest also has far lower costs than other airlines, which allows them to make profits on low-fare routes such as Dallas–Houston–Austin, which compete with car travel rather than with other airlines.) And to some extent, the big airlines' hub strategies help Southwest, by leaving many short nonstop possibilities open for Southwest to exploit.

HUBS: THE DOWNSIDE

Under the hub system, planes now carry 70% to 80% of their capacity, on average. Paul Hudson, executive director of the Aviation Consumer Action Project, says, "Mathematically, the hub-and-spoke system is more efficient for both the airlines and consumers — but only when the proper reserve capacities are in place." With such a highly interconnected network of very full planes, major carriers need: spare airports, in case one airport is out of commission; spare planes, in case a scheduled aircraft breaks down; and spare airline employees, in case pilots or flight attendants are sick.

Let's take, for example, that flight from Chicago to New York again, which gets its passengers from about 10 feeder planes coming in from mostly smaller airports. If eight of those feeders arrive on time and two are delayed, the airline is faced with a dilemma: Does it strand passengers on the tardy flights in order to depart on time, or does it wait for all 10 feeders to reach Chicago and depart late for New York? Either way, efficient operations are disrupted.

Hudson says that with the proper reserve capacities, the airline would have a second smaller plane waiting to pick up the late passengers. Although this strategy would save consumers time and make the whole system run more effectively, it also costs the airlines more money. So guess what usually happens to the passengers whose flights are delayed? Because the airlines would rather stretch their assets to the breaking point than "squander" profits on reserve facilities, delayed passengers are simply stranded and inconvenienced, with no legislation in place that would demand they receive compensation (see "Missed Connections," earlier in this chapter). Likewise, when technical difficulties occur, flights are often simply canceled. Without proper reserves, the system is so tightly wound that one little snafu produces a far-reaching ripple effect.

THE MONOPOLY GAME

Under the hub-and-spoke system, each major airline focuses its resources on a handful of cities around the country, and controls most of the business in that particular market. For instance, American Airlines controls nearly 70% of the

WORLD'S TOP 50 AIRPORTS
(Ranked by Passenger Numbers Jan–Dec 2000)

RANK	AIRPORT	TOTAL PASSENGERS	% CHANGE FROM 1999
1	Atlanta	80,171,036	2.8
2	Chicago O'Hare	72,135,887	-0.7
3	Los Angeles	68,477,689	5.1
4	London Heathrow	64,607,185	3.8
5	Dallas/Ft. Worth	60,687,122	1.1
6	Tokyo Haneda	56,402,206	3.8
7	Frankfurt	49,360,620	7.6
8	Paris Charles de Gaulle	48,240,137	11.6
9	San Francisco	41,173,983	2.1
10	Amsterdam	39,604,589	7.7
11	Denver	38,748,781	1.9
12	Las Vegas	36,856,186	9.5
13	Seoul	36,727,124	10.1
14	Minneapolis/St. Paul	36,688,159	5.3
15	Phoenix	35,889,933	7.0
16	Detroit Metro	35,535,080	4.6
17	Houston Intercontinental	35,246,176	6.5
18	Newark	34,194,788	1.7
19	Miami	33,569,625	-1.0
20	New York John F. Kennedy	32,779,428	3.5
21	Madrid	32,765,820	18.2
22	Hong Kong	32,746,737	10.2
23	London Gatwick	32,056,942	4.9
24	Orlando	30,822,580	5.6
25	St. Louis	30,546,698	1.2
26	Bangkok	29,621,898	8.5

passenger traffic at its hub in Dallas/Fort Worth. As a result, the top 20 airports control 55% of the nation's flights; the top 60 control 94%. Small airports often can't send you anywhere but to a few hubs.

This situation is only likely to get worse as airlines consolidate further. In May 2001, a federal judge threw out a case against American Airlines that attacked how American protected its Dallas hub. Although the judge said American

RANK	AIRPORT	TOTAL PASSENGERS	% CHANGE FROM 1999
27	Toronto	28,820,326	4.0
28	Singapore	28,618,200	9.8
29	Seattle–Tacoma	28,404,312	2.5
30	Boston	27,412,926	1.3
31	Tokyo Narita	27,389,915	6.7
32	Rome	25,921,886	7.5
33	Paris Orly	25,399,111	0.2
34	New York La Guardia	25,233,889	5.9
35	Philadelphia	24,900,621	4.7
36	Sydney	23,553,878	9.4
37	Munich	23,125,872	8.7
38	Charlotte	23,073,894	7.6
39	Honolulu	22,660,349	0.4
40	Zurich	22,649,539	8.4
41	Cincinnati	22,537,525	3.5
42	Beijing	21,659,077	19.1
43	Brussels	21,604,478	7.9
44	Mexico City	21,042,610	2.9
45	Milan	20,716,815	22.1
46	Osaka	20,472,060	2.9
47	Washington Dulles	19,971,449	1.6
48	Salt Lake City	19,900,810	-0.1
49	Pittsburgh	19,813,174	5.5
50	Barcelona	19,797,135	13.8

Source: Airports Council International via airwise.com.

used "brutal" tactics to drive Vanguard, Sun Jet, and Western Pacific airlines out of Dallas–Fort Worth (DFW) airport, he said the big airline's actions were perfectly legal.

American's tactic was this: when a smaller airline offered a route into DFW, American would flood that route with cheap, frequent, unprofitable service. Once the smaller airline backed off, unable to fill its planes, American would cut back on service and raise prices.

HOME IS WHERE THE HUB IS

CARRIER	HUB CITIES
Alaska/Horizon	Seattle, Portland, Anchorage
American	Dallas–Fort Worth, Miami, New York/JFK, St. Louis, Chicago O'Hare, San Juan
America West	Phoenix, Las Vegas, Columbus (Ohio)
Continental	Houston, Cleveland, Newark
Delta	Atlanta, Cincinnati, Dallas, JFK, Salt Lake City, LAX
Northwest	Minneapolis, Memphis, Detroit
Southwest	No hub; point-to-point system
United	Chicago O'Hare, Denver, Washington D.C. Dulles, San Francisco, LAX
US Airways	Pittsburgh, Charlotte (North Carolina), Philadelphia

With a win in Dallas under its belt, American is now following up by trying to kill off successful low-fare start-up JetBlue. In February 2002, the megacarrier announced new routes from New York to California's Oakland and Ontario airports, matching JetBlue's $299 one-way, walk-up fare.

Lest you think this is "fair competition," American also flies to San Francisco airport, 11.3 miles (18km) from Oakland. And what was the one-way, walk-up fare from New York to San Francisco in late February 2002? $1,221. That's a difference of more than $800 to fly into airports that are 11.3 miles apart. Either American's San Francisco route is vastly overpriced or they're losing money on every Oakland flight just for the purpose of stomping on JetBlue. American can't have it both ways.

The government is in the process of appealing the Dallas case, so this may not be the last word on "fortress hubs."

TAKING THE SCENIC ROUTE

For consumers, the hub system means fewer direct and non-stop flights. For instance, if you found a cheap flight on Northwest from New York to San Francisco, it's very likely you'd have to change planes in Memphis, one of Northwest's hubs — but far from the most direct route to the Bay Area.

So what's a consumer to do? You can try to book non-stop or direct flights whenever possible. You can use a low-fare airline based in your city, if that possibility is available. Or, you can console yourself by focusing on the fact that connecting flights are typically cheaper than direct routes.

6 Allied Forces: Codesharing & Partner Programs

COMPETITION MAY BE GOOD FOR TRAVELERS, but it isn't good for an airline's bottom line. Cooperation, on the other hand, lets airlines join together to reduce the number of pesky competitors who may try to lower prices — so it's no wonder that airlines join forces as much as possible.

Antitrust laws prevent all of America's major airlines from merging into one huge, indistinguishable mass. Although American Airlines swallowed TWA in 2001, government scrutiny prevented the "big seven" airlines from shrinking further to a "big five" by derailing a proposed merger between US Airways and United.

Short of mergers are **alliances** and **partnerships.** **Alliances** are business arrangements between airlines that allow seamless ticketing and other connections between them; your ticket on one airline may send you on another airline entirely.

An example: if you're flying from Allentown, Pennsylvania, to Hamburg, Germany, you can buy a ticket on United — even though United doesn't fly to either city. Part of your "United" ticket will be on Atlantic Coast Airlines, which is a member of the "United Express" alliance of small commuter airlines. Another part of the ticket will be on Lufthansa, the German carrier, which is part of the "Star Alliance" with United. You'll get United frequent-flier miles, and if you're an elite United flier you'll be able to use Lufthansa's first-class lounge in Hamburg.

Frequent-flier and codeshare **partnerships** are looser agreements than alliances. Frequent-flier partnerships are simply agreements by totally independent airlines to trade frequent-flier miles. If you fly a trip on Continental, for instance, you can get Alaska Airlines miles for that, even though the two airlines otherwise consider each other competitors.

Codeshare partnerships, like alliances, allow flights on one airline to "masquerade" as flights on another. But codeshares may not be as seamless as alliances otherwise; fliers may get fewer frequent-flier miles on a codeshare than on their "home" airline, or not have access to elite-class lounges.

Airlines call this "seamless ticketing" and "expanding options." Travel consultant and columnist Joe Brancatelli, on the other hand, calls it "lying." Rather than making flying easier, he says, codeshares are a bait-and-switch tactic where you may think you're buying one ticket, but you're delivered something completely different.

ALLIANCE PROBLEMS

The immediate danger of global alliances for fliers is that you'll get stuck flying part of your trip on a foreign airline with a weaker safety or on-time record than you expected. For instance, "American Airlines" tickets to Central America may be on Nicaraguense de Aviacion (part of TACA), an airline from a country that got a thumbs-down from the FAA for safety oversight.

Commuter-airline alliances spread responsibility in annoying ways; it may be difficult to figure out who is responsible if something goes wrong. One example: when pilots at Comair went on strike in 2001, many travelers holding "Delta" tickets found themselves suddenly without flights.

Protect yourself by asking your reservationist whether any part of your flight is a codeshare. Avoid codeshares with anyone other than trusted, large airlines if possible.

Consumer Reports Travel Letter warned several years ago about a now-common codesharing trap that should make travelers extra wary. On travel agents' reservation systems, nonstop flights appear first, followed by direct flights (a stop, but no plane change), flights with a change of planes on the same airline, and finally "interline" flights with two separate airlines.

Codeshares, though, make a two-airline flight appear like one airline by "hiding" the second airline's code behind that of the friendly partner. So your travel agent might pick that flight over another, cheaper interline connection, because it doesn't appear to be interline at all. (But it is!)

The only solution: be aware. When booking through a travel agent or airline, make sure there are no hidden codeshares in your ticket. If there are, *Consumer Reports* recommends you ask your travel agent if other interline connections may be cheaper — or if calling the codeshare partner directly may result in a cheaper fare for that leg of the flight. (Yes, different codeshare partners sell the same flight for different prices.)

The bottom line: Mergers, alliances, and partnerships increase frequent-flier networks. But the Justice Department and consumer watchdog organizations believe they stifle competition and raise prices, they may compromise your safety, and they certainly make flying more confusing by hiding what airline your trip is actually on.

WHO'S DOING WHAT WITH WHOM

At press time, the three big global alliances were OneWorld, Skyteam, and Star Alliance. A fourth alliance, called Wings, seems perpetually to be on the verge of formation.

- **OneWorld:** Aer Lingus, **American,** British Airways, Cathay Pacific, Finnair, Iberia, LanChile, Qantas

- **SkyTeam: Delta,** Korean, CSA Czech, Alitalia, Air France, Aeromexico

- **Star Alliance:** Air Canada, Air New Zealand, All Nippon, Austrian, bmi British Midland, Lauda, Lufthansa, Mexicana, SAS, Singapore, Thai, Tyrolean, **United,** VARIG

- **Wings: Continental,** KLM, **Northwest**

Each of the major airlines, and several minor ones, have codeshare and commuter partners as well:

- **Alaska:** Horizon, American, Continental, American Eagle, PenAir, Reeve Aleutian, Trans States, Era Aviation, Northwest

- **American: All OneWorld airlines plus** American Eagle, Business Express, Chautauqua, Executive, Trans States, China Eastern, EVA Air, Gulf Air, JAL, Kuwait, TACA, TAM, TAP, Air New Zealand, Turkish Air

- **America West:** Big Sky, Chautauqua, Mesa

- **ATA:** Chicago Express

- **Continental: All Wings airlines plus** Continental Express, CommutAir, Gulfstream International, bmi British Midland, Air Europa, COPA

- **Delta: All SkyTeam airlines plus** American Eagle, Atlantic Coast, Atlantic Southeast, Comair, SkyWest, Aerolitoral, Air Jamaica, British European, China Airlines (Taiwan), China Southern, Royal Air Maroc, South African

- **Frontier:** Great Lakes

- **Midwest Express:** Skyway Airlines, American Eagle

- **Northwest: All Wings airlines plus** Express Airlines, Mesaba, Trans States, Air China, Air Engiadina, Air Exel, Air UK, Alitalia, Eurowings, JAS, Kenya, Braathens, Korean, Malaysia, Transavia

- **United: All Star Alliance airlines plus** Air Wisconsin, Atlantic Coast Airlines, Great Lakes, SkyWest, UFS, ALM, Emirates, Spanair, Transportes Aeromar

- **US Airways:** CCAIR, Air Midwest, Colgan, Shuttle America, Chautauqua, Allegheny, Piedmont, PSA, Trans States, Deutsche BA

For a guide to frequent-flier partnerships, see chapter 8, "Sky Hounds".

7   QUESTIONS TO ASK BEFORE YOU BOOK

YOU CAN AVOID WASTING TIME AND MONEY IF YOU ASK a few key questions before you book your fare.

- **Confirmation and reconfirmation.** Must I reconfirm my reservation? How far in advance must I check in? Will my reservation be canceled if I fail to reconfirm or check in on time?

- **Delays and cancellations.** What does the airline owe me if my flight is canceled? Will I be guaranteed a spot on the next available flight at no additional charge? Will I be placed on another carrier if necessary at no extra cost? How much, if at all, will the airline pay for hotels, meals, and phone calls in the meantime?

- **Fares.** What are the penalties if I cancel? Am I able to get a refund if necessary? If so, what are the terms and conditions? How much extra will it cost if I lose or return my ticket, or if my ticket must be rewritten?

- **Baggage.** What are the rules regarding carry-on baggage and lost or mishandled luggage, beyond the federal guidelines for lost or mishandled luggage? (See chapter 4, "Lost in Space.") Will the airline be responsible for fragile checked items, such as skis or golf clubs?

- **Codesharing.** Will I fly any portions of my flight on a codeshare partner's aircraft? If so, how will that affect the principal airline's responsibility regarding confirmation and reconfirmation, cancellations and delays, fares, and lost or mishandled baggage? (For a discussion of codesharing and airline alliances, see "Allied Forces," earlier in this chapter.)

3

THE HOT SEAT: HOW TO PICK THE BEST SPOT ON THE PLANE

All airplane seats are not created equal. Even within the same plane, width and legroom can vary — never mind if you end up jammed between a smelly restroom and the food galley. Reservationists are supposed to ask your preference and offer you the best seats they can, but often they don't unless you speak up and request a particular seat or type of seat.

1 SITTING PRETTY: ADVICE FOR CHOOSING YOUR SPOT

TO HELP YOU PICK A PLACE FOR YOURSELF, THE SEATING plans for all major airlines are now online. You can dial up each airline's website, or alternately, About.com does a good job of collecting seat maps at http://airtravel.about.com/cs/airlineseatmaps/. If you don't know what kind of plane your flight is on, ask your travel agent or the airline.

KNOW YOUR TERMS: PITCH & WIDTH

The two most critical factors in airplane seating are **pitch,** otherwise known as legroom, and **seat width.** These vary from airline to airline, from plane to plane, and even from seat to seat on the same plane. For instance, on American Airlines Boeing 777 planes crossing the Atlantic, most of the seats in the rear cabin have 34 inches of legroom, but seats in the middle cabin only have 33. According to *Consumer Reports,* American Airlines has the best average legroom of the major carriers; United and Northwest have the worst.

Coach class seats generally vary from 17 to 18 inches in width—and that extra inch can make a big difference, comfort-wise. If that matters to you, fly Airbus planes with America West or American Airlines, 767s with United, or 777s with United and American.

LOOKING FOR LEGROOM?

Your best bet for legroom is the **emergency exit row.** Every plane has one or two, and the legroom can be vast. (However, in some plane models these seats do not recline; be sure to ask when you put in your request.) Emergency exit row seats are assigned first-come, first-serve at the airport to those who request them, though elite frequent fliers can usually reserve them in advance. In order to sit in the exit row, you must be over 15, fluent in English, and willing to help the crew in case of an emergency — which includes opening and hauling a 55-pound door.

Some aircraft have **magic seats,** which offer even more legroom than the usual exit-row seat. On a plane with two emergency-exit rows (usually 737s and 757s), the window seat of the second exit row often has no seat in front of it.

These are especially prevalent on America West, United, and Continental 737s, and even appear on Delta 727s. Check your airplane's seat map and look for a seat with a blank space in front of it. Then ask for that specific seat at the airport.

Bulkhead seats, in the front of the coach cabin or behind a partition, are a mixed deal. There's extra legroom *and*

You Don't Always Get What You Pay For

You'd think low-fare airlines would be cramped, but that's not always true. The seats on Southwest's 737-700 model planes and all Midwest Express planes are some of the roomiest coach seats in the industry, at 33 to 34 inches. Pan Am's seats are even more spacious, at 37 inches, but they have a very small route network. Other budget airlines match the big carriers' average, with 31 to 32 inches.

---

knee-room (no reclining seat in front of you), but there's no under-seat storage (so all of your goodies must go overhead), it may be difficult to see the in-flight movie, and most airlines seat babies and small children in the bulkhead area. Some planes, including Continental 737s and all Air Canada flights, have "soft dividers" in front of bulkheads that stop a little above the floor, giving travelers even more foot-level space.

American Airlines advertises "more room in coach," and they deliver — they've got the best legroom of any major domestic airline. **United**'s Economy Plus service for business travelers is even more spacious, but only elite frequent fliers and people with full-fare tickets can sneak into those seats.

DODGING THE MIDDLE

Middle seats are the bane of every traveler; you're often squeezed between two strangers and unable to stretch your legs or sleep. Of long-haul domestic planes, Boeing 767s have the fewest middle seats overall, according to *Consumer Reports Travel Letter;* 747s are chock-full of them.

But airlines leave middle seats empty whenever possible, giving window and aisle passengers more room to stretch out. Some aircraft layouts offer you a better chance of sitting next to an empty seat than others, according to *Consumer Reports.* If you're gunning to get two seats for the price of one, choose a plane with a 3-3, 3-3-3, or 3-4-3 configuration. Planes with

2-4-2 and 2-5-2 layouts offer the worst chance of having an empty seat next to you. If you end up in one of those planes, choose a **row with more than two seats** to maximize your chance of sitting next to an empty seat.

You can also try a **blocking strategy** to force an empty middle seat. If you're traveling with a friend in coach, ask for the window and aisle seats in a three-seat row. Even if the flight sells out, no one in his right mind would refuse a switch to an aisle or window so you can sit next to your companion.

On wide-bodied planes, try for **an aisle seat in a center section toward the back of coach,** as these seats are often assigned last, and you're more likely to score two for the price of one.

The only thing better than an empty middle seat is an empty middle seat with a raisable armrest, so you can really stretch out. (Armrests usually don't raise all the way, though, making it difficult for couples to cuddle up.) Of long-haul jets surveyed by *Consumer Reports Travel Letter,* Alaska Airlines Boeing 737 planes and all US Airways and American flights provide the most raisable armrests; all three have them on all rows except exit and bulkhead rows. (American's armrests are only on aisle seats; the other two airlines have them on all seats.) United and America West are by far the worst — United has no raisable armrests, and America West has one seat per plane, 6D. Airlines with raisable armrests will usually put you in one of those seats on request.

Window vs. Aisle Seating

This is the eternal choice. To go for the view or the easy escape?

- **In-flight snoozers** should pick window seats – they offer a solid surface to lean against.

- **Claustrophobes** and **people with small bladders** should choose aisle seats. Aisle seats have a bit more legroom, and you won't have to clamber over anyone else to get out.

WHICH IS THE SAFEST SEAT ON THE PLANE?

The short answer is, no magic seat will enable you to survive an accident. Because every crash is different, the government is unwilling to make generalizations. But safety experts have strong arguments that sitting in the rear of a plane may increase your chances of survival. The evidence:

- In an analysis of 30 fatal accidents between 1970 and 2000, Harro Ranter of aviation-safety.net found that rear seats were generally the safest — especially in landing-related crashes. (In takeoff-related crashes, front seats were just as safe.)

- The black box is in the rear of the airplane, notes Dan Rupp of Air Safety Online. "The tail portion of the airplane is most likely to survive" an accident, he says.

- Choosing an aisle seat near an exit (or in the emergency exit row) enables you to get out of the plane quickly in case of trouble, Rupp said.

STAYING SAFE & COMFORTABLE

Even if you've got an aisle seat, you can still have an uncomfortable flight if you're in the wrong part of the plane. Some seats don't recline, some are in high-traffic areas, and some are just more comfortable than others. A few tips:

- Exit row seats may have more legroom, but many do not recline. Seats in front of exit rows, and in the last row of any section, don't recline either. Your best bet is to ask for a reclining seat as close to the front of the plane as possible.

- The worst seats on the plane are **seats near bathrooms and galleys.** Even if you're flying with children, resist the temptation to get a seat near the bathroom, as the heavy traffic may outweigh the convenience. Instead, sit a few rows away on an aisle.

- Seats in the **rear of the plane** are noisier than those in the front, more prone to turbulence, and often smaller (if they're where the plane's body starts to narrow). Passengers sitting in the rear are also the last off the plane, which can be a problem if you're trying to make a tight connection.

- Seats with seat-back video screens, such as JetBlue's, are thicker than normal seats, according to Consumer Reports Travel Letter — so they cramp your style even more than usual when the person in front of you reclines.

2 SEAT ASSIGNMENT POLICIES FOR MAJOR DOMESTIC AIRLINES

AMERICAN

- **At booking:** Anyone can make a seat reservation; only elite members and non-elite status frequent fliers paying full coach fares may reserve seats in the front of the coach cabin, in an emergency-exit row, or in bulkhead.

- **At check-in** (up to 12 hr. before departure): Anyone can reserve any seat.

CONTINENTAL

- **At booking:** Anyone can reserve a seat; only elite members, the elderly, and disabled passengers can reserve bulkhead seats.

- **At check-in, 2 hours before departure:** Anyone may request emergency-exit or bulkhead seats.

DELTA

- **At booking:** Anyone can reserve a seat; exit rows are usually reserved for elite frequent fliers, but that policy is enforced at the gate agent's discretion. Bulkhead seats and those at the front of the cabin are held for passengers needing assistance or elite frequent fliers. Some seats are held back for day-of-departure assignment.

- **Four hours before departure:** Anyone can request a seat online or at the airport, though exit-row seats may only be requested at the airport.

NORTHWEST

- **At booking, if it's more than 90 days before the flight:** Only elite frequent fliers, disabled travelers, and travelers on full-fare coach tickets can request seats. Only disabled travelers and elite frequent fliers can request bulkhead seats; only elite frequent fliers can request exit-row seats.

- **90 days before departure:** Anyone can get a seat assignment. Some seats are held back for day-of-departure assignments.

- **At check-in (up to 6 hr. before departure):** Anyone may request any remaining seat.

SOUTHWEST

- There are no seat assignments on Southwest. Boarding group numbers are handed out an hour before the flight departs (though the line for group numbers begins forming much earlier). Passengers board in groups of 30.

UNITED

- **At booking:** Anyone can make a seat reservation, but only 60% to 70% of the seats on any given plane will be available to reserve. Other people will be stuck with an "aisle or window?" request. Bulkhead seats are usually reserved for disabled travelers, and only Premier Executive and 1K elite fliers can reserve exit rows.

- **The day before the flight:** At 6am, all seats except exit rows become available.

- **At check-in (up to 4 hr. before departure):** Anyone may request exit-row seats.

US AIRWAYS

- **At booking:** Anyone can make a seat reservation. Exit rows and the front of the coach cabin are reserved for elite frequent fliers. Some seats are held back for day-of-departure assignments.

- **At the airport, day of departure:** Anytime on the same day the flight is leaving, customers at the airport can receive seat assignments, including exit-row seats.

3 THE CLASS STRUGGLE

HOW WOULD YOU LIKE YOUR SEATS? GRIM AND tight — or plush and spacious?

The airlines would like you to think you get what you pay for. But of course that's not true. Rather, you get what you *fly* for. The cheapest tickets still garner the cheapest seats. But most first-class (and many business-class) passengers didn't pay more than coach fares for their lush accommodations. They upgraded — using miles, elite flier status, cash, or savvy negotiation when they were bumped. (See chapter 8, "Sky Hounds," for the upgrade policies of major domestic airlines.) Elite flier status, not wads of cash, is the way most domestic first-class passengers end up in their special seats, according to travel consultant and columnist Joe Brancatelli.

Moreover, paying more for a coach ticket certainly doesn't guarantee a nicer seat. Seats on budget carrier Southwest are roomier than many seats on full-fare airline Northwest. The plane model and the airline do matter; the amount you shelled out doesn't — unless you paid for a full-fare coach ticket, which can get you automatically upgraded to first class on US Airways or Continental.

Anyway, domestic first class is only a bit better than coach — not worth the extra money if you were going to pay for it, says Brancatelli. It's on international flights where class differences shine, and where you should save your frequent-flier miles for upgrades. Especially on foreign airlines, higher classes of international service offer amenities such as fold-down beds, private rooms, showers, extensive entertainment systems, and freshening-up lounges at your destination to make sure you arrive in top shape.

COACH: THE CINDERELLA CLASS

"Airbus" isn't just a European aircraft manufacturer. It's also a description of the way toward which coach-class cabins have been tending over the past decade. Seats have gotten tighter, service poorer, and the general experience closer and closer to riding Greyhound.

The reason is economic — although coach-class passengers are by far the majority of fliers, airlines feel like they don't make enough money on them to warrant treating them as anything more than cattle.

The truly sad folks are the business travelers in the coach cabin, who can find themselves paying $1,000 for the same cramped, miserable experience for which others pay $250. During the first quarter of 2002, for instance, passengers flying from Boston to Detroit could find themselves paying anywhere from $100 to $650 for a round-trip. Fliers heading from San Francisco to Washington, DC, paid anywhere from $150 to $1,200. The only difference between these fliers' experiences? Lighter wallets and a sense of dismay.

✐ NO-NONSENSE ADVICE FOR FLYING IN COMFORT

- **Dress sensibly.** Wear layers of comfortable clothes in natural fabrics. The climate in airplane cabins is unpredictable. You'll be glad to have a sweater or jacket to put on or take off as the on-board temperature dictates. Natural fabrics, as you probably know, breathe better than synthetics, and will help you adapt more readily to shifts in temperature. You'll also be better off in an emergency: Synthetics may melt and stick to the skin in the case of a cabin fire.

- **Choose comfy shoes.** For maximum comfort, you'll probably want to kick off your shoes before takeoff. Nevertheless, it's wise to wear comfortable footwear, since your legs and feet are bound to swell during air travel. If you have to squeeze back into stiletto pumps, surely you'll be pining for your Hush Puppies. (See "Economy-Class Syndrome" in chapter 6.)

- **Moisturize, brush, and lubricate.** Airplane cabins are notoriously dry places – with less humidity than air in the Sahara. Take a travel-size bottle of moisturizer or lotion to refresh your face and hands at the end of the flight. If you're taking an overnight flight (the red-eye), don't forget to pack a toothbrush. If you wear contact lenses, take them out before you get on board and wear glasses instead. Or at least bring eyedrops.

It's possible to escape from coach, if you fly quite a bit; most airlines allow frequent fliers to buy upgrades for miles or cash, and offer some sort of upgrade package for elite fliers.

- **Brown-bag it.** If you know your plane will still be airborne come mealtime, pack some food in your carry-on bag. You may cause a bidding war on the plane for your homemade sandwich and some truly fresh fruit – but many travelers would rather fight than digest airline food. If your preflight schedule won't allow you time for food preparation, leave yourself at least enough time to buy a sandwich at the airport.

- **Drink up.** Bring bottled water on board and drink plenty of it before, during, and after your flight. When you're on a plane, your skin evaporates as much as 8 ounces of water per hour. (For more information, see "Dehydration" in chapter 6.)

- **Keep your blood flowing.** Circulation slows when you sit for extended periods of time. Get up and walk around as often as you can while you're in the air. Try some stretching exercises near the lavatory, if there isn't a line. Also check out some of the neat little exercises you can perform inconspicuously from your seat. (See "Economy-Class Syndrome" in chapter 6.)

- **Try to catch some z's.** See "Snooze Boosters & Other Tools of the Flying Trade" in chapter 7, "Beat the Clock," for pillows, eyeshades, and other paraphernalia that will help you relax during your flight.

Things are a little brighter on international flights, where foreign airlines can deliver service that just might make you think they actually value you as a customer.

LEGROOM IN COACH ON DOMESTIC AIRLINES

PLANE MODEL	PITCH IN INCHES	WIDTH IN INCHES
Alaska		
737	32	17
MD-80	32	17.75
America West		
757-200	32	17-18
A319-100	32	18
A320-200	32	18
American		
767-200	33-34	17
777-200	31-32	18.5
A300-600	33-35	18
Continental		
767	32	17.9
777-200	31	17.9
DC-10-30	31	17.9
Delta		
767-200	31-33	17.7
767-300	31-33	17.7
767-300ER	31-32	17.7
767-400ER	31-33	17-18
777-200	31-33	17
MD-11	31-33	18

Virgin Atlantic was one pioneer of classy transatlantic discount coach service, with decent food, good music on the inflight stereo, and seat-back video systems with a wide selection of movies and Nintendo games. Airlines flying Boeing 777 planes, including United, American, and British Airways, have added seat-back video screens to coach class. Several Asian airlines, most notably Singapore, have award-winning service and a range of entertainment options in the coach section. But the seats will feel pretty cramped on those long trans-oceanic flights, and coach-class passengers should remember to get up and move around to prevent "economy-class syndrome" (see chapter 6, "Life Preservers").

PLANE MODEL	PITCH IN INCHES	WIDTH IN INCHES
Northwest		
747-200	31-34	17.17
747-400	31-32	17.17
DC-10	30-32	17.17
Southwest		
Most 737s	32-33	17.25
737-700	33-34	17.25
United		
747-400	31	17
767-200	32-33	18
767-300	31	18
777	31-32	18
US Airways		
767-200	31-32	17
A330-300	33-34	17

Source: Consumer Reports Travel Letter, July 2001; Southwest data from the airline.

So What's the Silver Lining?

Some carriers have taken pity on the poor peons in coach by supplying them with roomier seats or extra amenities. While no one's turning pumpkins into glass carriages just yet, these innovations make flying steerage a tiny bit more manageable.

DOMESTIC FLIGHTS When **American Airlines** says "more room in coach," they mean it. They ripped four rows out of each of their planes to give everyone else more breathing room. That's a daring and unmatched move — and space-sensitive fliers should reward them by jumping aboard.

Oddly, only two "budget" airlines — **Southwest** on their 737-700 planes and **Midwest Express** — come near

Entertain Yourself

To make coach a little more like business class, bring your own entertainment. InMotion Pictures (www.inmotionpictures.com) rents portable DVD players and movies at 14 U.S. airports and Vancouver, Canada. For $19.95 you get a player with 4 hours of battery life plus one movie (extra movies are $4). When you get to your destination, drop the player off at a UPS counter within 24 hours. Their cheaper in-airport-only rental plan is great for surviving long delays.

American's standard legroom. **United** established an "Economy Plus" class at the front of their economy cabins with more legroom, but the tickets cost extra.

JetBlue has gone another direction, aiming to distract passengers with seat-back satellite TVs at no extra charge.

INTERNATIONAL FLIGHTS This is where airlines have spent their money, and where you'll see the biggest changes if you haven't flown in a couple of years. **Seat-back video screens** are spreading like wildfire — they're built into Boeing 777 planes, and American, Continental, United, and US Airways all offer them on at least some planes of various makes and models. Foreign airlines are even farther ahead; British Airways and Virgin Atlantic offer 12 and 28 video channels, respectively, on their screens, and Virgin also offers Nintendo games.

Seatwise, British Airways' World Traveller Economy Class has footrests, an extra inch of knee space, contour in the lower back area to ensure extra lumbar support, and headrest wings to make it less likely that your noggin will flop around if you nod off. United is offering an S-back coach seat contoured for extra lower-back support and adjustable wings on its headrests so you can nap more comfortably, and American's roomier seats also have headrests.

BUSINESS CLASS: THE TOP BANANAS

Most domestic routes offer "two-class" service — coach and first — and domestic first class is inferior to international business class. (United and Delta offer three classes of service on cross-country flights.)

But airline consultant, travel columnist, and frequent flier Joe Brancatelli says the best domestic business class is the coach-class service on Midwest Express. The small, Milwaukee-based airline's award-winning food, quality service, and comfortable seats provide whopping value for money, he said. He gives a thumbs-down to Northwest, which charges business-class fares for seats that can be the same 34-inch pitch that Midwest Express and American offer in coach.

Internationally, of course, you'll see more plush accommodations. British Airways set a new standard in 2001 with fully-flat seats in business class, an idea also picked up by Singapore Airlines and Cathay Pacific. On long flights, these seats turn into beds, an amenity normally reserved for first-class passengers. But there's one peculiarity on BA's beds — fliers sit facing another person, and when both beds in a row are down, your head is directly opposite someone else's feet.

Even though most other airlines don't supply business-class beds, international business-class seats generally recline 150 to 160 degrees — enough for a good lie-down. Most international business-class sections give travelers 45 to 50 inches of legroom, compared to the usual 31 to 32 inches in coach. And business class seats are usually equipped with laptop power ports (though you need to buy a special adapter yourself).

Continental's international business class is the best of the U.S. airlines, Brancatelli said. That airline is part of the trend to eliminate first class in exchange for "BusinessFirst" service, which is either a roomy business class or a pathetic first class service, depending on how you look at it. Delta and Northwest have also dropped first class in exchange for beefing up business class.

Though business class costs less than first-class service, the price is still nothing to sneeze at. Business fares can cost as much as $550 to $800 for domestic hops under 500 miles (805km); $1,100 to $2,000 for cross-country domestic trips; and a whopping $5,000 to $6,000 for transatlantic travel.

FIRST CLASS: FIRST IN COMFORT

Nap time.

The big trend in international first class seats nowadays is the "full-flat" seat, which turns into a bed so travelers can get some serious ZZZs. Many airlines also provide privacy dividers, which turn first-class seats into their own little rooms. Laptop power ports, satellite phones, and multi-channel entertainment systems with at least 10 movies on demand are also de rigueur.

Food on international first-class flights is still reheated in the airplane's galley, but is often designed by world-class chefs and always served with better-caliber wines on "real" plates with actual utensils. First class menus on foreign airlines often feature delicious ethnic cuisine, one of many reasons to consider non-U.S. carriers for international trips.

Virgin Atlantic's Upper Class is an excellent example of an international first-class offering. Travelers are ferried to the airport in a complimentary chauffeur-driven car (or, because Virgin is a hip and happening airline, a complimentary chauffeur-driven motorcycle.) At the airport, Upper Class passengers relax in a reserved lounge with free food, drinks, and newspapers. On board, the Upper Class cabin is decked out with a step-up bar, a professional masseuse, and feather duvets on the full-flat seats. Feel peckish? You can ask for full meals any time.

Not to be outdone, British Airways outfits its similar first-class offering (called FIRST) with separate wine and cappuccino bars and a spa featuring washrooms, steam rooms, and a massage room.

The average first-class seat is usually at least 22 inches wide (4 in. more than coach seats), with between 60 and 90 inches of legroom — up to three times that of economy class!

But you get what you pay for — a first-class ticket on average costs 10 times more than an economy fare. That said, relatively few of the folks in first class actually *pay* for it. First class is a reward for elite frequent fliers, for regular frequent fliers who purchase upgrades, and for bumped passengers — which is the way you'll most likely see the comfort of a first-class seat.

Domestic first class is nowhere near international standards. First-class passengers generally get priority check-in, boarding, and baggage delivery after the flight. But the seats are generally inferior even to international business class. (United's transcontinental first class is an exception, with 60-in. seat pitch and a selection of 10 videos.) Most airlines have cut back on food service even in first class, and thanks to security restrictions, you'll be eating with plastic knives. At least the drinks flow free and fast. Even on US Airways' 20-minute Philadelphia–New York leg, which is such a short flight the plane never breaks 8,000 feet (2,400m), flight attendants manage to squeeze in both preflight and in-flight drinks.

4

Lost in Space: How to Cope with Baggage Snafus

Your luggage sits on the front lines in the war against terrorism — poked, prodded, and suspiciously analyzed now more than ever before. Stringent carry-on restrictions are inconvenient, and capricious enforcement of the rules can be infuriating. But believe it or not, there is an up side. Baggage regulations adopted post–September 11, 2001, may have been drafted to help make the U.S. skies safer for flying, but these measures have had unintended positive effects. Overhead bins are emptier thanks to fewer carry-on bags, and evidence indicates that the new rules will go a long way toward decreasing the number of lost or misrouted bags.

1 Today's Realities

MANY OF THE POST–SEPTEMBER 11TH BAGGAGE REGU-lations adopted in the U.S. have been in place at European airports for years. Though checked baggage did not play a role in the September 11th attacks, it has been used as a ter-rorist weapon before; a bomb in the cargo hold caused the crash of Pan Am Flight 103 over Lockerbie, Scotland, in 1988.

In the wake of that crash, the U.S. government began matching every bag on an international flight to a passenger who had boarded the plane, which they now do by checking computer records of baggage tags against records of boarding cards that were scanned at the gate.

WHAT'S BEING DONE?

In 2002, such bag matching procedures were extended to nonstop flights within the U.S. as well. This security measure is expected to reduce the number of lost and misrouted bags, because someone will be double-checking that you and your bag are on the same plane.

However, the plan does not yet extend to checking bags on multiple or connecting flights, which means there's as great a chance as ever of bags going astray if you change planes at any point during your trip.

By the end of 2002, all U.S. airports will be required to match bags with passengers on connecting flights and to check all bags for explosives, by using some combination of explosive-detection machines, X-ray machines, hand searches, or bomb-sniffing dogs. (Airports in Great Britain, Germany, and Israel have been doing this for years.) The newly created Transportation Security Administration (TSA) will work with individual airports to set the pace of the rollout. The law stipulates that by December 31, 2002, all bags must be screened for explosives *at least* by machine; other methods (like hand inspection and dog sniffing) will only be supplementary "second opinions" after the required machine check. TSA spokesman Paul Turk said in a March 2002 interview that while at least 75 of the nation's 429 commercial airports already have explosive detection machines, new system and procedures will be tested first in 15 airports: Anchorage, Atlanta, Boston Logan, BWI, Charlotte, Chicago O'Hare, Dallas–Fort Worth, Grand Rapids, New York JFK,

Louisville, Minneapolis, Mobile, Orlando, San Francisco, and Spokane.

But the practical implication of such a plan is providing to be a logistical and financial nightmare, According to a March 2002 Associated Press story, the nation's airports are looking at renovation costs in excess of $2 billion to make room for new machines. At press time, a bill was pending in Congress that would require the TSA to pay for the renovations, though it was unclear whether the proposal would actually make it through both chambers to become law. Whoever ends up footing the bill, airport executives (in conjunction with the TSA) have yet to decide where in the airports the machines will go and what the exact screening procedures will entail. And airport officials are adamant that it will be impossible to complete such sweeping changes by the December 31 deadline.

The airlines themselves warn that the new measures will likely cause extensive flight delays. But news reports and anecdotal evidence in the weeks and months following the initial post-9/11 security crackdown indicated that no appreciable rise in delays has been detected. In fact, delays fell below pre-9/11 levels simply because fewer flights were in the air. Even the institution of bag-matching procedures in February 2002 failed to significantly increase the number of delays. So whether these dire predictions will come true after another round of security changes is yet to be determined.

HOW WILL NEW LAWS AFFECT YOU?

Of the new regulations, two rules will most affect air travelers. One is the "one carry-on only" restriction. Another is the list of items prohibited from the passenger cabin.

Travelers are now restricted, nationwide, to **one carry-on bag per person.** (For more about carry-ons, see "Carry-on Conundrums," below.) International flights departing the U.S. are included in this rule. Though instituted to speed

TOP 5 CARRY-ON BAGS

MODEL	PRICE	DURABILITY	FEATURES	EASE OF USE
Atlantic Professional 2520*	$170	Excellent	Excellent	Very Good
Delsey Horizon 61274*	$170	Excellent	Excellent	Very Good
Victorinox Travel Gear Medium Mobilizer 34011	$335	Excellent	Very Good	Very Good
Tumi Fold-a-Way 2222	$450	Excellent	Good	Very Good
J.C. Penney Protocol Business Gear II 047-5353*	$125	Very Good	Very Good	Very Good

*Denotes a Consumer Reports *Best Buy*
Source: Consumer Reports, *December 2001.*

up security lines, it has the beneficial effect of minimizing competition for overhead bin space that was commonplace at a time when travelers boarded a plane juggling as many bags as they could sneak past the gate attendants.

Along with your carry-on, you may bring one "personal item," such as a purse, briefcase, laptop computer, child safety seat, diaper bag, or small holiday gift. Coats, umbrellas, canes, reading material, and things you stuff into your coat pockets don't count toward this allowance.

Expect to have your luggage searched at every turn, so pack in a way that makes repacking simple. Don't wrap gifts until you get to your destination — security officials might unwrap them during an inspection. (For more packing tips, see "Baggage Tips for Smart Travelers," and "The Well-Packed Bag," below.)

A long list of items — mostly cutting instruments and sports equipment — are newly banned from planes. (See "Banned Baggage," below.) Be smart; keep sharp or metallic toiletries in your checked luggage.

2 CARRY-ON CONUNDRUMS

FED UP WITH THE ESCALATING RATES OF LOST BAGGAGE, frustrated fliers at the end of the 20th century tried to haul as much as they could on board with them. No more — only one carry-on bag for you! Maximum carry-on sizes vary slightly by airline, but all will accept bags of 22×14×9 inches, including wheels and handles, that weigh no more than 40 pounds. Some commuter and prop planes require carry-on bags to be smaller; if you're flying on such a plane, ask your airline what the size and weight restrictions are.

Many airports now have templates at the X-ray machines that force carry-on bags to conform to the size requirements of the dominant carrier at that airport. At press time, these

---

TUNE IN, BUT KNOW WHEN TO TURN OFF

Airlines welcome "electronic devices" such as CD players, video games, and laptop computers aboard planes. But they tell passengers to turn them off during the takeoff and landing phases, for fear that radio signals leaking from the devices would interfere with navigational equipment. No instance of a CD player or Game Boy interfering with a plane has ever been reported, but the airlines take a "better safe than sorry" attitude.

Cell phones are another concern entirely. Designed to be used on the ground, they wreak havoc in the air, contacting several cell towers at once and potentially disrupting wireless calls for dozens of miles around. As radio transmitters, they have much more potential than CD players to cause havoc with a plane's systems. **Never make a cell phone call** on an airborne plane. Airline rules stipulate that you only turn on your phone when the plane is parked at the gate, but using it any time after landing won't cause damage.

---

restrictions included: 22×14×9 inches in Chicago (United); and 24×16×10 inches at Dallas Love Field (Southwest), St. Louis (American, formerly TWA), and Atlanta (Delta). Now that the federal government as assumed responsibility for airport security — the newly created Transportation Security Administration (TSA) assumed management in February 2002 — it's unclear what the feds will do with these templates.

The "one carry-on only" rule has made it easier to find space in overhead bins, but now that compact wheeled suitcases are the norm among frequent fliers, space still may be tight on your flight. If you're one of the last to board a full plane, toss your bag into the first empty coach-class overhead bin you see, even if it's not near your seat — you can always get it when you leave.

Crew members used to make exceptions to the carry-on guidelines, but the one-bag rule is now an FAA restriction, so despite erratic enforcement of the rule, expect no mercy.

3 BANNED BAGGAGE

AFTER THE EVENTS OF SEPTEMBER 11, A RASH OF items were banned from the passenger cabins of airplanes, as officials tried to prevent any potential weapons from getting on board. **All cutting instruments,** including those keychain-size Swiss Army knives, are now prohibited in carry-on baggage. If an item is confiscated at the security checkpoint, you'll never see it again, so if you have a knife or a cigarette lighter with sentimental value, put it in your checked baggage or leave it at home.

Unfortunately, despite the fairly straightforward FAA regulations, overzealous security personnel have been known to confiscate *specifically permitted* items like nail clippers and tweezers. To be safe, don't put anything with an edge on it or anything that could start a fire in your carry-on bag. Laptop computers, of course, should always be carried on, as they need to be treated gingerly.

The following items are specifically **permitted** in carry-on luggage:

- Nail clippers.

- Safety razors.

- Syringes (with an original pharmacy prescription label).

- Medication and medical devices, except oxygen.

- Tweezers.

- Eyelash curlers.

- Canes.

- Umbrellas.

- Cameras and film. It's always a good idea to take film in carry-on baggage, as the machines used to screen checked luggage may damage film. You are allowed to request a hand inspection of your film and cameras; photography experts recommend doing so if you're carrying film of 400 ISO speed or higher.

These items have been **banned** from the passenger cabin:

- Cutting instruments of any size, shape, or material.

- Corkscrews.

- Metal scissors.

- Metal nail files.

- Straight razors.

- "Strike-anywhere" matches.

- Knitting needles (even small, plastic "circular needles").

- Baseball bats, golf clubs, and pool cues.

- Mace or pepper spray.

- Any hand or power tools.

- Ski poles and hockey sticks.

- Toy weapons.

Many common household items that you use safely every day at home or in the office — paint, adhesives, bleach, and cigarette lighters, for example — become potentially dangerous cargo in an airplane cabin. During flight, shifts in air

---

✒ POST–SEPTEMBER 11 SUITCASES & HOW THEY WORK FOR YOU

Long waits at security checkpoints. Stricter carry-on restrictions. Luggage often unpacked and micro-inspected at the X-ray machine. Suitcase companies have been quick to recognize and respond to these new security issues with new and redesigned models that should make a post–September 11 traveler's life smoother.

Among the innovations are padded seats attached to carry-on luggage, see-through interior compartments for faster, tidier security inspections, and carry-on bags with built-in laptop cases, to get around that pesky "one carry-on only" rule. The Silhouette 7 Hardside Carry-On Upright Suiter With Comfort Seat, from Samsonite ($380; ☎ **800/262-8282** for a dealer near you) has inline-skate wheels for easy rolling and a padded seat that you can attach to the top of the upended bag when you need to take a load off. Travelpro's roomy Overnighter Expandable Carryon ($39.25 from QVC, Item #F28894; ☎ **888/345-5788** or www. QVC.com), comes with six clear plastic interior compartments. And the travel merchandise specialists at Magellan's (☎ **800/ 962-4943;** www.magellans.com) sell a wide assortment of packing supplies – anything from vacuum-sealed plastic bags for compressing clothes space to "packing cubes" that help organize items inside your suitcase.

pressure and temperature may cause these items to leak, generate toxic fumes, or ignite.

Other no-nos (some obvious, some not) include: fireworks, including signal flares, sparklers, and other explosives; fuel; cigarette lighters with a flammable liquid reservoir and lighter refills; household cleaners such as polishes, waxes, drain cleaners, and bleach; solvents; insecticides and pesticides; lighter fluid; poisons; flammable gases, liquids, or solids such as paint, paint thinners, lighter fluid, and adhesives; explosives; corrosives such as wet-cell batteries and acids; oxidizing materials; radioactive materials such as uninstalled pacemakers; mercury, including thermometers; briefcases with installed alarm devices; magnetic materials; pressurized containers such as tear gas, oxygen, scuba tanks, aerosol spray cans, butane fuel, CO_2 cartridges, self-inflating rafts, and propane tanks; mace; gun powder and ammunition; pepper spray; dry ice; camping equipment with fuel; and gasoline powered tools such as chain saws or lawn mowers.

Sporting guns are allowed in checked baggage, but they must be declared in accordance with international regulations. They also must be unloaded and packed in hard-sided containers or in a crush-proof case manufactured especially for shipment by air. Containers with handguns must be locked.

4 BAGGAGE TIPS FOR SMART TRAVELERS

FOLLOW THESE STEPS TO MINIMIZE BAGGAGE HASSLES and avoid misrouted luggage:

- **Take nonstop flights.** Your bag will be matched with your boarding pass on a nonstop flight, but if you're traveling before the end of 2002, it won't be matched on a connecting flight — giving it an opportunity to get lost.

- **Double-check your luggage tags** to make certain the flight number and airport code are correct. Make sure the stub you're given is accurate.

- In case your bags are lost, you'll increase your chances of recovering them quickly if you **mark them clearly with your name and a phone number** before you check them. But don't use your home address and phone number — thieves have been known to cruise airports, checking tags to see who's not home. An office address or wireless phone number is perfect.

- Get in the habit of **removing old tags** as soon you return from a trip, so your next destination is perfectly clear to frenzied luggage handlers.

- Confusion is all too likely in a crowded baggage-claim area. Avoid losing your goods in the shuffle by buying **brightly colored tags,** especially if your luggage is black — or better yet, opt for **brightly colored bags** — so you can identify your suitcases immediately and reduce the chance of a stranger walking off with them.

- **Don't bring your favorite things.** That $60 gold nail clipper may be confiscated by security, and heirlooms in your checked luggage may get stolen or lost.

- **Pack essential items** — a single change of clothes, prescription medications, anything that's not verboten — **in a regulation-size carry-on bag,** in case your checked luggage disappears.

Some tips for choosing a durable checked bag:

- You'll reduce the risk of damage to your luggage if you look for bags with **cushioned handles,** reinforced with **metal and double rivets.** Avoid bags with handles attached by single rivets.

- Avoid bags with loose stitching. The **tighter the stitches,** the more durable the bag.

- Look for luggage with **recessed wheels,** as these are least likely to snag or break.

TOP 5 LARGE WHEELED UPRIGHT SUITCASES

MODEL	PRICE	DURABILITY	FEATURES	EASE OF USE
Travelpro Platinum II 9926-01	$350	Very Good	Excellent	Very Good
Travelpro Crew4 7126-01*	$240	Very Good	Excellent	Very Good
Pathfinder TX2 9826	$340	Very Good	Very Good	Very Good
Delsey Horizon 61277 NO	$200	Good	Excellent	Very Good
Lands' End Check-Thru 6134-3AJ9	$250	Very Good	Very Good	Very Good

Source: Consumer Reports, *December 2001.*

Denotes a Consumer Reports *Best Buy*

Note: Consumer Reports *performed a series of trials to test each bag. Each was put in a large, rotating steel drum and tumbled 1,000 times to mimic the punishment it would get at the hands of baggage handlers. A test panel of two men and three women dragged each bag over carpet, concrete, and tile, and up and down curbs. Finally, each bag was scrutinized for features like pockets, handles, and expansion chambers.*

- **Check the bindings.** If space between the seam and binding is narrow, it's less likely to hold when stretched.

- **Zippers** that are **large and far from the edge** are less likely to break.

- While leather bags are beautiful, they're also weighty — not to mention expensive looking, and more likely to be stolen. A **good, sturdy nylon** is much stronger and lighter. Look for nylons with 430 denier or more, such as **bomb cloth, Cordura,** and **ballistic nylon.** Cheaper nylons or polyester are more likely to tear.

- If you want a shoulder bag, be sure to find one with a **wide, padded strap** for comfortable carrying.

- If you're looking for a carry-on with wheels, look for a **long handle.** Drag the bag around the store before you buy it, to make sure you can manage it comfortably. Place some things inside and turn a few corners to test maneuverability and balance.

- A **piggyback strap** on a wheeled bag will let you yoke your attaché or large purse to your suitcase and wheel it along.

- **Pockets,** both inside and outside, almost always come in handy. *Consumer Reports* especially recommends a waterproof pouch for soggy bathing suits.

5 THE WELL-PACKED BAG

CAREFUL WARDROBE PLANNING IS THE FOUNDATION of an efficiently packed bag. You'll get the most mileage from your selections if you stick to solid, neutral colors that you can mix and match. Keep prints and wacky colors to a minimum.

You may want to leave linen garments at home — unless you plan to spend a good part of your trip ironing. Obviously, it's best to stick to fabrics that won't wrinkle.

If your luggage barely holds the clothes you think you'll need, consider wearing your bulkiest shoes and clothes, so you won't have to squeeze them into your luggage. Carry your umbrella, coat, camera, and reading material outside your luggage. The airlines don't count these items as carry-ons, so you can tote them without forfeiting luggage space. Some carry-on bags, such as the Travelpro Rollaboard, feature a metal hook for items like these.

A PECK OF PACKING TIPS

- Pack your bag so it can be **easily repacked.** If you're pulled aside for a hand search of your luggage, you don't want your underwear flying into the air as if from a jack-in-the-box.

- **Leave gifts unwrapped** or security officers will likely unwrap them.

- If you can, use a **top-loading bag** with a frame. The shape of a top-loader lets stacked clothes stay stacked, keeping them neat. Unfortunately, top-loaders are expensive.

- Pack your bags on a **hard surface.** This will help you to fill corners and distribute the weight of your belongings evenly throughout the bag.

- **Fold shirts below the waist.** If they crease in transit, you can tuck the wrinkles away

- **Turn jackets or blazers inside out** before you pack them.

- To avoid wrinkles, **wrap your clothes in plastic.** Lay down a big plastic bag from the dry-cleaners, then lay down a folded garment on top of it. Fold or roll the plastic bag so it's encasing the garment. Do this with all of your clothes and put them in your suitcase so two garments are never touching; there's always a layer of plastic between them. Or, fold your garments around a large piece of tissue paper and put the folded garments into plastic bags.

- If you don't have plastic or tissue paper, **fold your clothes in overlapping layers,** so they cushion each other. For instance, lay pants on the bottom of the suitcase. Place the top half of a sweater over the top of the pants. Fold the bottom half of the pants over the sweater, and the bottom half of the sweater over the pants.

- If you can live with a few minor wrinkles, **roll your clothes.** You'll be able to pack them much tighter, and they will not crease.

- **Bring wrinkle-free clothing.** Tilley (☎ **800/363-8737;** www.tilley.com) and TravelSmith (☎ **800/950-1600;** www.travelsmith.com) are two companies who cater to this market. Image advisor Eve Roth of Savvy Style, who travels frequently between Hong Kong and the U.S. on business, says women should check out TravelSmith's "Indispensable Black Travel Dress" — it's comfortable and resists wrinkles.

- **Seal toiletries in resealable plastic bags.** Don't fill liquid bottles to capacity, or they'll be more likely to leak. Fill them partially and squeeze out the excess air before you close them, which will create a vacuum seal.

- **Pack accessories on the sides.** Put your socks in your shoes, and your shoes in a plastic bag. Pack underwear and scarves in plastic bags as well. Put shoes on the bottom or edges of your suitcase — never put the weight of shoes on top of your clothes. Place toiletries on the top edge of your suitcase, near the handle.

- If your suitcase isn't very full, consider **stuffing in a few towels** to fill up space and prevent contents from shifting.

- If you run out of space, zip your suitcase and **drop it on the floor.** Repeat this until the contents settle and free up space.

- If you absolutely must have neatly pressed clothing for your trip, consider purchasing a **travel iron. Travel Smart** makes a 1½-pound model with a retractable handle that folds flat and packs easily. It's available from Magellan's for $36.85 (☎ **800/962-4943;** www.magellans.com).

KEEPING YOUR BAG SECURE

If you really want to seal your bags, try shrink-wrapping them. Kiosks in the international terminals at Los Angeles, Miami,

San Francisco, Oakland, and San Jose and in Terminal 8 of New York's JFK airport offer a service whereby your bags are sealed in up to eight layers of cling wrap, with holes cut for handles and wheels. Wrapping costs $6 for most suitcases (but $10–$15 in Los Angeles). The plastic sticks to itself like Saran Wrap and protects hard-sided bags from scratches, dirt, and bursting in transit — not to mention from prying fingers.

Travelers who aren't using the above airports can wrap bags themselves. Buy industrial stretch film from a packaging store, a moving company, or an online shop such as PackagingPrice (☎ 888/236-1729; www.packagingprice.com). In theory, you could even use Saran Wrap, but industrial stretch film is much cheaper in large quantities. Beware that all of your luggage-wrapping efforts will be for naught if a security official decides to pull you out of the line to peer into your bag. Also, stretch wrap isn't exactly environmentally friendly.

Plastic film will only protect hard-sided luggage. Duffel or backpack owners can wrap their bags in steel mesh provided by Pac-Safe (☎ 800/873-9415; www.pac-safe.com). The reusable, $50 to $70 bag security kits are knife-proof and let you lock your bag to stationary objects while you sleep or go to the bathroom.

LOST LUGGAGE RATES BY AIRLINE

AIRLINE	BAGS LOST PER 1,000 PASSENGERS IN 2001
Alaska Airlines	3.00
US Airways	3.86
Delta Air Lines	4.11
Northwest Airlines	4.19
America West Airlines	4.22
Continental Airlines	4.29
American Airlines	4.60
Southwest Airlines	4.77
United Airlines	5.07

Source: Department of Transportation. 2001 data excludes Sept 11–30.

6   THE BOTTOM LINE: WHAT DO THE AIRLINES OWE YOU?

WHILE STILL LAMENTABLE, THE LOST-LUGGAGE SITUATION has improved from the awful years of 1999 and 2000. In 2000, major airlines lost or damaged one bag for every 189 passengers; by 2001, the rate had improved to 219 passengers per mishandled bag.

That's still too many bags going astray. Fortunately, if your luggage is lost, the airline is required to pay you for your missing property. But you'll rarely get the full value of your baggage back.

For most airlines, you must report delayed, damaged, or lost baggage to an airline representative at the airport within 4 hours of arrival; US Airways, United, and American give you 24 hours. If you can't find an airline representative, all the major U.S. airlines except Alaska and Southwest have "baggage hot lines" you can call to get help.

LOST & MISROUTED LUGGAGE

On flights within the U.S., airlines are responsible for lost-luggage reimbursement up to $2,500 per person; on international flights, airlines owe you a mere $9.07 per pound, with a ceiling of $640. (That rate was set by an international treaty in 1929.)

Beyond that, airlines owe you nothing for your most valuable items. Most contracts of carriage specifically exempt

---

AIRLINE BAGGAGE HOT LINES

America West	☎ 800/235-9292
American	☎ 800/535-5225
Continental	☎ 800/335-BAGS
Delta	☎ 800/325-8224
Northwest	☎ 800/648-4897
United	☎ 800/221-6903
US Airways	☎ 800/371-4771

from compensation things like antiques, art, books, documents, money, cameras, collectibles, electronics, or "fragile or perishable items." If you're traveling with anything you really care about, bring it in a carry-on or purchase additional luggage insurance.

If your luggage is delayed, airlines' customer service commitments require them to call you daily for at least 5 days while they search for the bags; they'll also deliver them to your house or destination free of charge (although this takes some arm-twisting sometimes — if they want you to come to the airport to pick the bag up, politely decline and remind them that they were in the wrong). Alaska and Continental will give you free toiletry kits if your bags are delayed. Alaska, Northwest, United, and US Airways will also reimburse some small clothing and toiletry expenses, usually $50 plus $25 per day for each day after the first, up to a total of $150. (US Airways throws in an extra $25 travel voucher; United only promises it will reimburse 50% of the price of "reasonable purchases.") Ask the airline representative at the airport for specific information.

After 5 days, responsibility for lost bags passes from the individual airports to the airlines' central baggage services. Request the new phone number from the baggage hot line; you may also have to file a request in writing within 21, 30, or 45 days to get your money. Don't wait; file it as soon as you can. If you don't have receipts to prove the value of the items you lost, airlines request that you provide a list of all items in the lost bag, when and where they were purchased, and how much they coast at the time of purchases. You'll also need to send copies of your ticket and baggage claim check.

Airlines' customer service policies also require that they respond to your lost-baggage claim within 30 days. If they haven't cut a check within a month of your claim, get on the phone with the airline's customer relations department. (See chapter 10 for tips on how to complain effectively.)

If you are flying in segments on two different airlines, the final carrier is responsible for lost or damaged luggage — even when they can prove the first airline is to blame. If your luggage is lost or damaged on international flights with a domestic segment, however, you will receive only the lower international reimbursement. When you're booking a segmented flight, allow yourself at least an hour between connections. Your bags, like you, will be more likely to reach their destination at the scheduled time.

The airlines are not responsible for the theft of individual items from checked luggage, though you can try filing a damaged-bag claim. Baggage handlers will hopefully receive additional scrutiny under the new security laws, but in the past there have been several incidents of airport employees helping themselves to travelers' goods. Lock your bag — and if you can, shrink-wrap it or enclose it in metal mesh (see "Keeping Your Bag Secure," above). **Magellan's Travel Supplies** (☎ **800/962-4943;** www.magellans.com) sells an exceptionally strong and reliable combination lock by Prestolock, for $9.85.

DAMAGED LUGGAGE

Airlines aren't responsible for "normal wear and tear" to luggage, and may try to interpret "normal wear and tear" as "Bruno the Baggage Handler tap-dancing on your suitcase." No offense to Bruno, but your best bet is to buy sturdy, dull luggage. (Flashy, expensive bags tend to be less durable and also make you a target for thieves.) If your bags are damaged in transit, alert the airline's staff to the problem before leaving the airport, They may require that their own staff inspect the damage within 24 hours of the bag's arrival.

LAST RECOURSES

If all of this has made you determined to never put a bag on an airport conveyor belt again, you can do one other thing to reassure yourself: buy additional insurance.

If you've purchased homeowner's or renter's insurance, you're probably already covered for the cost of goods lost or

Buy Back Your Baggage

After 3 months, airlines give up trying to match mystery bags with their owners. They ship unclaimed luggage to a warehouse in Scottsboro, Alabama, where bargain hunters from around the country poke around and get deals on discounted cameras, tennis rackets, and business suits. You can shop for unclaimed baggage online at www.unclaimedbaggage.com; or call ☎ **256/259-1525** for directions to the warehouse.

---

stolen during travel. Check your policy carefully before you make your next trip and purchase a rider for your existing policy if you travel a lot and aren't covered for lost or stolen bags. Most insurance providers require you to file a claim with the airline in order to be reimbursed. They will then cover anything in their policy that the airline did not reimburse you for.

Don't, however, buy insurance at the airport check-in counter; typically, it's overpriced, according to Ed Perkins, consumer advocate for the American Society of Travel Agents (ASTA) and former editor of *Consumer Reports Travel Newsletter.* Instead, buy it independently before your trip or from your travel agent. Coverage for lost bags is usually part of a comprehensive travel insurance package. But if you don't need a multifaceted policy, check to see if the company offers separate "baggage insurance." According to the American Society of Travel Agents, the following insurance companies are the largest providers, all of them reputable: **CSA** (☎ **800/873-9855;** www.csatravelprotection.com); **Travel Guard International** (☎ **800/826-1300;** www.travelguard.com); and **Access America** (☎ **800/284-8300;** www.accessamerica.com). Travel Guard is the only one of these three that offers separate baggage insurance, with a policy called "BagTrak". For more on insurance, see "Travel Insurance Demystified," in chapter 6.

In all cases, you'll need to file a police report describing your damaged or lost items as soon as you know about the problem, to get the money back from your insurer.

7 WHEN YOUR BAGGAGE HAS A PULSE: TRAVELING WITH YOUR PET

PETS DON'T LIKE TO FLY. THEY DON'T LIKE TO BE crammed into tiny kennels; they don't like the changes in air pressure, smell, and air quality that take place on a plane; and they certainly don't like to be tossed into a miserable, dark cargo hold. Many veterinarians advise that, especially on short trips, you should leave your pet home with a pet-sitter or a veterinarian's boarding service.

But if you insist upon flying with Fido, the safest way is to bring your pet as a carry-on item in a suitable carrier. Domesticated animals (see below for types and airlines) are allowed on flights within the United States, provided that you make an advance reservation for them. Be sure to ask the deadline when you book. In order to qualify for the cabin, animals must be at least 8 weeks old, fully weaned, under 20 pounds, and healthy. The airline will usually ask you to furnish a clean bill of health from a veterinarian, prepared within 10 days of your departure. On some airlines, you may be asked to present certification that your pet is vaccinated against rabies.

The airlines also ask you to feed your animal a small amount of food and water 4 hours before flight time. (A full stomach, however, isn't good for a traveling pet.) You are also expected to exercise and provide water for the pet before you stow it in the carrier. Book nonstop flights, if possible, to minimize the pet's discomfort. If your pet is traveling in the baggage compartment, book midday flights during the winter and early morning or late evening flights during the summer.

Regulations for taking pets on international flights vary widely both by airline and by destination. Many overseas

AIRLINE PET POLICIES

TYPE OF ANIMAL	WHO ALLOWS IN CABIN?*
Dogs, Cats	All major airlines
Rabbits	Alaska, Delta
Ferrets	Delta
Birds	All major airlines
Fish	Alaska
Hamsters, Guinea Pigs	Delta

* *Southwest Airlines does not allow pets on board.*

destinations, including the U.K., Italy, Germany, Hawaii, Japan, and China don't accept "tourist animals" at all. Check with your airline.

PETS IN THE CABIN

A small pet can ride in a carrier under the seat in front of you. Buy your carrier at a pet-supply store (or, if you're traveling on Continental, you can rent one for $30 per flight). The pet must remain under the seat at all times and never let out of the carrier mid-flight. (If this idea breaks your heart, leave your pet at home.) Most airlines charge $75 each way for a carry-on pet, although Continental charges $80 each way and US Airways, $100 each way.

You can even cram two puppies or kittens into one kennel, provided they're under six months old and the same kind of animal.

While soft carriers will usually fit under the seat more easily, the American Humane Society recommends hard-sided kennels for safety, as they offer your animal greater protection. The ASPCA recommends that you line the bottom of the crate with shredded paper or towels to absorb accidents.

Passengers with disabilities have the right to bring service animals (such as Seeing Eye dogs) on board on their standard leash or harness, provided they do not block aisles and emergency exits or otherwise hinder the safe and efficient passage of other travelers.

Pets will count as your one carry-on item (except on Continental and Northwest), and you must reserve a spot for your animal when you book your own flight. Along with your reservation comes the right to take precedence over allergic seatmates — nobody can force you to move your pet (see "What if You're Allergic?" below).

PETS AS CARGO

Larger pets must be checked as baggage or travel as cargo. Pets checked as baggage received the same treatment as any other bag — placed on the trolley, handled by the usual baggage handlers, and put in compartments with other bags. Airlines will assure you that these baggage compartments are pressurized and heated, but if the airline screws up you can't sue them: your pet qualifies only as damaged baggage. Using an airline's cargo service is more expensive, but generally provides a plusher experience for the pet. The cargo area is legally required to be pressurized and heated, and the pets are last on and first off the plane, so they spend less time on the tarmac than pets checked as baggage. Continental and United require that animals be shipped as cargo rather than checked; America West doesn't allow either option. Rates vary by the size and weight of the pet.

Unfortunately, many airlines no longer accept cargo from individual travelers — policies were changing as this book went to press, so you should check with the airline. If that's the case, you'll have to use a **professional pet shipper,** trusted by the airlines to get animals from Point A to Point B. Using a professional shipper is also the best way to transport a passel of poodles, a bevy of Burmese, or any large group of pets. Reliable pet shippers can be found though the Independent Pet and Animal Transportation Association International (IPATA) (☎ **903/769-2267;** www.ipata.com).

In all cases, your pet will ride in a compartment in the belly of the plane. You should use a USDA-approved, hard-sided kennel in this case. The crate should be large enough that your pet can stand, sit, and change position comfortably. You can purchase these from many pet-supply stores and sometimes from the airline itself.

Baggage compartments are climate-controlled, but airlines don't want to take their chances in extreme weather — and neither should you. American and Delta don't accept pets as checked baggage between May 15 and September 15, and no airline will (or should) take your pet on days where the mercury tops 85°. If it's below 45° on the ground, you'll have to get a certificate from your veterinarian certifying that the poor thing won't freeze to death while it sits on the tarmac waiting to be loaded on the plane.

WHAT IF YOU'RE ALLERGIC?

If you've ever thought that airlines treat you worse than a dog, well, you're right, in a way. While passengers with peanut allergies are attended to meticulously (see chapter 6), no such accommodation is made for passengers allergic to someone's precious little furball.

Alas, you can't get a pet kicked out of the cabin, even if you're gasping in asthmatic horror from the treacherous dander. The best you can ask for is to be moved to another seat, or put on another flight, which airlines will do (especially if they see you suffering; nobody wants a lawsuit). Be sniffly, be pathetic, and play upon flight attendants' or gate agents' sympathies.

If you're severely allergic to dogs or cats, tell the airline at the time you reserve your flight, and check again at the airport to make sure nobody's bringing one into the cabin. Bring your medication and inhaler, just in case.

Your other alternative: fly Southwest, which does not allow animals (other than service animals) on board.

Short-nosed dog and cat breeds require special care. Flatter facial structures mean these breeds take shorter breaths, and often have difficulty breathing in the lower pressures common at high altitudes. Alaska won't take these breeds at all; Continental requires special kennels; and Northwest bans them from any flight where the temperature will exceed 75°.

The ASPCA recommends that you write the words LIVE ANIMAL in letters at least 1 inch high, on top of the crate and on at least one side of the enclosure. Show the upright side of the kennel with prominent arrow indicators.

You should also write the name, address, and telephone number of the your pet's destination on the crate — even if you're on board the same flight. This information should be easy to read and secured on top of the carrier. Your pet should also be wearing identification tags on a collar. Cat collars should be elastic.

The ASPCA also recommends that checked pet crates be rigged with separate compartments for food and water. Some airlines require this. Some airlines also require that airline personnel have access to these compartments without having to open the kennel where the pet is stowed. The ASPCA recommends that you freeze the pet's water so that it doesn't splash out during loading but will melt by the time your pet is thirsty.

For trips that last longer than 12 hours, you should attach a plastic bag with dry food on top of the carrier with feeding instructions for airline staff.

The ASPCA also suggests that you acquaint your pet with the crate the day before the trip. You may want to place food and water inside, for instance, so your pet gets used to eating in there.

Be sure that the crate is securely closed, but do not lock it. Airline staff should to be able to open the crate in case of an emergency.

In the unlikely event that your pet is lost — a rare misfortune, but one that does occur from time to time — airlines will usually remunerate you according to the same rates used for lost luggage compensation. This may be a problem; you'll have to show the financial value of your pet.

Airlines, the ASPCA, pet shippers, and veterinarians all **warn against tranquilizing pets** in flight, especially if the animal is traveling as baggage or cargo. Dogs in particular control their body temperature by panting, not sweating. When tranquilized, dogs may be unable to pant, which leaves them no defense against temperature irregularities in the cargo hold, which obviously is not monitored like the airplane cabin on the same flight.

ANIMAL RIGHTS: THE ASPCA SPEAKS

According to Peter Paris, the ASPCA's vice president of public affairs, pet owners should think twice about checking their pets as baggage, even if they're traveling on the same flight. Conditions in the baggage compartments are far from ideal: Temperatures may vary, or the pilot may forget to turn on the air exchange. Paris says it's not uncommon for pets to die or suffer injury in the belly of the plane. Unfortunately, these mishaps are recorded as incidents of lost or mishandled luggage, and bereaved owners are due no more than the maximum compensation for a lost suitcase.

Paris says, "If your animal is worth more than $2,500 to you, think twice about sending it by air. If you can easily transport the animal by car, leave it with a friend or relatives, or place it in a kennel while you're away, don't risk putting it on a plane for your own convenience."

If you must transport your pet by air, Paris says you should make your best effort to travel on the same flight. Publicize the fact that you are traveling with an animal. Paris says that concerned pet owners should go so far as to poke their heads in the cockpit when boarding to let the pilot know there's an animal in cargo, so he's sure to turn on the air exchange.

5

WHITE KNUCKLE COMBAT: HOW TO CONQUER THE FEAR OF FLYING

Even in 2001, air travel was by far the safest form of transportation in the United States.

People who fear flying may feel that the events of September 11 have confirmed their decision never to set foot on a plane. The death of 266 air passengers was televised live that awful morning, part of a greater national catastrophe. But let us not overlook the widespread reality that more than 40,000 people die in highway accidents every year. While those deaths are rarely witnessed on such a global scale, the damage done is every bit as real.

Fear of flying, also known as aviophobia, is the second-most common fear in the United States, according to the National Institutes of Mental Health. Two out of every ten Americans are "afraid" of flying, according to a January 2002 CBS News poll — and another three are "bothered slightly."

But you're far more at risk when you hop in your car to fetch a stick of butter from the supermarket. Most people don't think twice about settling into their cars, betting on the fact that they will be transported safely from point A to point B. Yet car accidents account for more than 90% of transportation fatalities and are the leading cause of death for people aged 6 to 27, according to the U.S. Department of Transportation.

Planes are safer than cars mile by mile, passenger by passenger, or any other way you want to analyze it. During the year ending September 2001 (and taking into account the September attacks), 0.05 people died on planes per 100 million paid passenger miles. On America's highways in 1999 (the most recent year for which data is available), 1.6 passengers and drivers were killed per 100 million vehicle miles.

1 Profile of an Aviophobe

IF YOU SUFFER FROM AVIOPHOBIA, TAKE CONSOLATION in the fact that you're in good company. Despite the fact that Stanley Kubrick's most brilliant pictures feature obsessively recurrent flight imagery — the fighter plane in *Dr. Strangelove,* the space ship in *2001: A Space Odyssey* — the late director was deathly afraid to fly. Aretha Franklin turns down concerts that require air travel. The notoriously phobic Danish director Lars Von Trier is so acutely fearful of flying that he refused to travel to Cannes when his 1996 film *Breaking the Waves* was nominated for the Palm D'Or.

According to statistics from the National Institute of Mental Health, aviophobes tend to be successful, perfectionist, and intelligent — certainly smart enough to know that flying is safer than driving, but nonetheless unable to conquer the irrational fear. Some frequent fliers spend half their lives on planes for years on end and suddenly find themselves overcome with aviophobia out of the blue, so to speak.

WHAT CAUSES THE FEAR?

Fear of flying may stem from a variety of influences. Some aviophobes — perhaps the most justified of all — suffer from post-traumatic stress disorder when they set foot on an aircraft because they actually survived a plane crash. Other aviophobes fear flying as an extension of phobic disorders such as claustrophobia (fear of enclosed spaces), acrophobia (fear of heights), the fear of losing control, panic attacks — even guilt. The tendency to suffer from these fears is often inherited.

People who suffer from severe phobias unconsciously use their fear as a sieve for perceiving information. Aviophobes believe so firmly that they will die by setting foot on a plane that they are far more likely to remember information that supports their belief and discard information that refutes it — namely, say, the well-known fact that air travel is safe in comparison to other forms of modern transportation.

Many aviophobes who tremble at the mere thought of airplanes are fearless in the face of bigger threats to their health and safety. For instance, many people who refuse to set foot on a plane don't hesitate to drive in treacherous, icy conditions, with no more fear than the healthy amount that inspires caution. Many an aviophobe puts his life at risk by smoking two packs of cigarettes a day, without giving more than passing thought to the certifiably lethal threat of lung cancer.

SYMPTOMS OF AVIOPHOBIA

As you probably know, when you perceive danger, the brain responds by signaling the hypothalamus gland to prepare for action, to kick into the "fight-or-flight" response and allow you to escape from the perceived threat. This instinctive defense mechanism may be fueled by a real fear — say, a stranger in the window with a gun and a stocking over his head — or an imagined danger.

Fear of air travel is not entirely imagined; no form of travel is 100% safe. But nervous flying becomes aviophobia when rational thought gives way to irrational reflex, and no list of statistics or comforting argument can quiet the beast of fear within your chest.

✐ AFRAID OF TERRORISM?

September 11 sent many aviophobes into new paroxysms of fear. Fear-of-flying therapists saw their caseloads diminish throughout September and October, as terrified patients stayed away, not willing to fly under any circumstances. Dr. Duane Brown, who counsels fearful fliers in Chapel Hill, NC, suspended his small practice entirely.

Fliers afraid of terrorism, Dr. Brown says, should focus on the good news – and there's a lot of it. Every day brings new news stories about stepped-up airline and airport security. Fearful fliers should get a friend to clip those stories and start a file on how U.S. airlines aren't just getting safer, they're the safest they've ever been. (This isn't just reassuring – it's also true.)

Fearful fliers should also go gently on their fear, Dr. Brown said. If they wish to avoid nonstop, cross-country flights, or work with smaller airlines with perfect safety records such as Southwest and JetBlue (both of which have never had a fatal crash, and which have lower international profiles than major airlines), there's nothing wrong with that.

The fear engendered by September 11 seems to be dying down, as of press time. Comparing a November 1999 ABC News poll to a January 2002 CBS poll, only 6% more Americans are "afraid" of flying than they were in '99 – and only 2% more than in 1999 fit into the next category, "bothered."

Once a severe phobia develops, physical reactions make the fear harder to beat. The fight-or-flight response releases hormones into the bloodstream that inspire a range of physiological symptoms, many of which serve to magnify the fear.

In aviophobes, the response to air travel — even the very idea of flying on a plane — ranges from sweaty palms to severe hysteria. Mild aviophobes can sometimes manage to psych themselves through a plane ride with nothing more than a case of hives, but in severe cases aviophobes must either refrain from air travel or undergo therapy.

As with any irrational fear, aviophobia usually manifests first as a siege of racing, irrational thoughts regarding the fear. The mere mention of air travel can unleash a parade of worst-case scenarios to fly past the mind's eye. In response to the perceived danger, brain activity actually shifts from the cerebrum, the center of conscious thought, to the brain stem, a very primitive part of the brain that hosts mental activity when a person is in "survival mode." Consequently, your access to information stored in the cerebrum may be cut off entirely. Memory is severely impaired. Concentration may become next to impossible. Dizziness may set in and make it difficult to walk or even speak.

The victim's heart will also respond to the fear. In the face of a threat, a person's heart rate escalates from 72 beats per minute, the average resting pace, to more than 140 beats per minute. The heartbeat may become irregular, and palpitations may occur. Blood vessels constrict, and blood pressure skyrockets. Sensing danger, the body responds by releasing blood sugars into the bloodstream. This usually serves to intensify fear and convinces many victims that they are having a heart attack.

In the face of fear, the body also requires more oxygen in order to escape from the perceived danger. Normally a person takes 6 to 15 breaths per minute, but when someone is intensely scared, that rate may increase to 20 or 30 or more breaths per minute.

A frightened person will also breathe from the thorax, the upper part of the chest, which allows the body to consume oxygen and dispel carbon dioxide much more quickly than when breathing from the diaphragm — the healthy, relaxed way to breathe, which fills the lungs to capacity from the bottom up. When a person breathes too much oxygen, the pupils may dilate and cause vision to blur. Dizziness may set in from the shortage of carbon dioxide. If someone gasps for shallow breath from the upper part of the chest for a long enough time, that person may start to feel a sort of choking sensation and eventually will pass out. This is how the body manages to overcome fear and ensure that a healthy level of carbon dioxide is restored to the respiratory system.

The stomach also responds to fear by secreting more acid. Someone who is very scared may also draw more than the normal level of oxygen into the stomach. These two effects, solo or combined, may cause stomach upset or diarrhea or both.

Fear of flying usually also makes for sweaty palms. The victim's lips, hands, and feet tingle and go cold. The face flushes. Hands may tremble and make it impossible to hold a glass.

Taking Things to an Extreme

Fear can make people do bizarre things. Dr. Rob Reiner, who treats fear-of-flying cases, recounted one story of a high-powered New York attorney who was in control of herself until she boarded a plane. While flying one day, she saw two obese women snacking in front of her and imagined that their bulk was tilting the plane to the side. (On a commercial airliner, that's utterly impossible.)

She tried to contain her worry, but eventually her fear got the better of her. Against her better judgment, she walked up the aisle and told the two women that they were clearly too fat and were tilting the plane. Could they move to opposite sides of the aisle? Needless to say, they were offended and refused to move. So the normally cool attorney became hysterical and flight attendants had to restrain her.

There's a happy ending: after several sessions with Dr. Reiner, she now flies regularly for business – and keeps her opinions of the other passengers to herself.

Muscles tense up in response to flight fright, especially in the lower jaw, shoulders, lower back, calves, and legs. If leg muscles tense for an extended period of time, the legs may begin to tremble conspicuously or even give out. A person may have trouble standing up if the fear is severe enough. In the worst instances, aviophobes experience such great muscle tension that they may feel the urge to attack a flight attendant or fling open the emergency exit doors — which, by the way, is impossible while the plane is in flight.

2   So What Can Be Done About It?

DR. DUANE BROWN, WHO TEACHES COUNSELING AND counseling psychology at the University of North Carolina, Chapel Hill, and used to lead American Airlines' fear-of-flying program, offers a fairly simple, drug-free program for coping with the fear of flying. It attends to both the psychological and the physiological aspects of aviophobia. His book *Flying Without Fear* (New Harbinger Publications: Oakland, 1996) is very user-friendly and offers a host of techniques you can try on your own, without any formal workshop or seminar training.

The program teaches you how to curb the irrational, involuntary thoughts that make your heart pound and your teeth chatter. It also shows you how to curb these physiological symptoms of fear, which undeniably aggravate the phobia and make it harder to overcome. The program also emphasizes the importance of reeducation and offers a new information base about the safety of air travel. These facts are sometimes at odds with the media's terrifying treatment of airplane disasters. They also challenge the natural human fear of the unknown, which allows so many aviophobes to tremble in the sky yet feel entirely comfortable racing along the freeway at killer speeds.

CURBING THE INVOLUNTARY "FIGHT-OR-FLIGHT" MECHANISM

To some extent, the fear of flying is an involuntary response. You cannot control the thoughts that enter your mind, and once the idea of a plane crash enters an aviophobe's head, a series of physiological responses is triggered, which usually serves only to intensify the fear. In *Flying Without Fear,* Dr. Brown suggests that you can actually curb your initial fear and reduce or eliminate the more advanced stages of flight fright.

The first step is to **identify your fear** and decide you don't want to live with it anymore. Brown recommends that you actually wear a thick rubber band over the palm of your hand on the day of your flight. The minute you have second thoughts about flying or you start to imagine a crash scene, a cabin fire, or your funeral, he recommends that you snap the rubber band. It will hurt, but not as greatly as the pain you'll experience if you panic and your imagination goes into overdrive. Next, he recommends that you actually command your fear to go away. You must not be hard on yourself as you command your fear to flee; keep your anger trained on the fear itself.

The shortness of breath and heart palpitations that usually accompany scary thoughts about air travel may set in within a fraction of a second after you first entertain the fear. This response is involuntary, so even if you snap the rubber band and try to quell your anxiety, your body will have already started secreting fight-or-flight hormones, your heart will have already started pounding in your chest, and your breathing will quicken and become shallow. You can take action, however, to retard these somewhat automatic responses even after they've set in.

CONTROL YOUR BREATH

The minute after you snap your rubber band, you should **focus on your breathing.** Make an enormous effort to breathe slowly and deeply from your diaphragm. Place your hand on your stomach and take a deep breath. If your belly compresses when you inhale, you are breathing correctly, diaphragmatically. If not, you are probably breathing from the chest, which will intensify your response to the terror.

Keeping your hand on your belly, **practice slow, deliberate inhalation,** sucking your belly in as you fill your lungs with air. After several long, deep breaths, you will begin to perceive an overwhelming sense of calm. As you probably know, deep, diaphragmatic breathing is the cornerstone of ancient relaxation strategies like yoga. Think of your breath as an instrument of healing that will help to cure you of your fear.

If you still feel light-headed after breathing deeply, your chest muscles are probably too worked up to relax entirely. In this case, Dr. Brown recommends that you **grab a plastic bag** — if you're already on the plane, use the air sickness bag in the pocket behind the seat in front of you. Cover your nose and mouth with the bag, pressed against your face so that no air escapes, and breathe normally. Eventually, the air you're breathing will become pure carbon dioxide, which will curb your dizziness once it is restored to its normal levels. Be sure, however, that you remove the bag as soon as your symptoms disappear. Also be sure not to seal the bag over your nose and mouth; just hold it there. Children should not try this.

CONTROL YOUR HEART RATE

You can also slow a pounding heart with a technique called the **Valsalva Maneuver.** Please be aware, however, that only people with healthy cardiovascular systems should try this exercise, as it can altogether stop the heart of someone who has suffered a heart attack or stroke. If you have even slight doubts about the healthiness of your cardiovascular system, consult a doctor before trying this procedure.

If you're convinced your ticker is strong and healthy, try the following steps the minute you can feel your heartbeat speed up and intensify. Sit up straight in your seat. Breathe slowly and deeply from your diaphragm. As you are filling your lungs, pull in your stomach. When your lungs feel full, hold your breath. Use your stomach muscles to push down on your lower intestines, as you would if you were suffering from constipation. As you are bearing down, count 5 seconds: one one-thousand, two one-thousand, and so on. Exhale and release the tension. Your heart rate should slacken by about 20 beats per minute. Repeat the process three or four times, until your heart is beating at a normal pace.

Now, focus all your attention on your breathing, drawing in long, deep breaths from the diaphragm and exhaling slowly. This will keep your heart beating at a normal, relaxed rate.

RELAX TENSE MUSCLES

You will also need to work on relaxing your muscles, focusing on those that are most susceptible to stress: the trapezius, which are the large shoulder muscles that support the neck; the jaw muscles; and the leg muscles.

To eliminate stress in the shoulders, try an exercise called **the turtle.** Sit up straight in your seat. Shrug your shoulders at the same time that you pull in your neck, as though you were a turtle. Aim to touch your ears with your shoulders. Hold the position and count out 5 seconds as you rotate your head to massage the muscles in your shoulders. At the count of five, release the tension. Let your shoulders relax completely, and then repeat this exercise three to five times.

To eliminate stress in the jaw, try **the piranha.** Stick out your lower jaw as far as you can. Try to extend it beyond the teeth in your upper jaw. Hold the position as you count out 5 seconds. Release and allow your jaw to slacken. Repeat three to five times.

To eliminate stress in the legs and prevent them from trembling, try **the ballerina.** Slide your feet as far under the seat in front of you as you can. (This exercise works best in coach, where you won't have much room for your legs.) Lift one foot off the floor, arch your foot, and point it toward the front of the plane. Count out 5 seconds. Then rotate your foot so your toe is pointing toward you. Try to point your foot toward your chin and count out 5 seconds. Drop your foot to the floor and relax. Repeat this exercise three to five times with each leg. You can also try walking to the back of the plane, where you'll have more room to stretch your legs. The walk will also do you good.

3 EASE YOUR ANGST: UNDERSTANDING GOVERNMENT SAFETY ENFORCEMENTS

DR. BROWN BELIEVES THAT ANOTHER WAY TO EASE angst about the perceived precariousness of air travel is to become familiar with the government's monitoring of safety standards. The U.S. government regulates domestic air travel far more rigorously than car travel. The Federal Aviation Administration monitors every aspect of airline safety, from mechanical inspections to pilot training to air traffic control to airport management. (For a discussion of safety standards on foreign carriers, see chapter 1, "A Whole New World.")

Under FAA regulations, every commercial plane in the United States is subject to two preflight inspections before it can legally get off the ground. First, an in-service mechanic thoroughly scrutinizes both the exterior of the plane and the cockpit, cross-checking his own observations and findings against the information recorded in the aircraft's logbook, also required by the FAA. Each time an airline disaster introduces a safety glitch that goes unaddressed by the current guidelines, the FAA revises its standards and requires mechanics to look out for the problem in the future.

Before they are hired, airline mechanics undergo rigorous, FAA-approved training. Throughout their careers, they are subject to annual retraining and random drug tests.

Often, the preflight mechanic has few corrections to make, since planes and their engines are also subject to strict, routine maintenance overhauls. Also, the minute pilots enter

So How Did It Happen

Fearful fliers may ask: with all of these safety enforcements, how did September 11 happen?

First of all, what failed on September 11, 2001, was U.S. intelligence, law enforcement, and security at airports – not the planes themselves, nor the pilots, nor the mechanics.

The airport security lapses that led the hijackers to board planes are the focus of intense government and industry scrutiny right now. New regulations and even entire new government agencies (namely the Transportation Security Administration) are helping fix the flaws from that end.

But the hijackers also counted on passengers not fighting back. Since September 11, passengers have mobilized to subdue potential threats on planes – and no hijacker with a knife can stand up to the force of 100 angry fliers.

---

crew members detect a mechanical problem, they dispatch a report before the plane even lands. This way, if new parts are needed, mechanics can see to it that they're ready the minute a plane lands. If mechanics make a repair, they indicate that the aircraft is fixed and ready to fly by signing and recording an employee number in the plane's logbook. A supervisor then checks the repair and also signs the logbook with an employee number.

After the mechanic signs off on an aircraft, indicating that the plane has passed preflight inspection, the pilot and copilot conduct a second inspection of more than 100 items both inside and outside the plane. During the inspection process, baggage is unloaded; gas, food, and drinking water are replenished; and waste is expelled in preparation for the next flight.

It would be naive to assume that aircraft inspectors and mechanics adhere perfectly to every aspect of their job descriptions. Because one small goof can lead to catastrophe, however, the government levies strict fines against airline employees who get sloppy on the job. If a repair proves to be faulty, both the mechanic and the supervisor who signed off on the work are held responsible. Each may be fined as much as $5,000 out of pocket — with no help from the airline.

(For a more detailed discussion of airline safety, both domestic and international, see chapter 1, "A Whole New World.")

HOW FLIGHT PLANS ARE PREPARED

Two hours before a scheduled departure, an airline's dispatchers, who are licensed by the FAA, prepare a flight plan. In light of weather conditions, temperature, and wind velocity, they evaluate the plane's route and determine optimal cruising altitude (typically 35,000 ft./10,500m) and speed (typically 500 mph/805kmph at cruising altitude). They determine how much fuel to load by weighing the fastest possible flight time with the most economical amount of fuel. Every commercial plane that leaves the ground carries enough fuel to transport the plane to its destination, surplus fuel for expected delays and reroutings, 1 or 2 hours' worth of "hold fuel" for unexpected delays, and a minimum of 45 minutes' worth of "reserve fuel," required by the FAA.

Bye-Bye Birdie

In the past, a significant hazard to flight safety was – believe it or not – birds. Planes could suffer serious engine damage if they happened to crash into a flock of birds or even a single bird, if it was large enough.

Now, however, engines are designed to ingest birds after a tangle, so they can continue functioning normally after the encounter. In fact, airplane mechanics test new engines by firing dead chickens into them. In order to pass FAA inspection regulations, an engine must be able to sustain the impact of an 8-pound bird.

> ### Heavy Traffic
>
> According to the Department of Transportation, between eight and nine million scheduled passenger flights have taken off in the U.S. each year since 1995.

HOW AIR TRAFFIC IS CONTROLLED

Once the dispatchers establish the flight plan, they run it by air traffic control. The plan is not official until the FAA's central computer in Washington approves it, and then it is filed electronically and available to every air traffic control tower responsible for a plane along its route.

From their glassed-in towers at the airport, controllers command the skies, monitoring both the sky above their own airport and landing conditions at the destination terminal. If they anticipate congestion when the plane is scheduled to land, controllers at the departure airport have the power to postpone the flight.

Via computerized video screens, each controller monitors a tier of the airspace around an airport. Throughout a flight — on average every 3 to 4 seconds — air traffic controllers maintain direct communication with a plane's pilot via headphones. Each plane appears as a blip as it travels over a variety of digital maps on screens.

The pilot first makes contact with a controller 15 minutes before takeoff. The plane is transferred from one controller to another as it moves from the gate to the runway to the air. Once the plane leaves a control tower's jurisdiction, it is transferred to controllers at other towers en route.

HOW PILOTS ARE TRAINED

Every commercial U.S. airline flight has three pilots in the cockpit: a captain, a first officer, and a second officer. Pilots must have 2,000 hours of experience in the air and pass a rigorous series of tests before commercial airlines will consider hiring them.

Pilots usually receive their training from either a military service academy (such as the Air Force Academy), an undergraduate military ROTC (Reserve Officers Training Corps) program, or a college or university program that focuses on airline technology. Pilots receive a variety of flying licenses en route to earning their commercial pilot's license.

Once hired, a pilot undergoes another battery of strenuous training; both written and oral testing; flight simulation; and at least 25 hours of flight time, supervised by the FAA, on the type of aircraft he will be flying. A pilot is retrained each time he switches aircraft. New pilots must demonstrate that they know how to perform every aspect of their job before they're allowed to fly. New hires also hold probationary status for 1 year and undergo monthly evaluations by fellow crew members. Captains, flight engineers, and first officers are retrained every year. If they cannot perform satisfactorily with each retraining, they are dismissed.

The FAA also appoints doctors who examine captains twice a year and first officers and flight engineers once a year. Pilots over 40 must receive an EKG. On each flight, the captain and first officer are served different meals, in the "off" chance that the airline food is bad and causes food poisoning.

Air Traffic Violations

The next time you're about to complain about a $150 speeding ticket, be glad you're not a pilot. Commercial pilots have a steep incentive to listen to air controllers, the traffic cops of plane travel. Planes flying at an altitude below 10,000 feet (3,000m) are not allowed to exceed 281 miles per hour (452kmph). If a plane exceeds the speed limit, the captain can be fined $10,000. If a pilot deviates from the minimum distance allowed between planes, he may receive a fine of up to $10,000.

In both these instances, the pilots themselves are responsible for coming up with this cash; the airline doesn't bail them out.

Near Misses: So Close & Yet So Far

For commercial aircraft flying at altitudes under 29,000 feet (8,700m), air traffic controllers space planes 1,000 feet (300m) apart vertically and 3 to 20 miles (5km–32km) apart horizontally. For commercial aircraft flying above 29,000 feet (8,700m), air traffic controllers space planes 2,000 feet (600m) apart vertically and 10 miles (16km) or more apart horizontally. Near misses are registered every time a plane deviates from this minimum space allowance. Certainly, from 10 to 20 miles (16km–32km) away, you are in no danger of a midair collision, just because a flight was called a near miss.

In fact, only two midair collisions have occurred on commercial air carriers between 1990 and 2002, resulting in 506 fatalities. While any loss of life is too much, more people die each week in car accidents on U.S. highways than have died in midair collisions during the past decade.

Pilots also undergo random drug testing throughout their careers, and no-notice checks at the hands of FAA officers and airline supervisors.

DO INTERNATIONAL GUIDELINES EXIST?

International carriers are not subject to FAA safety requirements, but all nations' safety standards are rated by the Montreal-based International Civil Aviation Organization (ICAO). Fearful fliers may want to use solid northern European flag carriers such as Lufthansa and British Airways while traveling abroad — they're widely considered to be safer than U.S. airlines, in part because of their nations' past experiences with terrorism. For a detailed description of ICAO rules and a list of which foreign nations have inadequate safety standards, see chapter 1, "A Whole New World."

FLYING BLIND

A flight from San Francisco to Los Angeles was delayed for 45 minutes after passengers had already boarded the aircraft. Needless to say, nearly everybody on board was feeling irritable by the time the flight departed. To make matters worse, the plane had to make an emergency stop in Sacramento. With no further explanation, the flight attendant announced that there would be another 45-minute delay there. As minor consolation, she added that passengers could disembark, provided they return in 30 minutes.

Everybody got off the plane except one gentleman who was blind. It seemed pretty clear that he had flown before. His Seeing Eye dog lay quietly underneath the seats in front of him throughout the entire flight, as though he had done so many times before. The pilot approached the man as though he were no stranger, and finally even called him by his first name. He said, "Keith, we're in Sacramento for almost an hour. Would you like to get off and stretch your legs?"

Keith replied, "No thanks, but maybe my dog would like to stretch his legs."

Picture this: All the disgruntled passengers were hanging around the gate area when the pilot — who also happened to be wearing dark sunglasses — walked off the plane with the Seeing Eye dog. First the passengers, en masse, froze. Then they started scattering! Not only did many of them try to change planes; some tried to change airlines!

4   KNOW YOUR METEOROLOGY: WEATHER DANGERS DEMYSTIFIED

FEARFUL FLIERS TEND TO FRET NEEDLESSLY OVER WEATHER patterns in the air that seem to herald danger. In fact, such occurrences pose little threat to air travelers. Some weather events certainly do make for hazardous flight conditions, but the FAA prohibits takeoff under these circumstances. Again, here Dr. Brown recommends educating yourself about some of the most commonly feared weather phenomena, and the actual threat they pose to air safety.

TURBULENCE

Turbulence, one of the scariest aspects of flight, happens to be relatively innocuous. The biggest threat posed by turbulence is injury inside the cabin if you happen to be standing or sitting without a seat belt when the plane encounters especially rough turbulence, which does jostle the plane. Turbulence is essentially streams of air in motion. Picture what happens when you insert a running hose into a pool of water: The hose water runs as a current, moving faster than the rest of the water and displacing it, sending the displaced water elsewhere. The air moves similarly. When a stream of cold wind, say, encounters warmer air, it runs right through it, cold air being more highly pressurized than warm air, and causes the warm air to rise and go elsewhere. These crashing streams of air are obstacles for airplanes, which manage to fly right through them, but not without some resistance. Air travelers experience this resistance as turbulence. Flying through turbulence is comparable to, and no more dangerous than, driving over gravel in a truck.

A common misnomer for severe turbulence is "air pockets." Air pockets are like the Loch Ness monster of air travel — no more real and no more of a threat, despite their mythic proportions in the aviophobe's mind. The misleading term was coined during World War I by a journalist who was merely trying to describe turbulence. Contrary to popular myth, air pockets cannot cause planes to drop out of the sky or fall hundreds of feet. They are nothing more than a severe form of turbulence.

Turbulence is hard to predict, but it tends to occur near thunderstorms, over mountain ranges, and over very warm areas like Florida. The most dangerous type of turbulence is called clear-air turbulence. As its name suggests, it occurs unexpectedly in otherwise calm, clear skies. Clear-air turbulence poses a mild threat only because the plane will encounter it unexpectedly. If you happen to be walking about the cabin at that moment, you may fall or bang into something. If you're traveling on a smooth flight, and the pilot turns on the FASTEN SEAT BELTS sign, it is usually because he is expecting some clear-air turbulence. When this happens, follow the flight crew's instructions. You might want to stop drinking hot beverages until the light goes off. It's also wise to wait a minute if you were planning to use the restroom or pull belongings down from the overhead bin.

Flight attendants are actually at greatest risk when the plane encounters turbulence, since they move about the most during a flight. When a pilot asks the flight attendants to sit, it is usually not because the plane is in grave danger, but because the flight path is passing through choppy skies.

Pilots will often try to escape turbulence by ascending or descending to another altitude, where the air may be less agitated. This, too, does not mean the plane is endangered, but rather that the pilot is simply trying to give his passengers a smoother ride. Nor is he struggling to maintain control of the plane, another popular misperception of turbulence. In fact, many captains navigate rough skies on autopilot, which is better able to anticipate shifts in temperature and air pressure.

THUNDERSTORMS

Thunderstorms do pose a danger to air travel. Flight plans are devised to help pilots avoid them, and the FAA prohibits planes from flying in the perilous core of a storm. Commercial aircraft must remain 20 miles (32km) away from this turbulent center of high winds, hail, and heavy rain. When a plane does enter a windy, rainy part of the sky, it must stay within the storm's outer reaches — where the biggest threat is turbulence. Most pilots try to avoid thunderstorms altogether, however, to provide passengers with a smoother ride.

Even lightning, contrary to popular belief, cannot "strike" an airplane and electrocute passengers, because the plane is not grounded. Lightning hits planes almost every day and does no damage to the aircraft or to travelers, because it passes right through the plane. If lightning hits your plane, the worst you'll suffer is a ringing in your ears from the subsequent thunderclap.

WIND SHEAR

Wind shear is essentially a sudden change in wind speed or direction within a short distance. When it occurs, it usually accompanies a thunderstorm. The most severe form of wind shear is called a "microburst," which starts off as a strong head wind followed by a tail wind, torrential rain, and a fierce down draft that can literally run a plane into the ground if it is flying at low altitudes.

Although wind shear poses no threat at high altitudes, it can be dangerous to planes flying at lower levels. In the entire history of flight, however, only two planes have crashed because of it. Since the most recent incident, in 1994, pilots have been required to receive special training in flight simulators to detect wind shear and avoid it. After the initial training, pilots must take refresher courses every 6 months. Several newfangled wind-shear detection devices have also been invented since then. Most airports are equipped with mechanisms that measure wind speed and alert air-traffic control when wind shear is detected. Doppler radar is also able to detect wind shear in advance.

FOG

If fog happens to cloud the runway when a plane is scheduled to depart, air traffic control will delay the flight until visibility improves. Controllers don't always have the leisure, however, to postpone a plane's landing indefinitely. Because of this, planes are required to travel with enough fuel to allow them to postpone landing if visibility is poor.

Through Rain & Snow & Dark Of Night

When a ValuJet plane crashed in Florida in 1996, it became public knowledge that ValuJet pilots were paid by the flight. If inclement weather forced the airline to cancel a departure, the scheduled pilot would be out of luck.

ValuJet pilots, however, had enormous say over whether their flight would be grounded in poor weather. In practice, this meant that many ValuJet flights got off the ground under hazardous weather conditions that would have prompted any major carrier to cancel the flight without question, because pilots didn't want to lose money.

All airlines now pay pilots by the minute, according to Aviation Information Resources, a career-placement service for pilots. If a hailstorm forces an airline to delay a flight, the pilots make more money, not less.

Under certain conditions pilots are allowed to land, with help from electronics and computers, in even 0/0 visibility. The term "0/0 visibility" means that the plane has no ceiling — it's less than 300 feet (90m) above the ground — and the pilot can't see farther than 600 feet (180m) ahead. If the runway has an instrument called an "electronic glide slope," the pilot can use instruments to "see" ahead and land safely. Likewise, some planes are equipped with devices to make a safe 0/0 landing possible. Newer pilots, however, are sometimes prohibited from landing until visibility improves.

ICE

In freezing weather, airport runways are systematically inspected for ice and closed the minute ice is detected. Planes are also equipped with antilock and antiskid brakes as further protection against icy conditions.

The planes themselves are thoroughly de-iced almost immediately before a flight and coated with a substance that prevents ice from forming. Once a plane is airborne, ice cannot develop on jets, because the engine, which is naturally very hot, distributes hot air to areas of the plane that may develop ice.

5 Other Ways to Treat Aviophobia

DR. BROWN'S PROGRAM MAY NOT WORK FOR SEVERE aviophobes, or those who need a professional hand to hold while they work through their fears. The first step in most professional treatments is to help the patient discover the true root of his or her fear. Is it claustrophobia? Lack of control over the situation? Or fear of not knowing what's going on in the cockpit and in the workings of the plane?

Patients then learn relaxation techniques to calm the physiological symptoms of irrational fear, do homework assignments on the safety of air travel to build up rational defenses against fear, or attack the fear from both rational and physiological angles.

After a few sessions addressing the underlying psychological issues, therapists then put the patient on an airplane — in a real ("in vivo") or imaginary ("in vitro") context.

No U.S. airlines currently run fear-of-flying clinics; most are organized by independent therapists or ex-pilots. Clinics at the Seattle (☎ **206/772-1122**; www.scn.org/health/fofc/) and San Francisco (☎ **650/341-1595**; www.fofc.com/) airports are run by an organization of female pilots and focus on spending time on airplanes.

VIRTUAL REALITY THERAPY

One of the hottest approaches at press time was virtual reality therapy, in which patients don a 3-D headset and sit in a chair that vibrates to simulate takeoff, flight, turbulence, weather problems, and landing. (See "Flying in the Virtual World," above.) Thirteen clinics in nine states currently use the VR system, which was developed by Virtually Better,

C FLYING IN THE VIRTUAL WORLD

I'm not a nervous flier, but I decided to take a spin on Virtually Better's virtual plane in Dr. Rob Reiner's New York office to see what the fuss was about.

I sat down in a comfortable, business-class-style chair and donned a wraparound headset. Suddenly, I was in a plane similar to a 727, sitting in a window seat. If I craned my head, I could see the discarded magazine on the next seat and peer out into the deserted aisle. (Future versions of the software will include other passengers, Virtually Better says.)

The graphics required a bit of suspension of disbelief — the edges of objects are a touch jaggedy — but as the sound effects kicked in and the chair vibrated to simulate takeoff, I found it pretty easy to imagine myself flying.

Eventually, the sky outside my virtual window became dark — I was flying through a thunderstorm. My chair shook. I was startled by brilliant, realistic flashes of lightning. When I took off the headset, Dr. Reiner revealed his personal twist on the VR software: The lightning was created by him flashing his digital camera near my head.

Inc. (☎ 404/634-3400; www.virtuallybetter.com). Therapists like VR systems because they give the doctor complete control over the flying situation, so a session can focus on a particular facet of flying (such as takeoff or weather problems).

VR therapy is costly — think $65 to $300 per session, depending on where you're taking the treatment and how much you can afford to spend — but many medical plans cover it, especially if you can prove that flying is necessary to your job.

A 2000 study in the *Journal of Consulting and Clinical Psychology,* a respected peer-reviewed medical publication, found VR therapy to be as successful as exposure to a real-life plane — both VR and exposure therapies had a 93% success rate. (However, two of the researchers performing the study were being paid by the VR firm.)

But there are differences in approach even between clinics using Virtually Better.

Dr. Rob Reiner of Behavioral Associates in New York (☎ 212/860-8500; www.behavioralassociates.com) combines virtual reality therapy with biofeedback, where computers monitor a patient's vital signs to provide an objective measure of fear. He teaches a breathing technique called "respiratory sinus arrhythmia" which forces the body to calm down when anxious. Using the biofeedback monitor, patients can watch themselves calming down.

The exposure therapists at **Boston University's Center for Anxiety and Related Disorders** (☎ 617/353-9610; www.bu.edu/anxiety/), however, view relaxation techniques as avoidance tactics that prevent patients from really grappling head-on with their fears. Dr. Curtis Hsia of the center says fliers should be as aware of their surroundings as possible so as to have a sense of control over their flying experience.

FLOODING

Flooding, a more intensive variation on exposure therapy, is another popular treatment for fear of flying. Not for the faint of heart, flooding forces clients to face their fears all at once, in an airport or on an airplane. Clearly it's a faster way to deal with, and perhaps overcome, the fear of flying; in fact, the approach seems tailored to the kind of people who dive head-first into ice-cold water rather than wade in slowly. But while many clients do manage to confront their fears at first, existing data regarding the long-term benefits of flooding are still inconclusive.

6 SIMPLE REMEDIES FOR MINOR AVIOPHOBIA

IF YOU'RE LEAVING ON A JET PLANE TOMORROW, OR for some other reason don't have time to embark on an intensive treatment program, there are simple safeguards you can take to curb anxiety before you board a plane.

- **Eat a nutritious meal before boarding.** If you go too long without food, your body will try to compensate for your low blood sugar level by releasing adrenaline. This chemical reaction will make you feel stressed and anxious.

- **Avoid refined sugars** (candy bars and other junk foods), **caffeine** (a stimulant), and **alcohol.** While doctors sometimes prescribe one-time doses of anti-anxiety drugs like Xanax for aviophobia, the side effects can be a problem (drowsiness, withdrawal symptoms). Ultimately, it's a Band-Aid solution that doesn't get at the root cause of the phobia. Alcohol is an even worse idea, as it can spur irrational behavior and "air rage."

- Try to **get to the airport early.** The last thing you want to be when you step on a plane is nervous and anxious.

- **Pay attention to good news, not bad.** If you suffer from untended aviophobia, you will tend to seek out information that supports your fear. Avoid reading about the airline industry in the news and have friends clip stories about how security is improving.

- **Sit over a wing,** rather than in back, for a smoother ride. While turbulence is for the most part harmless — provided that you're seated and wearing a safety belt at the time it occurs — it is jarring and can easily fuel your fear if you're not in full control of your phobia.

- **Splurge on a first-class or business-class ticket** if your fear of flying stems from claustrophobia; it will guarantee you more space. If you must fly coach, try to book a bulkhead seat or check in early and reserve an emergency exit row seat. Or try to fly American Airlines, which offers an inch or 2 more legroom in coach than other major airlines do.

- **Fly at off-peak times** such as midday and midweek. Emptier planes are less stressful, and staff are often friendlier because they have to deal with fewer passengers.

- **Avoid sitting in a window seat** if your fear of flying stems from acrophobia (fear of heights); that way you won't be able to look down and see how high you're flying.

- Finally, **take charge of your situation.** Make choices that give you a feeling of control. Some airlines have better safety records than others, and some countries have more rigorous safety enforcement procedures than others. See chapter 1, "A Whole New World," for a full discussion of safe-flying strategies.

6

LIFE PRESERVERS: STAYING HEALTHY WHEN YOU FLY

Airplanes are not healthy places. Thin, recirculated air incubates disease, and cramped spaces are unkind to those who need a little more room. Travelers with health problems — even just a cold — may find a long flight difficult to bear. Children and pregnant women are especially vulnerable to airborne health problems, and wheelchair users often find themselves at the mercy of flight attendants for hours at a time.

Travelers can do little to combat stale cabin air. But informed fliers can assert their rights for a "healthier" flight — whether that's the right to dignified treatment as a disabled person or the right to keep a child flying solo as safe as possible. And some airborne health hazards, such as "economy class syndrome," may be avoided or minimized by taking precautions during flight.

1 Health in the Air: Common Problems & Ailments

EVEN IF YOU'RE A LOW-MAINTENANCE GLOBETROTTER, needing only the air that you breathe to feel content and alive, you may find yourself feeling cruddy and in need of some pampering soon after you board an airplane.

Many travelers experience flu-like symptoms on planes that persist through the duration of a flight. Mistakenly, they attribute their temporary unwellness to jet lag, when in fact they may be suffering from dehydration, mild altitude sickness, or the in-the-air variation of "sick building syndrome."

A National Academy of Sciences study in late 2001 raised concerns about cabin air quality. Commissioned by two members of Congress, the study noted that low cabin air pressure and high levels of ozone in cabin air may cause respiratory difficulties, but that there's no way for passengers to complain and that there's no national air-quality standard for commercial aircraft.

"SICK AIRPLANE SYNDROME"

If you work in a poorly ventilated, highly populated office space, you're probably familiar with the occupational hazard known as sick building syndrome. Fewer public places are as prone to this condition as an airplane cabin — where strangers are packed, elbow to elbow, with no access to fresh air, for extended periods of time.

Cabin air on almost every domestic aircraft is now recycled, which exacerbates the problem. For years, airlines pumped fresh air into their aircraft cabins from outside. At cruising altitude, air temperature is about −65°F, so fresh air was pumped through the aircraft's jet engine compressors, which heated it to about 400°F, then chilled to comfortable temperatures by air conditioners and heat exchangers.

In recent years, however, airline executives discovered that they could curtail fuel expenses and boost profits by mixing 50% fresh air with 50% filtered, recycled cabin air. In fresh air, the oxygen you inhale contains under 1% carbon dioxide. The air you exhale, on the other hand, contains 4% carbon dioxide. When many people share a poorly ventilated, enclosed space for extended periods of time, the carbon dioxide level rises. Carbon dioxide, as you may know if you work in a poorly ventilated office space, is the primary culprit in sick building syndrome.

And although recirculated cabin air is usually passed through air filters that trap allergens, skin flakes, and bacteria, very little new air is being circulated. About 6 to 10 cubic feet per minute of outside air comes into the economy-class cabin — as opposed to the legal minimum of 15 to 20 cubic feet per minute in buildings, and the 50 or more cubic feet per minute the pilots get in the cockpit. This keeps gases, especially carbon dioxide, from being ventilated out of the cabin.

In general, the more time you spend in an enclosed, highly populated, poorly ventilated space like an airplane cabin, the more likely you are to experience headaches, sluggishness, sore throat, coughing, and dry or watery eyes. To boot, the air at high altitudes is dryer than the atmosphere above the Sahara Desert, so you may find your symptoms compounded by dehydration.

Furthermore, evidence suggests that more travelers develop colds in airplane cabins than in other enclosed, highly populated public spaces. This is partly because dehydration diminishes the immune system; but it's also because, as mentioned, few other public spaces keep people in such close quarters for such an extended period of time.

Fortunately, symptoms of poor cabin air tend to vanish soon after you take leave of the offending space. Unfortunately, there's not too much you can do to help yourself. Some suggestions:

- If your budget allows, **fly in first or business class,** where fewer people share air space.

- Don't leave home without your inhaler if you have asthma.

- Where possible, try to **avoid flying with a cold** (see "Flying with a Cold," below).

- If you're on a connecting flight, **try to get as much fresh air** as you can between connections.

- Clear your head with a **steaming hot shower** when you land.

- **Avoid smoke-filled bars** when you reach your destination or while you wait for a connecting flight.

DEHYDRATION

While the earth's desert regions have a 20% to 25% humidity level, the cabin of a plane flying at cruising altitude (35,000 ft./10,500m) has a mere 15% humidity content. In this arid environment, your skin evaporates as much as 8 ounces of water per hour. This is why your eyes burn, your lips dry out, your head hurts, and you feel generally sluggish, light-headed, and cranky while you're on a plane.

It's absolutely imperative that you drink lots of water before, during, and after your flight to maintain your body's fluid reserves. Not only will you feel much better, you'll help ward off a host of other maladies. The effects of dehydration compromise the immune system, so you're far more likely to catch the complimentary cold that comes with air travel if you don't drink enough water. Dehydration will also aggravate the symptoms of jet lag.

Even if you don't feel thirsty, drink up. Thirst doesn't necessarily precede the symptoms of dehydration, which can set in without warning. Experts recommend that you drink at least two 8-ounce glasses just before departure and 1 liter for every hour you spend in the air — in addition to the beverages you drink with meals.

Pack a travel-size bottle of skin lotion to replenish moisture in your face and hands during air travel. If you're taking an overnight flight, don't forget to pack a toothbrush, which will help you at least to *feel* fresher and less dry. Before you prepare to land, visit the lavatory and wash your face and hands, rinsing with cold water.

If you don't want your morning flight to feel like the red-eye, trade your contact lenses for glasses before you board, to keep your eyes from drying out, itching, and turning red. If nothing comes between you and your lenses, you should at least pack some rewetting drops in your carry-on bag.

PRESSURIZATION

If you've lived your whole life at sea level, you're likely to feel wobbly on a long-distance flight. When cruising at their maximum level of 40,000 feet (12,000m), commercial aircraft are pressurized to an equivalent of 8,000 feet (2,400m), according to Judith Murawski, an industrial hygienist for the Association of Flight Attendants. That means there's only about three-quarters as much oxygen in the (already somewhat stale) air as there is at sea level.

The pressure level is built into the design of commercial aircraft, according to Murawski. Thickening the air beyond existing levels would require a tougher, heavier skin so the pressure differential doesn't pop the plane like a balloon. A heavier plane means greater fuel expenses. (The Concorde, which flies at 60,000 ft./18,000m and is pressurized to a comfortable 6,000 ft./1,800m, is just that kind of tougher plane — and tickets on the Concorde cost thousands of dollars.)

The thin air in most planes isn't lethal — millions of people around the world live at altitudes of 8,000 feet (2,400m) or greater and are quite healthy. But 8,000 feet (2,400m) is the threshold at which some people begin to develop mild altitude sickness, otherwise known as Acute Mountain Sickness, according to Rick Curtis of Princeton University's Outdoor Action Program. The symptoms of mild Acute Mountain Sickness are headache, dizziness, fatigue, shortness of breath, loss of appetite, nausea, disturbed sleep, and a general feeling of malaise.

And the thin air on board makes flying an anathema to people with heart and lung problems (see "Grounding Conditions," later in this chapter).

There's nothing you can do about pressurization levels on board, and it's ultimately harmless if you're otherwise healthy, but it's also unpleasant.

PESTICIDES

The cabins of planes traveling to or from certain countries are subject to spraying with pesticides, a controversial practice that has brought complaints from the flight attendants' union and class-action lawsuits filed in 2001 by passengers and flight attendants who say that the bug spray made them sick.

Australia, Fiji, New Zealand, Barbados, Jamaica, and Panama require planes to be sprayed while empty; India, Grenada, Kiribati, Trinidad and Tobago, Madagascar, and Uruguay require actual passengers to be sprayed while on board. The most highly publicized complaints come from passengers and attendants on United Airlines flights from Los Angeles to Sydney, Australia.

Permethrin, one pesticide used in Australia, has ingredients similar to those in lice shampoo. It's banned for use in aircraft cabins in the U.S. because of safety concerns, according to the Association of Flight Attendants.

The World Health Organization and the airlines say that the pesticides are safe. But they haven't been approved by the U.S. Environmental Protection Agency for airline use, and 12 U.S. senators wrote letters to the Bush administration during the summer of 2001 asking that the Department of Transportation force airlines to halt the spraying. In a letter dated June 11, 2001, Transportation Secretary Norman Mineta said the government was "preparing a response."

As the spraying is government-mandated in foreign countries, it's hard to avoid. Cover your nose and mouth during in-flight spraying, immediately report any odd smells in the cabin, and write to your congressional representatives if you want it stopped.

FLYING WITH A COLD

Next to jet lag, the most ordinary health problem to worry about when you travel by plane is the common cold or flu. During takeoff and landing, even the healthiest travelers experience slight ear discomfort as pressure in the inner ear adapts to rapidly shifting air pressure in the plane cabin. When your mucous membranes are swollen from a cold, the eustachian tube, which connects the sinus cavity to the inner ear, is congested. There's very little room for air to reach the inner ear soon enough to avert severe discomfort — or worse. In the worst instances, you may suffer permanent damage to your eardrums if inner ear pressure can't match cabin pressure at a healthy clip.

If your cold is severe, you should consider postponing your flight. If you simply must fly, however, use a decongestant

Kids with Colds

It's even more difficult for kids to make their ears pop during take-off and landing. The eustachian tube is especially narrow in children; the passage is even tighter when mucous membranes are swollen. This can make ascent and descent especially painful – even dangerous – for a child with congested sinuses. If your little one is suffering from a cold or the flu, it's best to keep him grounded until he recuperates, if that's an option. (If you simply must travel with your child as scheduled, give him or her an oral child's decongestant an hour before ascent and descent or administer a spray decongestant before and during takeoff and landing.)

or nasal spray before takeoff and landing to minimize pressure buildup. Read the label of your decongestant carefully and time your preflight dose so that you'll be able to take another about 1 hour before you're scheduled to land, as sinus and inner-ear pain tend to be most severe during descent.

When you start to feel pressure build in your ears, you can make them pop with a "modified Valsalva maneuver." It's very simple: Pinch your nostrils closed and breathe in deeply. Then breathe out through the nose, as though you were trying to blow your fingers off your nostrils. Blow out in short, firm bursts until you feel your ears "pop." Yawning, drinking liquids, or chewing gum also help to minimize pressure buildup during takeoff and landing.

Antihistamines are even more effective than decongestants, but they will also cause drowsiness. If you're driving yourself from the airport to your destination, it's best to avoid them.

"ECONOMY-CLASS SYNDROME"

Rare but potentially lethal, economy-class syndrome is a result of sitting in cramped conditions for long periods of time. The combination of a sitting position, inertia, and pressure on leg veins reduces blood flow in the lower limbs by two-thirds, according to Dr. Luis Navarro, director of New York's Vein Treatment Center. Stagnant blood in the legs can clot, leading to a condition known as deep vein thrombosis (DVT). If those clots break off and move to the lungs, they can cause a fatal pulmonary embolism like the one that killed British traveler Emma Christofferson in 2000.

Christofferson was flying from Singapore to London — and DVT has most often been reported in people who've taken flights of 8 hours or more. The elderly, pregnant women, women taking hormone therapy or birth control, and people who have recently undergone surgery, have varicose veins, smoke, or have a history of blood clots are most at risk, according to Dr. Navarro.

Economy-class syndrome isn't exclusive to air travelers. Two million Americans suffer from DVT each year, according to Dr. Navarro. In a study published in the medical journal *Chest* in 1999, French physicians looked at 160 DVT patients. Only about a quarter had taken long trips recently, and of that group, most had been on long car journeys rather than in the air.

The syndrome isn't exclusive to economy class, either. Former Vice President Dan Quayle got DVT in 1994, and his doctors suspected a flight-heavy schedule was the culprit. (Former vice presidents generally don't ride in coach.)

If one of your feet, ankles, or legs swells or aches for longer than 24 hours after you board a plane, seek medical help immediately — from an emergency room, if necessary. The standard treatment for DVT is an injection of Heparin, followed by an oral anticoagulant. This remedy thins the blood and will dissipate the clot — and possibly save your life.

There's fortunately a simple solution to DVT: *Move.* Get an aisle seat and walk around the cabin every 60 to 90 minutes, to shake up the blood in your legs. Take off your shoes, put your feet up if possible, and don't cross your legs. Drink lots of water to stay hydrated and avoid caffeine and alcohol, which dry you out.

The truly worried, obese, pregnant, or elderly should consider wearing compression stockings, which promote blood flow. They're available at medical supply stores for around $15. Put them on before your flight, while lying in bed, and wear them all day.

You can also stimulate blood flow by doing these leg exercises in your seat:

- **Flex and point.** From a sitting position, raise your feet slightly off the floor in front of your seat. Flex your left foot while you point your right. Then switch: point the left and flex the right. Try to perform 10 to 25 repetitions every hour.

- **Round the clock.** With your legs still elevated slightly, rotate both your feet outward in a full circle from the ankle — as though they were hands on a clock, one moving clockwise, the other moving counterclockwise. Then switch: rotate them inward. Try to perform 10 to 25 repetitions every hour.

C FLYING WITH AN ALLERGY

For the severely allergic, flying can be Russian roulette. Fortunately, the airlines are willing to work with passengers – to some extent. Folks with peanut allergies are protected by a federal regulation requiring three-row, peanut-free "buffer zones" on request. Most airlines will go a bit further and remove peanut-based snacks from entire flights at the request of a passenger with a peanut allergy, although they warn that they can't control what other passengers bring aboard.

If you need to bring an injector or other medical device, make sure you have a note from your doctor and the prescription label from the pharmacy. It's illegal for airport security to take these devices away from you, if they're properly documented.

Peanut-allergic passengers may also want to book business class, where many airlines serve almonds rather than peanuts – and where the air supply won't be contaminated by coach-class snack fumes.

Airlines are less sympathetic to passengers with pet allergies; instead of removing pets from the cabin, they'll remove you from the cabin. Animal-allergic passengers generally have a choice of being reseated away from the pet or taking a different flight at no charge.

Finally, anyone with any sort of food allergy should avoid airline food. You don't know what's in it. Bring your own snacks.

- **Stair master.** With your left foot on the floor, raise your right leg a few inches off the floor. Lower it, then raise your left leg to the same height. Repeat this motion, as though you were climbing a flight of very low steps. Try to perform 10 to 25 repetitions every hour.

- **Seated knee lifts.** With your left leg on the floor, raise your right knee as close to your body as you can comfortably manage. Return your right foot to the floor and raise your left knee the same way. Return your left foot to the floor. Try to perform 10 to 25 repetitions every hour.

Magellan's travel suppliers (☎ **800/962-4943;** www. magellans.com) sells an **Exercise and Support Cushion** ($9.85) that stimulates leg and foot joints and improves circulation when inflated. From a sitting position, you can use your feet to force air through special passages and chambers to relieve the restless sensation you experience when your legs are squeezed in the confines of most airline seats, particularly in coach.

2 Obtaining Medical Assistance While Airborne

WOE TO THE TRAVELER WHO HAPPENS TO FALL seriously ill while in an airplane cabin. The airlines are under no obligation to provide medical assistance to passengers. In the absence of federal guidelines, most airlines simply hope there's a doctor in the house if a passenger suddenly needs medical attention.

Unfortunately, this default strategy is hardly foolproof. For fear of malpractice suits, many doctors are reluctant to provide assistance to strangers in the event of an emergency. Only one airline, Air Canada, provides full legal protection to doctors who come to the aid of passengers in need.

Doctors are especially afraid to get involved in in-flight emergencies when traveling to or from countries in the Middle East. Under Islamic law, an individual who is deemed responsible for a Muslim's death must pay blood money to the spouse of the deceased.

One doctor recently pressed charges against American Airlines after he intervened in a midair emergency. According to *Condé Nast Traveller*, Dr. John Stevens, a British psychiatrist aboard an American Airlines flight in early 1999, assisted a fellow passenger who suffered from a blood clot on the plane. While he may have saved the passenger's life, he apparently found the experience less than fulfilling and ended up suing the airline for $900 — on the grounds that his vacation had been interrupted.

GROUNDING CONDITIONS: WHEN ARE YOU TOO UNHEALTHY TO FLY?

Because medical facilities on board most aircraft are limited, the American Medical Association advises you not to fly on large jets if you have certain medical conditions. Some of these maladies are more severe than others, but all of them are adversely affected by changes in air pressure or the lack of oxygen at high altitudes.

You should seriously consider postponing your flight if you suffered a heart attack within the last month or a stroke within the last 2 weeks, if you have severe high blood pressure or heart disease, or if you are beset with any other condition that weakens the heart.

You should also remain on land if you have severe respiratory illnesses, such as pneumothorax (air outside the lung), cysts of the lung, or severe lung disease.

People with chronic heart and lung problems should use supplemental oxygen at all times when flying over 22,500 feet (6,750m). (The average cruising altitude is 35,000 ft./10,500m.) Be aware, however, that most airlines do not allow passengers to bring their own supplemental oxygen on board, as it is hazardous at high altitudes.

Unfortunately, most airlines charge extra for the oxygen they provide. And be aware that some carriers require that you order oxygen in advance.

You should also try not to fly with the flu, a cold, allergies, acute sinusitis, or middle ear infections. (See "Flying with a Cold," earlier in this chapter.)

If you underwent abdominal surgery within 2 weeks of your scheduled flight, you should postpone your trip. You should not fly if you have acute diverticulitis, ulcerative colitis, acute esophageal viruses, acute gastroenteritis, or an intestinal virus.

If you have epilepsy you should not fly, unless your condition is under sound control or you know that you will be flying at altitudes below 8,000 feet (2,400m). If you are overcome by violent or unpredictable behavior, or suffered a recent skull fracture or brain tumor, you should stay on the ground.

If you have severe anemia or hemophilia with active bleeding, you shouldn't fly. If you have sickle cell anemia, you shouldn't fly over 22,500 feet (6,750m).

If you underwent recent eye surgery or had your jaw wired shut, you shouldn't fly.

If you are more than 240 days pregnant (8 months) or if miscarriage is a serious threat, you shouldn't fly.

You should not fly if you went scuba diving 24 hours before departure. You may suffer from the "bends," from the rapid decrease in air pressure after time spent in a compressed air environment. Symptoms include difficulty breathing, neuralgic pains, and paralysis; and death can occur.

If you have questions regarding these guidelines, call the **American Medical Association**'s help line (☎ **312/ 464-5000**).

BE PREPARED: GET ON BOARD
WITH ALL THE INFO

It's up to the passenger to take precautions against a midair medical emergency. If you suffer from a chronic illness,

⏾ THE "SMOKING" GUN

Stock up on that nicotine gum. Smoking is banned on all flights to, from, and within the United States, except on Aeroflot and Egyptair — and those two carriers have worrisome safety records.

Most international airlines have also banned smoking in the air; now the only smoking-allowed carriers are a motley collection of third-world airlines, two low-fare European airlines (Air Europa and Condor), the Western European carrier with the area's worst fatal accident record (Olympic), and two airlines belonging to official U.S. enemies (Cubana and Iran Air). The best pick of this bad bunch for long-haul flights outside the U.S.? Malaysia Airlines and Kuwait Airways, which have relatively solid safety records according to airsafe.com.

According to the Department of Transportation and other sources, the following airlines have some smoking flights: Aero California, Aeroflot, Aeroperu, Air China, Air Europa, Air India, Avensa, China Eastern, Condor, Cubana, Gulf Air, Iran Air, Kuwait Airways, Lloyd Aero Boliviano, Malaysia Airlines, Olympic Airways, Pakistan International Airlines, Philippine Airlines, Royal Air Maroc, Royal Air Nepal, Royal Jordanian, Saeta, TAROM Romanian, and Uzbekistan Airways.

The situation in airports is only slightly more comforting for smokers. Many airports allow smoking in designated bars, smoking lounges, and frequent travelers' clubs. Nicotine addicts should stay away from the airports in Detroit, Minneapolis, Houston, and San Francisco, though, where smoking is entirely banned.

---

consult your doctor before your departure. If you must fly with a condition such as epilepsy, diabetes, or heart disease, wear a **Medic Alert Identification Tag** (☎ **800/825-3785;** www.medicalert.org), which will immediately alert doctors to your condition and give them access to your records through Medic Alert's 24-hour hot line. Membership is $35, plus a $15 annual fee.

If you suffer from a dental problem during a domestic flight, a nationwide referral service known as **1-800-DENTIST** (☎ **800/336-8478**) will provide the name of a nearby dentist or clinic when you land.

3   TASTELESS: DEALING WITH AIRLINE FOOD

MOST AIRLINES HAVE CUT BACK ON FOOD SERVICE recently — and even if you do get a "meal" on a domestic flight, it's likely to be a limp turkey sandwich. Your best bet is to brown-bag homemade sandwiches. Unlike fruit, for example, they have no leftover parts to throw away, and you won't have to tussle with airport security over silverware. But if you insist on eating economy-class cuisine, some tips:

- **Order a special meal.** Most airlines allow coach-class passengers to order from a range of special meals, including low-fat, low-cholesterol, vegetarian, and children's meals (the latter usually a hamburger or hot dog). These meals aren't necessarily fresher than the standard ones, but at least you'll know what's in them. Call your airline 2 days before your flight to secure your meal. Then double-check when you check in.

- **Become a vegetarian.** Dieticians and frequent fliers say vegetarian and vegan meals are often better than standard airline fare. Vegan meals skip cheese and sweets, leading to a healthier but more spartan platter.

- **Fly a tasty airline.** The Zagat organization rates airline food annually. For 2001, Midwest Express had the best economy-class meals (including fresh chocolate-chip cookies and real plates), while America West rated the worst of the airlines that actually serve meals (think that aforementioned turkey sandwich).

Alcohol-Free Flights?

Drinking while flying isn't just a bad idea – it's several bad ideas. Alcohol dehydrates you, for one thing, and appears to exacerbate "air rage" and misbehavior on planes. But wary of potential traveler revolts and hoping to keep income flowing in from onboard drinks, no U.S. airline has dared to offer "dry" flights. To avoid alcohol, you'll have to fly Kuwait Airways or Saudia – because the religion of Islam bans alcohol, those two airlines offer sweet fruit juices to soothe your soul instead.

In general, coach-class passengers now only get meals on flights crossing two-thirds of the country or more; everyone else gets peanuts or other mini-bags of snacks. (Continental and Alaska are welcome exceptions, but 'meals' on Continental flights under 3½ hours are of the dreaded turkey sandwich variety.)

Most low-fare airlines generally only serve snacks (except for Midwest Express), even on cross-country flights. But some offer better snacks than others. Southwest offers a non-yummy bag of salted peanuts. But JetBlue serves up classy blue potato chips, and Frontier goes even further with chicken wraps and specialty bagels.

THE ECONOMY-CLASS MEAL POLICIES OF MAJOR AIRLINES

- **Alaska:** Food served on flights of 2 hours or more. Meal times: Breakfast 6 to 8:30am; Lunch 10:30am to 1:30pm; Dinner 4 to 7pm.

- **America West:** Food served only on flights between the East Coast and Phoenix. Breakfast 6 to 9am; Lunch 11am to 1pm; Dinner 5 to 7pm.

- **American:** Food served only on nonstop, transcontinental flights. Breakfast 5 to 8:30am; Lunch 12 to 1pm; Dinner 5:30 to 7pm.

- **Continental:** Food served on flights of 2 hours or more. Breakfast 7 to 9am; Lunch 11am to 1pm; Dinner 5 to 7pm.

- **Delta:** Food served only on flights of more than 1,750 miles (2,818km). Breakfast 5 to 8:30am; Lunch 12 to 1pm; Dinner 6:30 to 7:30pm.

- **Northwest:** Food served only on flights between Detroit/Minneapolis/Memphis and the west coast. Breakfast 6 to 9:45am; Lunch 11am to 1:15pm; Dinner 4:30 to 7:15pm.

- **United:** Food served only on flights of more than 1,635 miles (2,632km). Breakfast 5 to 9:59am; Lunch 11am to 1:29pm; Dinner 4:50 to 7:29pm.

- **US Airways:** Food served only on nonstop, trans-continental flights. Breakfast 6 to 10am; Lunch 11am to 1pm; Dinner 4 to 7pm.

ZAGAT'S TOP-RATED AIRLINE MEALS

ECONOMY CLASS

1.	Midwest Express
2.	Alaska Airlines
3.	National Airlines (tie)
	United Airlines
5.	Hawaiian Airlines

PREMIUM CLASS

1.	Hawaiian Airlines
2.	Alaska Airlines (tie)
	Continental Airlines
4.	United Airlines (tie)
	American Airlines

Source: 2001 Zagat Airline Survey, found at www.zagat.com

4 TRAVEL INSURANCE DEMYSTIFIED

THE DISASTERS ON SEPTEMBER 11, 2001, MADE TRAVEL insurance more necessary than ever. The right policy can protect you financially against an airline going bankrupt or a terrorist attack shutting down an airport, as well as provide the usual refunds if you get sick and have to cancel your trip.

But it's also become more important to be a smart insurance shopper. Several major insurers are reducing or eliminating coverage for "carrier default," otherwise known as bankruptcy. Policies were in flux as this book went to press, so you'll have to call around and compare prices and coverage when you book your trip.

BEFORE YOU BUY

Before you buy any travel insurance policy, figure out what your existing insurance policies cover. Your homeowner's or renter's insurance may cover lost or stolen baggage. Your credit card company may insure you against travel accidents or plane crashes. And your existing health insurance should cover you if you get sick while on vacation — although if you belong to an HMO, you should investigate whether you are fully covered when away from home.

If you need hospital treatment, most health insurance plans and HMOs will cover out-of-country hospital visits and procedures, at least to some extent. Most make you pay the bills up front at the time of care, however, and you'll get a refund only after you've returned and filed all the paperwork. Members of **Blue Cross/Blue Shield** can now use their cards at select hospitals in major cities worldwide (☎ **800/ 810-BLUE** or www.bluecares.com and click on "BlueCard Doctor & Hospital Finder"). You should have some type of medical coverage while you travel, though, so you may want to consider purchasing some if your home policy doesn't cover travel — or if you're altogether uninsured.

TRIP CANCELLATION INSURANCE

Trip cancellation insurance will reimburse you for the money you lose if you can't go on the trip or if you have to return home early. A wide variety of reasons may be covered — from the U.S. State Department telling Americans not to go to your destination country, to being unable to go because you lost your job and have to look for work. Buy this insurance to go with tickets purchased well in advance, because you may not know your personal situation — or the state of the world — several months in the future. Without insurance, if you cancel a trip far in advance, you may lose just a pittance, but if you must back out at the last minute, the fees can be astronomical. Likewise, if you purchased discounted tickets, you may lose the entire ticket value if you decide not to travel and don't have coverage. Most policies will reimburse you for the following:

- Extra costs incurred by sickness (this can apply to some preexisting conditions as well), injury, or death suffered by you or a travel companion before departure or during your trip.

- Costs incurred by canceling or interrupting your journey because a close family member suffers illness, injury, or death.

- Costs of cancellation if you suffer a flood, accident, or fire at home; if you have to serve on jury duty; if you miss a flight because of a natural disaster, an act of terrorism, or a strike.

- Costs of cancellation because the U.S. State Department has advised Americans not to travel to your destination country.

- The costs of a single supplement, should your traveling partner have to cancel.

- The cost of rescheduling a flight if you are forced to postpone a trip.

- The cost of returning home if you must interrupt your trip.

- The cost of outside help if it is warranted by sudden sickness or an accident during your trip.

- The price of your ticket if your airline or tour operator goes out of business.

Unfortunately, several major insurers (even a few mentioned under "Recommended Agents," below) have been backing out of protecting against airline and tour company bankruptcies, according to *Consumer Reports Travel Letter* of January 2002. CSA Travel Protection's policies skip "carrier default" entirely. Travel Guard requires you buy your policy within 7 days of buying your trip, only covers claims if the supplier doesn't collapse within 2 weeks of the trip payment, and specifically doesn't cover certain airlines including National, Aer Lingus, and Thai. Access America only covers a narrow list of airlines — it's missing Alaska and America West among the majors, has few low-fare airlines, and covers no foreign carriers. When you call to buy a policy, inquire whether you'll be covered if your airline goes bankrupt.

EMERGENCY MEDICAL-EVACUATION INSURANCE (EME)

Emergency medical-evacuation insurance will cover the exorbitant cost of emergency transportation if an emergency situation forces you to return home or visit a hospital far from the scene of an accident. It is often sold as part of a "bundled" coverage policy, in conjunction with trip cancellation insurance. It's especially useful for "outdoorsy" or third-world trips where getting to a quality hospital means more than an ambulance ride down the block.

OTHER BITS OF THE BUNDLE

Most insurers push bundled policies, with cancellation and medical components as well as a bunch of other protections. It's up to you whether travel delay insurance (which gives you a bit of dough if you're stuck overnight in the airport), missed cruise connection insurance, or rental car insurance is worth it. Usually, these extra features are the icing on the cake, and shouldn't make or break your insurance shopping.

Insurance companies are **not** the same. At press time, policies were changing frequently to reflect the shaky travel marketplace. Compare prices, and especially the conditions of your cancellation insurance, before buying.

RECOMMENDED AGENTS

These major insurers have been recommended by *Consumer Reports Travel Letter* in the past:

- **Access America,** 6600 W. Broad St., Richmond, VA 23230 (☎ **800/284-8300;** www.accessamerica.com).

- **CSA,** P.O. Box 939057, San Diego, CA 92193-9057 (☎ **800/873-9855;** www.csatravelprotection.com). *Consumer Reports* rated this provider a "Best Buy," but they don't cover against airlines or tour operators going bankrupt.

- **International SOS Assistance,** P.O. Box 11568, Philadelphia, PA 11916 (☎ **800/523-8930** or 215/244-1500; www.internationalsos.com).

- **Travel Guard International,** 1145 Clark St., Stevens Point, WI 54481 (☎ **800/826-1300;** www.travelguard.com).

- **Travel Insured International,** 52-S Oakland Ave., P.O. Box 280568, East Hartford, CT 06128-0568 (☎ **800/243-3174;** www.travelinsured.com). Travel Insured coverage is especially generous in regard to preexisting medical conditions.

- **Travelex Insurance Services,** P.O. Box 641070, Omaha, NE 68164-7070 (☎ **800/228-9792;** www. travelex-insurance.com). Travelex covers an especially broad range of causes.

- **Worldwide Assistance,** 9200 Keystone Crossing, Ste. 300, Indianapolis, IN 46240 (☎ **800/821-2828;** www.worldwideassistance.com).

5 Advice for Passengers with Special Needs

TRAVELERS WITH DISABILITIES

Since it became law in 1986, the Air Carrier Access Act has revolutionized domestic air travel for persons with disabilities. In essence, the law attempts to prohibit the airlines from discriminating against travelers on the basis of a physical disability by recognizing the obstacles they face, by introducing new technologies and services to accommodate them, and by training airline personnel in how best to attend to their particular needs.

It's wise to verse yourself in your rights, however, if you need to fly with a disability, as the law leaves a few points open for interpretation. Unfortunately, if you read the ombudsman section of any travel publication, you will still hear plenty of horror stories regarding the violation of the Air Carrier Access Act. So be sure to know your rights before you fly.

If you feel your rights as a disabled traveler have been violated, you should by all means file a complaint with the airline and the **Department of Transportation** (Aviation Consumer Protection Division, 400 7th St. SW C-75, Washington, DC 20590; ☎ **202/366-2220** or 202/755-7687). See chapter 10, "The Squeaky Wheel," for advice on how to complain effectively.

The Letter of the Law

Fundamentally, the **Air Carrier Access Act** states that:

- An airline may not refuse to transport a passenger solely on the basis of a disability.

- An airline may not limit the number of individuals with disabilities on a particular flight.

- All trip information made available to other passengers must also be made available to passengers with disabilities.

- An airline must provide transport to a person with a disability that might affect his appearance or involuntary behavior, even if this behavior may offend, annoy, or inconvenience crew members or other passengers (for example, passengers who may suffer from Tourette's Syndrome).

- The airline may refuse to transport a person with a disability if doing so endangers the health or safety of other passengers or otherwise violates FAA safety rules.

- Airline personnel are not required to carry a special-needs passenger on board by hand. If the plane has fewer than 30 seats, the airline may refuse to transport the passenger if the plane has no lifts, boarding chairs, or other devices to help the passenger board.

- The airline may refuse to transport special-needs passengers if it cannot do so without seating them in an emergency-exit row seat. By law, these seats must be occupied by able-bodied adults who can assist other passengers in case of an emergency.

  The law has its fine points as well. The airlines are also not allowed to require advance notification of a passenger's disabilities. They may, however, require 48-hour notice if they will be expected to transport an electric wheelchair or respirator.

New planes with more than 29 seats — meaning aircraft that have started flying since April 5, 1992 — must have movable armrests on at least half the aisle seats to accommodate passengers with disabilities. As older planes are refurbished, they must be retrofitted with movable armrests as well. New wide-body planes must be equipped with accessible bathrooms and an onboard wheelchair. Ramps or mechanical lifts must be available for most aircraft with 19 through 30 seats at larger domestic airports and at all airports with more than 10,000 passengers annually.

Airline personnel are required to show passengers where to find these accommodations and how to operate them.

Airlines may not require a person with a disability to fly with an attendant, except in limited circumstances: if a person needs to travel in a stretcher; if a person is unable to comprehend or follow safety instructions because of a mental disability; if a person is unable to assist in his or her own evacuation from the aircraft in case of emergency; or if a person has both severe hearing and vision impairment and would not be able to comprehend or follow safety instructions in case of an emergency.

In these situations, when the airline does have the right to insist that such a passenger fly with an attendant, they cannot charge for the companion's passage. If the flight in question does not have room for an attendant, the passenger with a disability is entitled to denied boarding compensation.

The airline is also under obligation to assist the traveler with a disability while boarding, disembarking, and making

Some Disassembly Required

If you travel in a large, powered wheelchair, be prepared to take it apart. On some planes such as the popular MD-80 series, the cargo opening is only 26 inches high, so anything bigger will have to be dismantled to fit into the plane. Bring your owner's manual and plenty of patience.

connections. Flight attendants must help passengers move to and from seats, open and identify food, get to and from the lavatory, and load or retrieve carry-on items. This may involve assisting the passenger with a walking support or an onboard wheelchair.

Wheelchairs and other assisting devices must be given priority over other items as checked baggage if a passenger with a disability preboards. Carriers must accept battery-powered wheelchairs, including the batteries, which might otherwise be classified as hazardous material. If necessary, the airline must also provide hazardous-materials packaging for the batteries. (If a wheelchair or assisting device is lost or damaged on a domestic flight, the airline is liable for a value up to $2,500. On international flights, no special exceptions are made for assisting devices. See chapter 4, "Lost in Space.")

Disabled passengers have the right to bring service animals on board, such as Seeing Eye dogs, provided they do not block aisles and emergency exits or otherwise hinder the safe and efficient passage of other travelers. If a passenger objects to being seated near a guide dog (because of an allergy, for instance), the objecting passenger — not the guide dog — must be moved or removed.

Usually, passengers may not bring their own oxygen on board, but the airlines must provide aircraft-approved oxygen. Disabled passengers must ask for this in advance, however, and should be prepared to pay a fee. You must also ask in advance for an incubator, respirator hookup, and accommodations for a stretcher.

Disabled passengers are under no obligation to provide airlines with advance notice that they will be traveling on board. You should be aware, however, that some carriers require 48 hours' notice for the following services: transportation for an electric wheelchair on an aircraft with under 60 seats; hazardous materials packaging for an electric wheelchair battery; accommodations for 10 or more passengers with disabilities flying as a group; and an onboard wheelchair, for aircraft with lavatories that would be inaccessible without the chair. Passengers with electric wheelchairs may also be asked to check into the airport an hour earlier than other passengers, so batteries can be properly packaged and stowed.

If an airline refuses to carry you because of a disability, demand an explanation in writing. The law requires the airline to provide you with one. The statement must include a rationale for why the airline thinks that transporting you would compromise the health and safety of other passengers.

If you believe your rights have been violated, consult immediately with a Complaints Resolution Official (see "Complaining 101," in chapter 10, "The Squeaky Wheel"). By law, all airlines are now required to have one immediately available, even if only by phone, to resolve disagreements on the spot. If you are still not satisfied, you may take up the case with the Department of Transportation and seek enforcement action. (See chapter 10 to investigate the proper channels for complaint.)

More in-depth information on the legal rights of travelers with disabilities is available on the Department of Transportation website at **www.dot.gov/airconsumer/ horizons.htm**.

PREGNANT WOMEN

Because sudden changes in air pressure can induce labor, airlines advise that any woman in her last month of pregnancy check with her doctor to see if it's safe for her to travel.

Airlines will deny boarding to any woman showing signs of labor (for obvious reasons), and most require a doctor's note for very pregnant women to travel. The note must be signed and dated within 72 hours of the flight, and United requires theirs in triplicate.

The American Medical Association advises against flying if you have a history of miscarriages, or if miscarriage is a serious threat otherwise.

Pregnant women should not use scopalamine ear patches, Dramamine, and other antihistamines. Studies have

AIRLINE REGULATIONS FOR FLYING WHILE PREGNANT

AIRLINE	DATE AFTER WHICH DOCTOR'S NOTE IS REQUIRED TO FLY
Alaska	No restriction
American	4 weeks before due date
America West	7 days before due date
Continental	7 days before due date
Delta	No restriction
Northwest	30 days before due date
Southwest	After the 38th week of pregnancy
United	4 weeks before due date
US Airways	7 days before due date

indicated these drugs can be passed to the child in utero and result in birth defects.

PETS

The ASPCA offers helpful safety guidelines for flying with pets. See "When Your Baggage Has a Pulse," in chapter 4, "Lost in Space."

6   TRAVELING WITH CHILDREN

SAFE SEATS FOR KIDS

The practice of allowing children younger than 2 to ride for free on a parent's lap may be prohibited by the time you read this. At press time, the FAA was writing a rule that would require all children under 40 pounds to have their own tickets and be secured in a child seat.

All the major American airlines except Delta now offer discounted infant tickets for children 2 years of age or younger, to make it more affordable for you to reserve a separate adjacent seat for your baby and a restraining device.

(Most airlines require than an infant be 2 weeks old to travel — bring a birth certificate. American and Continental only require that the child be 7 days old. Alaska lets babies fly as soon as they're born.)

For now, if a seat adjacent to yours is available, your lap child can sit there free of charge. When you check in, ask if the flight is crowded. If it isn't, explain your situation to the agent and ask if you can reserve two seats — or simply move to two empty adjacent seats once the plane is boarded. You might want to shop around before you buy your ticket and deliberately book a flight that's not very busy. Ask the reservationist which flights tend to be most full and avoid those. Only one extra child is allowed in each row, however, due to the limited number of oxygen masks.

On international journeys, children already can't ride free on parents' laps. On flights overseas, a lap fare usually costs 10% of the parent's ticket (see "Minor Policies of Major Carriers," below, for each carrier's policy). Children who meet the airline's age limit (which ranges from 11–15 yr. old) can purchase international fares at 50% to 75% of the lowest coach fare in certain markets. Some of the foreign carriers make even greater allowances for children.

Children riding for free will usually not be granted any baggage allowance.

All airlines offer child meals, if requested in advance. Ticketed babies can get "infant meals" on America West, Delta, and US Airways; and all major airlines except Alaska and Southwest will warm bottles on request.

CHILD SEATS: THEY'RE A MUST

According to *Consumer Reports Travel Letter,* the National Transportation Safety Board says that, since 1991, the deaths of five children and injury to four could have been prevented had the children been sitting in restraint systems during their flights. Even in the event of moderate turbulence, children sitting on a parent's lap can be thrust forward and injured. When you consider that a commercial aircraft hits a significant amount of turbulence at least once a day on average, you'd do well to think about investing a few hundred dollars for a safety seat.

The FAA recommends that children under 20 pounds ride in a rear-facing child-restraint system, and says children that weigh 20 to 40 pounds should sit in a forward-facing child restraint system. Children over 40 pounds should sit in a regular seat and wear a seat belt.

All child seats manufactured after 1985 are certified for airline use, but make sure your chair will fit in an airline seat — it must be less than 16 inches wide. You may not use booster seats or seatless vests or harness systems. Safety seats must be placed in window seats — except in exit rows, where they are prohibited, so as not to block the passage of other travelers in the case of an emergency.

The airlines themselves should carry child safety seats on board. Unfortunately, most don't. To make matters worse, overzealous flight attendants have been known to try to keep safety seats off planes. One traveler recounts in the November 2001 issue of *Consumer Reports Travel Letter* how a Southwest attendant attempted to block use of a seat because the red label certifying it as safe for airline use had flaked off. That traveler won her case by bringing the owner's manual and appealing to the pilot — you should do the same.

The Custody Trap

Because of concern about parental abductions, special requirements exist for children flying to many foreign countries, including Mexico. If they're with one parent, they must bring a notarized consent document from the other parent – even if the missing parent is the one waving goodbye at the airport! A decree of sole custody or parental death certificate will also do. Minors traveling alone to these countries must bring either two consent forms, a decree of sole custody and one consent form, or applicable death certificates. Ask your airline what's required when you book the ticket.

Getting safety seats on an international flight may be even more difficult. Ask to make sure you can use your safety seat when you book a flight on a foreign airline.

Until the new FAA rule comes into effect, if you can't afford the expense of a separate ticket, book a ticket toward the back of the plane at a time when air travel is likely to be slowest — and the seat next to you is most likely to be empty. (See chapter 3, "The Hot Seat," for tips on picking seats with extra space in mind.) The reservationist should also be able to recommend the best (meaning the least busy) time for you to fly.

CHILDREN TRAVELING SOLO

Although individual airline policies differ (see "Minor Policies of Major Carriers," below, for details), for the most part children ages 5 to 11 pay the regular adult fare and can travel alone as unaccompanied minors on domestic flights only with an escort from the airlines — a flight attendant who seats the child, usually near the galley, where the flight crew is stationed; watches over the child during the flight; and escorts the child to the appropriate connecting gate or to the adult who will be picking up the child. Unaccompanied minors typically board first and disembark last.

On domestic flights, the service costs between $30 and $75, depending on the airline and whether the child will have to change planes. On all the major airlines, several children traveling together from the same family will only have to pay one fee.

Unaccompanied children are never left alone; escorts stay with them until turning them over to an escort on the connecting flight or to a designated guardian. Airlines require attending adults to furnish a name, address, and government-issued photo ID. The adult who drops the child off at the airport must designate then the name and address of the adult who is authorized to pick the child up. At the destination city, the airline will not release the child to anyone but the authorized adult, after receiving a signature and seeing a photo ID.

Children ages 5 to 7 generally may travel unaccompanied on direct and nonstop flights only; in other words, they're not allowed to change planes for connecting flights at that age. (Northwest and Delta allow all children to travel on connecting flights.) Children ages 8 to 11 may make connecting flights with an escort, with the exception of Southwest and America West, which do not allow any unaccompanied child under the age of 12 to take a connecting flight. America West's policy is relatively new, started in 2001 after two embarrassing incidents where the airline sent one child to the wrong destination and neglected to tell a parent about another child's flight delay.

Children over the age of 12 are considered adults and may travel without an escort on every major carrier but Northwest, which requires escorts until age 14. They still qualify for assistance from the airline for the extra fee. Southwest is the only airline that does not allow children to use the escort service once they are able to fly without one, at age 12.

Because airlines want to avoid the responsibility of having to shepherd children overnight, minors are usually not allowed to take the last connecting flight of the day, when the risk of missed connections is greatest. Minors are usually not allowed to travel on standby, and they must have confirmed reservations.

On connecting flights, ask when you book if the child will be flying on more than one airline. (With the new airline alliances, your child may end up on a Northwest aircraft, even though you booked the flight through Continental. See "Allied Forces," in chapter 2, "Ticketing Pitfalls.") If so, make sure you know each airline's policy for unaccompanied minors. Once you receive the ticket, review it yourself to make sure the city of origin and the destination are accurate. Review the ticket carefully with your child and explain simply how it works.

If you're booking a flight for your child, the airlines will request your name, telephone number, and address — along with the name, number, and address of the guardian who will meet your child at the destination city. An adult guardian must accompany the child to the gate or plane, furnish reasonable proof that another adult will meet the child at the final destination, and remain at the airport until the plane is in the air. The accompanying adult at the destination will have to sign a release form and furnish government-issued photo identification, such as a license or passport. If a child is unusually big or small, it's wise to bring a birth certificate to the airport as proof of age.

Solo Minors on International Flights

Major carriers' policies for minors traveling alone are basically the same for both domestic and international travel, although fees are higher on international flights. Children may be prohibited from boarding an international flight under poor weather conditions that could require that the plane be rerouted.

Parents should seriously consider using European airlines for international trips, because of the extra services they provide for kids. British Airways has a toy chest on its planes, and Virgin Atlantic treats kids like royalty, with special entertainment channels, toys, and treats.

If you're booking a ticket for a minor on an international flight, you should call the consulate of the destination country to find out about visas and other special entry requirements.

Minor Orientation

With increased security measures at airports, parents must now get a pass from the ticket agent for permission to escort their children to the departure gate. (Adults picking up unaccompanied minors at arrival gates also need this permission slip.) If your child has never flown before, it makes sense to show up at the airport a little early to wander around, watch other planes take off and land, and prepare your child in advance for how flying is going to feel. Be sure to discuss the danger of talking to strangers — even if you have had the same discussion before. You will be allowed to escort your child to the gate, but not onto the plane. It's wise to stick around until departure to ensure that the plane is not delayed.

Some airlines allow unaccompanied minors to board first, so the flight crew has more time to meet the child, orient the child to the location of bathrooms and emergency exits, store carry-ons, review safety procedures, and — kids love this part — introduce the child to the cockpit crew. Make sure minors understand that they should contact an attendant in case of any type of problem — from sickness, to a malfunctioning headset, to a bothersome neighbor. If you can't make it all the way on to the plane, be sure to introduce your child to the gate attendant and ensure the child will receive help boarding if necessary.

Some airlines offer special meals for children, such as hamburgers, hot dogs, or peanut butter sandwiches, which must be ordered in advance, when you make the reservation. It's still wise to send your child off with a bagged lunch, snack, and drinks. Also pack books and other entertainment in a carry-on and make sure your child knows how to get at them on board the plane.

Make sure your child has cash and knows how to make a collect phone call. In one place, record your child's name, your own name, address, and phone number, along with the names and phone number of your child's hosts at the final destination. Review the information with your child and place it in a safe purse, pocket, or neck pouch. Be sure, however, that your child knows not to share this information with strangers — not even a friendly neighbor in the cabin.

If your child is taking medication, it may be wise to postpone the trip unless you are certain your child is responsible for self-administering dosages properly. Flight attendants are not allowed to administer drugs to minors.

Minor Policies of Major Carriers

ALASKA

- Unaccompanied children 5 to 11 must travel with escort.

- Escort is $30 each direction for nonstop and direct flights, $60 each way for connecting flights.

- Children 5 to 7 may not travel on connecting flights.

- Children 8 to 11 may travel on connecting flights.

- Children 12 and over are no longer considered unaccompanied minors, though escorts are available to them.

- One fee applies for up to three children.

- Children below the age of 13 are not allowed to travel on the last flight of the day, or on any flight leaving between 9pm and 5am.

AMERICA WEST

- Unaccompanied children 5 to 11 must travel with escort.

- Escort is $30 each direction.

- Children 5 to 11 may only travel on nonstop flights.

- Children 12 and over are no longer considered unaccompanied minors, though escorts are available to them for the fee.

AMERICAN

- Unaccompanied children 5 to 11 must travel with escort.

- Escort is $30 each way on nonstop and direct flights, $60 each way on connecting flights.

- Children 5 to 7 may not travel on connecting flights.

- Children 8 to 11 may travel on connecting flights, as long as the connection is within the same airport terminal.

- Children 12 to 17 are no longer considered unaccompanied minors, though escorts are still available to them for the fee.

CONTINENTAL

- Unaccompanied children 5 to 12 must travel with escort.

- Escort is $30 each direction (connecting flights $60 each way; direct or through $30 each way).

- Children 5 to 7 may not travel on connecting flights, late flights, or red-eye flights.

- Children 8 to 11 may make connecting flights.

- Children 12 to 17 are no longer considered unaccompanied minors, even on connecting flights, though escorts are still available to them for the fee.

- International travel: Escorts are $60 for nonstops and direct flights, $90 for connecting flights.

- Continental has special club rooms in Cleveland, Houston, and Newark for unaccompanied minors.

DELTA

- Unaccompanied children 5 to 11 must travel with escort.

- Escort is $40 for nonstop and direct flights (connecting flights are $75 one-way).

- Children 5 to 11 may travel on any flights with escort.

- Children 12 and over are no longer considered unaccompanied minors, though escorts are available to them for the fee.

- International travel: Same policy, except the escort fee is $60 for nonstop and direct flights, $90 for connecting flights on flights outside the U.S., Canada, and Mexico. (Flights to Canada and Mexico are $30 for nonstops, $60 for connecting.) Unaccompanied minors will not be permitted to board international flights in bad weather conditions that could require the plane to be rerouted.

Northwest

- Unaccompanied children 5 to 14 must travel with escort.

- Escort is $40 for nonstop and direct, $75 for connecting flights.

- All children ages 5 and older may fly on connecting flights.

- Children 14 and under may travel on connecting flights but may not be on the last flight of the day.

- Children 15 to 17 are no longer considered unaccompanied minors, though escorts are available to them for the fee.

- International travel: Same policy, but escort service beyond Canada and Mexico costs $60 for nonstops, $90 for connecting one-way flights.

Southwest

- Unaccompanied children 5 to 11 must travel with an escort and may not take connecting flights.

- Escort service is free.

- Children 12 and over are no longer considered unaccompanied minors and may travel alone, even on connecting flights; escort service is not available to children over 12.

UNITED

- Unaccompanied children 5 to 11 must travel with escort.

- Escort is $60 each direction.

- Children 5 to 7 may not travel on connecting flights.

- Children 8 to 11 may travel on connecting flights with escort.

- Children 12 and over are no longer considered unaccompanied minors, though escorts are available to them for the fee.

- International travel: Same policy.

US AIRWAYS

- Unaccompanied children 5 to 11 must travel with escort.

- Escort is $40 each way ($75 for connecting flights).

- Children 5 to 7 may not travel on connecting flights.

- Children 8 to 11 may travel on connecting flights with escort.

- Children 12 and over are no longer considered unaccompanied minors, though escorts are available to them for the fee.

- Special children's lounges are available in Charlotte, Philadelphia, and Pittsburgh.

- International travel: Same policy.

EASING TRAVEL WITH THE TOTS IN TOW

Several books on the market offer tips to help you travel with kids. Most concentrate on the U.S., but two, ***Family Travel & Resorts: The Complete Guide*** (Lanier Publishing International; $19.95) and ***How to Take Great Trips with Your***

Kids (The Harvard Common Press; $9.95), are full of good general advice that can apply to travel anywhere. Another reliable tome, with a worldwide focus, is *Adventuring with Children* (Foghorn Press; $14.95).

Family Travel Times (☎ **888/822-4FTT;** www.family traveltimes.com) is an excellent online newsletter updated twice monthly. Subscriptions are $39 a year, $49 for 2 years. Sample articles are available on the newsletter's website.

If you plan carefully, you can actually make it fun to travel with kids.

- If you're traveling with children, you'll save yourself a good bit of aggravation by **reserving a seat in the bulkhead** row. You'll have more legroom, and your children will be able to spread out and play on the floor underfoot. You're also more likely to find sympathetic company in the bulkhead area, as families with children tend to be seated there.

- Be sure to **pack items for your children in your carry-on luggage.** When you're deciding what to bring, ready yourself for the worst: long, unexpected delays without food, bathrooms without changing tables, airline meals that feature your children's least favorite dishes.

- Have **a long talk with your children** before you depart for your trip. If they've never flown before, explain to them what to expect. If they're old enough, you may even want to describe how flight works and how air travel is even safer than riding in a car. Explain to your kids the importance of good behavior in the air — how their own safety can depend upon their being quiet and staying in their seats during the trip.

- **Pay extra careful attention to the safety instructions** before takeoff. Consult the safety chart behind the seat in front of you and show it to your children. Be sure you know how to operate the oxygen masks, as you will be expected to secure yours first and then help your children with theirs. Be especially mindful of the location of emergency exits. Before takeoff, plot out an evacuation strategy for you and your children in your mind's eye.

- Ask the flight attendant **if the plane has any special safety equipment for children.** Make a member of the crew aware of any medical problems your children have that could manifest during flight.

- **Be sure you've slept sufficiently** for your trip. If you fall asleep in the air and your child manages to break away, there are all sorts of sharp objects that could cause injury. Especially during mealtimes, it's dangerous for a child to be crawling or walking around the cabin unaccompanied by an adult.

- **Be sure your child's seat belt remains fastened properly,** and try to reserve the seat closest to the aisle for yourself. This will make it harder for your children to wander off — in case, for instance, you're taking the red-eye or a long flight overseas and you do happen to nod off. You will also protect your child from jostling passersby and falling objects — in the rare but entirely possible instance that an overhead bin pops open.

    In the event of an accident, unrestrained children often don't make it — even when the parent does. Experience has shown that it's impossible for a parent to hold onto a child in the event of a crash, and children often die of impact injuries.

    For the same reason, sudden turbulence is also a danger to a child who is not buckled into his own seat belt or seat restraint. According to *Consumer Reports Travel Letter,* the most common flying injuries result when unanticipated turbulence strikes and hurtles passengers from their seats. (See "Child Seats: They're a Must," above, for suggestions regarding FAA-promoted child-restraint systems.)

- **Try to sit near the lavatory,** though not so close that your children are jostled by the crowds that tend to gather there. As mentioned in chapter 3, seats near the lavatory are often smaller, less comfortable, and in a noisy (and potentially smelly) area. But the advantage of sitting near the bathroom will come in handy if your children need to visit it often — and urgently. Consolidate trips there as much as possible.

- Try to **accompany children to the lavatory.** They can be easily bumped and possibly injured as they make their way down tight aisles. It's especially dangerous for children to wander while flight attendants are blocking passage with their service carts. On crowded flights, the flight crew may need as much as an hour to serve dinner. It's wise to encourage your kids to use the restroom as you see the attendants preparing to serve.

- Be sure to **bring clean, compact toys.** Magnetic checker sets are a perfect distraction, and small coloring books and crayons also work well, as do card games like Go Fish.

  Visit the library before you leave home and check out children's books about flying or airplane travel. Geography-related books and coloring books that include their departure point and destination will also help engage them during air travel.

  A Walkman with a few favorite recordings will also come in handy — especially if you throw in some sleepy-time tunes. By all means, don't leave home without a favorite blanket or stuffed animal — especially if it's your kid's best friend at bedtime.

- Some airlines **serve children's meals first.** When you board, ask a flight attendant if this is possible, especially if your children are very young or seated toward the back of the plane. After all, if your kids have a happy flight experience, everyone else in the cabin is more likely to as well.

- You'll certainly be grateful to yourself for **packing tidy snacks** like rolled dried fruit, which are much less sticky and wet and more compact and packable than actual fruit. Blueberry or raisin bagels also make for a neat, healthy sweet and yield fewer crumbs than cookies or cakes. Ginger snaps, crisp and not as crumbly as softer cookies, will also help curb mild cases of motion sickness. And don't forget to stash a few resealable plastic bags in your purse. They'll prove invaluable for storing everything from half-eaten crackers and fruit to checker pieces and matchbox cars.

- **Juice or cookies** will not only keep kids distracted during ascent and descent — often the scariest parts of flight for a child — they will also help their little ears pop as cabin air pressure shifts rapidly. Juice (paper cartons travel best) will also keep them swallowing and help them to stay properly hydrated. Avoid giving young children gum or hard candies, since sudden turbulence may cause them to choke.

- If your children are very young, **bring pacifiers.** The act of sucking will keep their ears clear. By the same logic, takeoff and landing are the perfect time for feedings. Your kids will be distracted from the deafening cabin noise, and their ears will pop more easily. If your schedule won't allow this, try placing drops of water on an infant's tongue, to facilitate swallowing. Don't forget to pack bottles and extra milk or formula as well, as these are unavailable on most aircraft. Many airlines prohibit flight attendants from preparing formula, so it's best to pack your baby's food premixed.

7

Beat the Clock: How to Minimize Jet Lag

The human body functions like clockwork. Your patterns of eating and sleeping, working and resting are scheduled by a clock in your head, a steady circadian rhythm in rough sync with the earth's cycles of night and day.

When you travel by plane, especially from east to west, you change the time of day without resetting your body's clock. Suddenly, it's 5pm outside but your body insists it's 11pm and time to go to bed. The dissonance between external events (sunlight, meal times, work routines) and the comfortable routine to which your body is accustomed throws you into a time warp, a dizziness, a physical illness known as jet lag.

The human body can slowly adapt to new time zones, but waiting for that to happen can ruin a short break or a business trip. Fortunately, there are strategies that speed up your acclimation to a new time zone. A few have been scientifically studied and proven to be effective. Others have strong anecdotal evidence behind them. The effectiveness of such treatments as herbal or homeopathic remedies is still unknown.

If you're taking a very short trip — just for a meeting, say, or a weekend vacation break — you may not want to deal with the hassle of jet lag at all. Just schedule your business and activities for the times you'd normally be awake, and keep your body on "home time."

1 WHAT IS JET LAG?

JET LAG MAKES YOU FEEL DISORIENTED, FORGETFUL, and absentminded precisely because your body *is* disoriented; your brain, nervous system, and reflexes think they're someplace else, and they're inclined to do the things they would have been doing back home. Body functions that operate cyclically — hormone levels, blood pressure, body temperature, digestive enzymes, kidneys, bladder, heart, and brain waves included — all lapse into a sort of temporary state of confusion.

Let's say you fly out of New York just after lunch at 3pm. When it would have been time for your dinner at 7 o'clock, your stomach is going to release enzymes and stomach acids in anticipation of food, but when you touch down in San Francisco, it's only going to be 4pm — too late for lunch, too early for supper. Three hours later, when you would have been curling up with a book for the evening and your bodily functions would have started shutting down in anticipation of sleep, you'll be nodding off in your gazpacho as your California business associates are plying their wits and picking at their martini olives.

JET LAG SYMPTOMS

The first stages of jet lag may include stomach upset, deep fatigue, fuzzy-headedness, absentmindedness, slow-wittedness, poor concentration, weakness, disrupted bowel movements, and changes in the frequency of urination. At more advanced stages, you may experience diarrhea or constipation, headache, loss of appetite, poor motor coordination, impaired night vision and peripheral vision, decrease in sexual appetite, muscle tremors, vertigo, and fainting.

WHAT CAUSES JET LAG?

One of the most common misconceptions regarding jet lag is that it results from flying in general — in particular, from traveling at high altitude. In fact, jet lag is caused only by long-distance travel across time zones. For example, if you were to fly from Montreal to Santiago, Chile — a hefty transcontinental trek of 5,434 miles (8,749km), but on the same north-south axis — you might feel some of the symptoms commonly associated with jet lag: headache, fatigue, a slight dizziness. Since you didn't cross a time zone, however, your discomfort would more likely be the by-product of dehydration, as airplane cabins are literally drier than the Sahara; shifts in air cabin pressure, which can throw off the normal function of your sinuses and lead to low-grade headaches, earaches, and sinus congestion; sitting cramped in the same position and close quarters for hours on end; and the exhausting stresses and strains that all too often accompany airplane travel, like simply getting to the airport on time, waiting in line, schlepping your carry-ons and worrying about airport security. With a sound night's sleep, lots of water, and a few healthy meals, you'll probably be back in fighting trim by the following day — or the one after that, at the most — if you have traveled on a north-south axis, no matter how great the distance.

On a trip that requires a 5- to 8-hour time change, however, jet lag may keep you from feeling your best for 2 days to 2 weeks. How you're affected depends on your personal disposition, age, physical fitness, and a host of other factors — the most important of which is whether you've traveled from east to west or from west to east. East-to-west travel is much easier on your internal time clock. Why? The human body cycle is actually approximately 25 hours long, rather than 24. When you travel west, you're required to stay up late, which is more acceptable to your body than going to bed early.

Your heart rate, normally faster during the day than at night, may take from 5 to 6 days to return to its normal cycle. Your output of urine, which usually slows at night, can take up to 10 days to function regularly. Your gastrointestinal system, which governs the bowels, may not normalize for as many as 24 hours for each time zone you cross. Your body's response to light and your ability to perform mathematical equations may stay out of whack for anywhere from 2 days to 2 weeks. And your physical coordination may be under par for 5 to 10 days. If you're traveling from east to west, your recovery will usually take 30% to 50% less time. You will still experience some disruption of your circadian rhythms, but the fact that you're gaining time — and therefore gaining sleep — will put you ahead of the game, so to speak, and hasten your recovery.

WHO WINS, WHO LOSES?

Most night-owl types tend to adapt faster to the new time frame on a trip out west. They are less prone to sleep deficiency and can extend the sleep period more easily when necessary. When traveling east, on the other hand, night owls tend to adjust far more slowly, and it's the early birds who get the worm. Likewise, "morning people" are more readily able to rise and shine at any hour, even if it means cutting short the sleep period for a few hours each day.

Several other personality factors figure into your capacity to cope with east-west travel. Gregarious types, who love to meet new people, mix among various social groups, and travel in a pack, tend to cope better with jet lag than people who reach a destination and retreat to their rooms with a book or remote control. This is because the more you expose yourself to external stimuli in your new environment, the faster the necessary chemical changes will take place in your brain to help you adapt to your new surroundings.

Alcohol, Drugs & Jet Lag

As a general rule, if a substance picks you up or brings you down, it will interfere with your body's ability to adapt to a new time frame. If you are taking prescribed medications, consult your doctor before traveling. Be sure to tell him or her where you're going, how many time zones you will be crossing, what sort of activity you have planned for your trip, and whether you anticipate other drastic changes in your diet. If you plan to use any other jet lag remedy, be sure to say so.

Surprisingly, regimented types — people who wake up, go to bed, eat breakfast, eat lunch, and sit down to dinner at the same time every day — will adjust more quickly to a new time and place than the sort of person who wakes and eats at whim and goes with the flow every day. The person accustomed to following the clock will have less trouble following a new schedule in a new time zone.

Calm, stable types will also do better, in either direction, than neurotic types who are readily frazzled by disruptions of circumstance. Nervous types secrete hormones and neurotransmitters that unsettle body rhythms and make it even harder to establish temporary new ones.

If you are traveling under pressure — conducting business, attending many social engagements, or otherwise traveling according to a rigorous, demanding timetable — you will also do better than someone who is traveling strictly for relaxation, with no firm commitments or social and professional obligations. By having to keep up, the busy traveler will typically recover faster from jet lag — simply because he must. Like the gregarious traveler, the busy person will also encounter a greater profusion of external stimuli in the new environment, which will induce more rapid adaptation.

Age is also a factor in your ability to cope with jet lag. While even infants experience jet lag, they recover very quickly. The elderly seem to have the hardest time recovering. This is largely because 40% of men and women over the age of 65 already experience difficulty sleeping. When seniors cross time zones, they are requiring an already compromised system to work double time. The good news is that a new body rhythm, once it is finally established, may be accompanied by a new vigor, which will allow for sounder sleep.

As you might guess, healthy people cope better with jet lag than people in poor health, whose body rhythms have already been disrupted. Jet lag will make you feel even worse if you travel while ill. If you must take prescription drugs during your trip, be aware that jet lag may impair their effectiveness, as timing is usually crucial to their proper functioning. Even common or social drugs — such as coffee, cigarettes, or alcohol — alter your body rhythms enough that they usually aggravate the symptoms of jet lag and slow the recovery process.

2 How to Cope with Jet Lag

IT SEEMS LIKE EVERYBODY'S GOT A CURE FOR JET LAG. Diets. Light. Drugs. Herbal remedies. Completely crackpot ideas like the "Cylinders of the Pharaohs" that swear by minerals and magnets. As there's been very little peer-reviewed scientific research into many of these treatments, travelers often rely on anecdotal evidence — what's worked for themselves and their friends.

But three approaches have evidence to beat the others. The hormone **melatonin** has been shown to actually reset the body clock, providing a powerful aid for jet lag sufferers. Other scientific studies have shown that the body uses light to cue its clock, so **light-based treatments** have the backing of sleep experts. And for years, Argonne National Laboratories in Illinois has been offering a **special diet** which has plenty of anecdotal, although little scientific, backing for success.

If you're crossing more than a few time zones or traveling to attend an important business engagement, you may want to consider one of the more intensive strategies for beating jet lag listed below. For brief trips, however, you can curtail the symptoms of jet lag without having to take any drugs or follow any complicated diet regimens. Try the following tricks the next time you fly.

- **Drink lots of water before, during, and after your flight.** Experts recommend that you drink at least two 8-ounce glasses just before departure and 1 liter for every hour you spend in the air — in addition to beverages you drink with meals. Even if you don't feel thirsty, drink up. Thirst doesn't necessarily precede the symptoms of dehydration, which can set in without warning.

- The minute you step into the airplane cabin, **adopt the hour of the time zone you're traveling to.** Reset your watch and start to think according to the new time zone.

- **Avoid drinking alcohol** or ingesting other depressants, such as Dramamine or other motion-sickness drugs, before and during your flight.

- **Exercise, sleep well, and eat as healthily as you can** during the few days before your trip. With your body in peak condition you'll be better able to conquer jet lag.

- **Eat more lightly** than you are accustomed to before your flight and while you're in the air.

- If you're traveling west to east, it's to your advantage to **schedule business meetings over a late dinner,** during the first day or two of your trip, when you're likely to be the most alert member of the dining circle.

- Once you reach your destination, **don't sleep longer than you normally would** to try to "catch up." You'll feel much better the faster you can acclimate yourself to the new time zone.

- Travelers who have trouble sleeping on planes like to **fly to Europe on a morning flight,** so they arrive in the evening, eat supper and find a room at a reasonable hour, and get a good night's sleep. The problem with this routine is that you waste a full day on the plane and will still likely suffer the effects of jet lag, at least for a few days after you arrive. You will most likely forfeit a day on the plane at the tail end your trip as well, since most U.S.-bound flights depart from Europe in the early afternoon.

3 MELATONIN: JET LAG PILLS

ONE OF THE CHEAPEST, EASIEST, AND MOST EFFECTIVE means of treating jet lag is through the use of synthetic **melatonin,** which has become increasingly more popular and available in recent years.

Melatonin is a hormone that occurs naturally in the body, secreted by the pineal gland in the forebrain, and induces sleep. Daylight curbs the natural production of melatonin, but when night falls the pineal gland releases the hormone into the bloodstream and triggers the sleep cycle. Although the pineal gland was long thought to have outgrown any useful purpose in the human body, René Descartes called it the "seat of the soul." Though Descartes, in the 16th century, didn't need to concern himself with jet lag, he obviously understood how crucial sound sleep is to proper mental functioning. The last job he had before he died was to serve as personal tutor to Queen Christina of Sweden; she required him to administer her lessons every day at 5am.

Melatonin not only induces sleep but improves sleep quality as well. Taken 2 hours before bedtime on an eastbound trip, a dose of melatonin will trick your body into thinking that night has fallen earlier. Dr. Timothy Walter of the Eastside Sleep Diagnostic Center in Columbus, Ohio, recommends 2 milligrams of melatonin as a proper dose. Researchers say that melatonin can help the body adjust to a new time zone at twice its normal rate. Dr. Steve Lamm, a professor of medicine at New York University, recommends that travelers skipping five or more time zones heading east experiment with dosages up to 5 milligrams of melatonin. The hormone is less useful, but still might be helpful for travelers traveling two to four time zones east, he said.

Travelers who have trouble adapting to traveling westward — waking up at 2 in the morning, for instance — should take melatonin when they wake up, Dr. Walter said.

But melatonin must be combined with a comprehensive program of adapting to the new time zone. No matter how sleepy you feel, don't nap when you reach your destination (unless it's late at night). Take a walk instead. Sightsee a bit. Stay awake until it's time for bed in the new time zone.

Be careful not to go overboard and take too much melatonin, or you may suffer a hangover and feel addled the following day. But taken in small quantities, clinical tests have shown melatonin to be nonaddictive, nontoxic, and safe, and it causes very few side effects.

Make sure to get melatonin from your doctor or a trusted pharmacist — although sold over the counter, the quality of melatonin is completely unregulated, so there's no guarantee that what you buy at the health food store is actually melatonin!

In the past, doctors were hesitant to prescribe sleeping pills for jet lag because of their addictiveness and "hangover" effects, which can do as much harm as good to someone trying to adapt to a new time zone. But a new medication, Ambien, has broken that pattern. If you need to sleep on the plane or force yourself to sleep early, taking Ambien at bedtime was shown by a recent study in the journal *Aviation, Space, and Environmental Medicine* to be even more effective than melatonin for reducing jet lag discomfort.

The downside? Ambien is more likely than melatonin to cause side effects like nausea and confusion upon waking up in the morning. And travelers should never combine Ambien and melatonin — they're less effective together than Ambien is alone, and the combination can make you very drowsy in the morning.

4 LIGHT THERAPY: SEEING THE LIGHT

THE OTHER CLINICALLY TESTED WAY TO RESET YOUR body clock is with light. Your body uses the sun's rise and set to figure out when it should be awake and asleep, and studies at Rockefeller University and elsewhere have supported light-based therapies for easing jet lag.

"The timing of light and timing of darkness — that's the most powerful environmental cue that changes our sleep-wake clock," said Dr. Russ Rosenberg of the Northside Hospital Sleep Medicine Institute in Atlanta.

At the web page for Outside In (www.bodyclock.com), a British light-therapy company, you can get a free, customized plan of when to seek and avoid light while traveling across a certain number of time zones. The timings aren't what you'd guess off the bat — just getting sunlight according to your destination's schedule may be helpful, but it's not ideal.

"If you're traveling from the east coast [of the U.S.] to the western portion of Europe you would want to avoid morning light and get late morning and afternoon light," Rosenberg said.

Avoiding light is easy enough — bring a sleep mask, wear dark sunglasses, or stay indoors, in dim light, during the hours you need to dodge the rays. (If you nap, keep it to less than 30 min.) Movies are a great "avoid light" activity.

Any outdoor daylight, even on cloudy days, works during "seek light" hours. But light therapies can be difficult to pull off if they require you to get lots of light at night — as most hotel rooms don't have enough lighting to reset your body clock. Outside In's managing director, Steve Hayes, says truly aggressive indoor lighting may be able to do the trick. If an outdoor camera can work without a flash, the lights are high enough.

For travelers interested in making sure they get the proper light, BioBrite (☎ **800/621-LITE;** www.biobrite.com) sells a $339 kit with a lighted visor that delivers the appropriate amount of white light and a calculator to figure out when you'll need to turn it on for the best benefit.

If you're keeping your body on "home time," schedule your periods of light and darkness to correspond with your original time zone — or you'll end up with jet lag when you head back.

WHAT THE SLEEP DOCTORS SAY

Getting a good night's sleep in a foreign place is about more than just jet lag. Your body may be upset by unfamiliar sounds, smells, and textures and by the dehydrating, deoxygenated rigors of air travel. Some things sleep doctors suggest may help lull you to sleep when you arrive at your destination:

- **A comfortable pillow.** Some hotels provide a selection to choose from. An even better idea: bring yours from home, as it has a familiar smell and texture.

- **White noise.** Unfamiliar sounds can prevent you from getting to sleep. Consider picking up a sound generator like Sharper Image's Travel Soother ($39.95) or just turning on the fan in the room.

- **Boredom.** Obsessing about your inability to sleep isn't going to get you anywhere. Get out of bed and watch incomprehensible foreign TV or read a really boring

ⓒ SNOOZE BOOSTERS & OTHER TOOLS OF THE FLYING TRADE

The following products from **Magellan's** (☎ 800/962-4943; www.magellans.com) will help you rest more soundly on a plane, in an unfamiliar hotel bed, or at odd hours when you're trying to adapt to a new time zone. **Rand McNally** (☎ 800/627-2897), **Brookstone** (☎ 800/926-7000; www.brookstone.com), and **Walkabout Travel Gear** (☎ 800/852-7085; www.walkabout travelgear.com) are also reliable vendors of travel-related gadgets, gizmos, and gear, and you can always find basic travel gear at airport shops.

Hearos' foam ear plugs ($4.85 for a set of four) shrink to half their normal size so you can slide them deep into your ear. Then they slowly expand to fit snugly and provide maximum, yet comfortable, insulation against environmental noise.

Magellan's **eyeshade** ($3.85), specially designed for travel, features adjustable straps and a nose bridge to keep light from filtering in underneath.

Cloud-Soft Inflatable Pillow ($9.85) wraps around your neck in a horseshoe shape to support the back of your neck, so you can tip back and nap, and prevents your head from bobbing side to side. The pillow inflates as easily as it packs when it's deflated. The soft poly-cotton cover is comfortable year-round and zips off for easy washing.

---

magazine for a little while. Then go back to bed and think about the utterly boring topic until you doze off.

5 Light Therapy: Sample Schedules

THE TIMING OF LIGHT THERAPY IS BASED ON TWO factors: your normal wake-up time and the distance of your

Bucky ($29.85) is the **travel pillow** many frequent fliers swear by. Made from buckwheat hulls, the pillow conforms more closely to your neck and shoulders than an inflatable pillow. The removable cover, made of soft, cozy Polartec, is machine washable. Bucky **eyeshades** ($29.85) are made from 100% cotton blackout cloth and come with earplugs that fit into their own pocket.

Folding Footrest ($24.85) unfolds to a 4-inch height, so you can stretch your legs to sleep, improve circulation, prevent cramping in the back of your thighs, and relieve pressure on the lower back. Folded, the footrest measures a nifty $4 \times 8^{1}/_{2} \times ^{3}/_{4}$ inches for easy packing.

NoiseBuster Extreme ($49) counteracts the low rumble of airplane engines and helps you sleep. This high-tech device analyzes sound waves, duplicates their frequency inthe opposite phase, and sends a signal to cancel out the offending noise in your headphones. NoiseBuster is very light (6 oz.) and will run for 100 hours on two AAA batteries. The headphones come with a stereo jack so you can plug them into your Walkman or CD player during the active phase of the jet lag program.

trip. We give some sample schedules here, but Outside In's managing director Steve Hayes warns that it's important to get an exact schedule for your trip — or you'll throw your body even further off. His website (www.bodyclock.com) has a customized light therapy calculator.

We've chosen to show examples for five to nine time zones because many popular trips span those distances.

Bodyclock.com covers distances up to 12 time zones. All times are given in the time at your destination — reset your watch as soon as you get on the plane. The recommendations that follow are tailored for someone who generally wakes up around 7am.

CROSSING FIVE TIME ZONES

Traveling West

Seek bright light between 20:30 (8:30pm) and 23:30 (11:30pm), then switch to **avoid light** until 03:30am or later.

Traveling East

Avoid light between 04:30am and 09:30am, then switch to **seek bright light** until 12:30pm.

On day 2, **avoid light** between 01:30am and 06:30am, then switch to **seek bright light** until 09:30am.

CROSSING SIX TIME ZONES

Traveling West

Seek bright light between 19:30 (7:30pm) and 22:30 (10:30pm), then switch to **avoid light** until 02:30am or later.

On day 2, **seek bright light** between 22:30 (10:30pm) and 01:30am, then switch to **avoid light** until 05:30am or later.

Traveling East

Avoid light between 05:30am and 10:30am, then **switch** to **seek bright light** until 13:30 (1:30pm).

On day 2, **avoid light** between 02:30am and 07:30am, then switch to **seek bright light** until 10:30am.

CROSSING SEVEN TIME ZONES

Traveling West

Seek bright light between 18:30 (6:30pm) and 21:30 (9:30pm), then switch to **avoid light** until 01:30am or later.

LIGHT THERAPY FOR TRAVEL ACROSS TIME ZONES

TRIP	TIME ZONES CROSSED
East Coast USA–UK	5
East Coast USA–Hawaii	5
East Coast USA–Europe	6
Central USA–UK	6
Central USA–Europe	7
Mountain USA–UK	7
Mountain USA–Europe	8
West Coast USA–UK	8
West Coast USA–Hong Kong	8
West Coast USA–Europe	9

On day 2, **seek bright light** between 21:30 (9:30pm) and 00:30 (12:30am), then switch to **avoid light** until 04:30am or later.

Traveling East

Avoid light between 06:30am and 11:30am, then switch to **seek bright light** until 14:30 (2:30pm).

On day 2, **avoid light** between 03:30am and 08:30am, then switch to **seek bright light** until 11:30am.

CROSSING EIGHT TIME ZONES

Traveling West

Seek bright light between 17:30 (5:30pm) and 20:30 (8:30pm), then switch to **avoid light** until 00:30 (12:30am) or later.

On day 2, **seek bright light** between 20:30 (8:30pm) and 23:30 (11:30pm), then switch to avoid light until 03:30am or later.

Traveling East

Avoid light between 07:30am and 12:30am, then switch to seek bright light until 15:30 (3:30pm).

On day 2, **avoid light** between 04:30am and 09:30am, then switch to **seek bright light** until 12:30pm.

CROSSING NINE TIME ZONES
Traveling West
Seek bright light between 16:30 (4:30pm) and 19:30 (7:30pm), then switch to **avoid light** until 23:30 (11:30pm).

On day 2, **seek bright light** between 19:30 (7:30pm) and 22:30 (10:30pm), then switch to **avoid light** until 02:30am or later.

Traveling East
Seek bright light between 10:30am and 13:30 (1:30pm), then switch to **avoid light** until 17:30 (5:30pm).

On day 2, **seek bright light** between 13:30 (1:30pm) and 16:30 (4:30pm), then switch to **avoid light** until 20:30 (8:30pm).

6 THE ARGONNE NATIONAL LABORATORY'S ANTI-JET-LAG DIET

WHEN A TRIP ABROAD IS GOING TO HAVE FAR-REACHING effects on global politics, government officials — from White House staff members to the U.S. Army Rapid Deployment Force — use the Three-Step Jet Lag Program, developed by Dr. Charles F. Ehret at the Argonne National Laboratory. Promoted by the U.S. Olympic Committee, the program is elaborate but inexpensive and requires no drugs or special equipment. It lasts anywhere from 1 to 3 days before departure, depending on the number of time zones involved, and ends the second day of the trip.

Unlike with melatonin and light, there haven't been studies in peer-reviewed scientific journals proving the diet's effectiveness, and scientists are sharply divided as to whether it works. But there's plenty of anecdotal evidence that the diet helps with jet lag, and it has powerful backers.

HOW DOES IT WORK?

The full Argonne jet lag plan combines light therapy, physical activity, environmental cues, and the Argonne diet to help you build up a resistance to jet lag before you depart and help you lick what few symptoms you may experience soon after you reach your destination.

The program breaks down into three stages: preflight, in-flight, and postflight. The full treatment is tailored to the number of time zones you'll be crossing.

During the **preflight** step, you feast and fast on a special diet of foods that will either help you sleep or keep you awake. The objective of this step is to allow your body's reserves of glycogen to run low before your flight by fasting and eating sparingly for 1 to 3 days before your trip. When your body's store of glycogen is drained, you become hypersensitive to influences — light and darkness, certain foods, and methylated xanthines such as caffeine — that trick your body clock into shifting more rapidly than it normally would.

During the **in-flight** step, you simulate the time zone of your final destination by drinking coffee and tea at certain times, adhering to specific periods of light and darkness, and subjecting yourself to particular periods of rest and inactivity.

During the **postflight** step, you eat foods that will provide maximum energy during the day and maximum restfulness at night. The dietary premise of the program is that feasts on high-protein foods such as red meats, eggs, and fish activate the body. Feasts on high-carbohydrate foods, such as pastas, breads, and potatoes, induce sleep. Fasting on low-calorie, low-carbohydrate foods such as soups, salads, and fruit depletes the body's glycogen reserves, which makes it easier to reset your body clock.

Essentially, you fight jet lag through the strategic use of light, nutrition, stimulants like coffee or tea, and physical and mental activity.

HOW DOES FOOD HELP?

High-protein foods such as lean meats, fish, eggs, and dairy products will rev up your adrenal pathways — the combination of chemicals in the body, most active during the day, that give you energy and keep you active and alert. To the contrary, high-carbohydrate foods such as pastas and whole grain breads, will fuel your indoleamine pathways — the combination of chemicals in the body, most active at night, that slow down your body functions, make you drowsy, and ultimately put you to sleep.

On the anti-jet lag diet, you will generally aim to eat a high-protein breakfast and lunch, as each will supply you with a solid 5 hours' worth of energy. At dinnertime, you will aim to eat a meal high in carbohydrates, which will tire you out and signal to your body that it's time to shut down and sleep. While this is not a very complicated or difficult regimen, it does go against the standard travel diet. Most hotels serve a continental breakfast high in carbohydrates. A sticky bun, fruit, and coffee may give you a rush of energy right after you've eaten, but within an hour you'll start to drag and feel tired — and maybe even feel as though you need to take a nap. This is deadly when trying to adjust to a new time zone.

Get with the Jet Lag Program

You can receive a free wallet-sized version of the Argonne Three-Step Jet Lag Program if you send a self-addressed, stamped envelope to Public Affairs, Argonne National Laboratory, 9700 S. Cass Ave., Argonne, IL 60439 (☎ **630/252-5575**). The complete program is also laid out in Dr. Ehret's book, written in conjunction with Lynne Waller Scanlon, ***Overcoming Jet Lag*** (Berkeley Publications, 1993, $11.95). A quick read, this slim volume is available in the travel section of many major bookstores.

The careful, strategic use of caffeine will also dramatically help reset your body clock — especially when taken in concert with the program of feasting and fasting (eating lightly) on either high-protein or high-carbohydrate foods. When you fast as prescribed by the jet lag diet, you drain your body's reserves of glycogen, which makes you ultra-sensitive to stimulants like caffeine, food, and light. The jet lag regimen repeatedly replenishes and drains your body's supply of glycogen, allowing your internal body clock to adjust more rapidly. (The chart on the next page shows the comparative caffeine levels of various common foods, beverages, and over-the-counter stimulants.)

THE PHYSICAL FACTOR

You can also help psych yourself into a new time frame by staying active during daylight hours and exposing yourself to maximum social stimulation in your new environment. If you're still on a plane during what would be the active phase of the daily cycle in your new location, get up, walk around, or talk to fellow passengers. On your first day in town, don't linger over the newspaper in your hotel room, even if your body seems to be telling you that you need a few more hours of rest. Get up and set out right away and stay as active as possible over the course of the day. The mere act of rubbing shoulders with other people will cause your body to secrete neurotransmitters that will help keep you alert until it's bedtime in your new locale.

MIND-BODY ACTIVATION: GET YOUR SYSTEM JUMP-STARTED

Part of the Argonne Program focuses on rousing your whole body once you've pried open your eyes. You want your heart to speed up from its sleepy pace, your blood to circulate faster, your joints to loosen up, and your mind to clear itself from the cobwebs of sleep.

CAFFEINE CONTENTS OF BEVERAGES & OVER-THE-COUNTER MEDICATIONS

PRODUCT	QUANTITY	CAFFEINE LEVEL (IN MILLIGRAMS)
Coffee		
decaffeinated	5 oz.	2
instant, regular	5 oz.	53
percolated	5 oz.	110
drip	5 oz.	146
Tea		
1-minute brew	5 oz.	9 to 33
3-minute brew	5 oz.	20 to 46
5-minute brew	5 oz.	20 to 50
canned iced tea	10 oz.	22 to 36
Cocoa & Chocolate		
milk chocolate	1 oz.	6
cocoa mix (with water)	8 oz.	10
baking chocolate	1 oz.	35
Nonprescription Stimulants		
Caffedrine capsules	standard dose	200
NoDoz tablets	standard dose	200
Vivarin	standard dose	200
Nonprescription Pain Relievers		
plain aspirin	standard dose	0
Anacin	standard dose	64
Midol	standard dose	65
Excedrin	standard dose	130
Nonprescription Diuretics		
Pre-Mens Forte	standard dose	100
Aqua-Ban	standard dose	200
Permathene	standard dose	200
Nonprescription Cold Remedies		
Coryban-D	standard dose	30
Dristan	standard dose	32
Nonprescription Weight Control Substances		
Dietac	daily dose	200
Dexatrim	daily dose	200
Prolamine	daily dose	280

Source: Consumer Reports, October 1981, p. 599.

It doesn't take much to rev up your system after it has been at rest. You can do the following exercises in very little space — even within the cramped quarters of an airplane, near the lavatory, or at the back end of the aircraft.

1. Take five long, deep breaths from the diaphragm. If you're breathing properly, your abdomen should rise and fall instead of your chest.

2. Stand on your tiptoes and reach for the ceiling. Do this slowly 5 to 10 times, breathing deeply with each stretch.

3. Slowly, while breathing deeply, roll your shoulders forward and back. Roll each shoulder separately five times. Then roll each shoulder back, one by one, five times.

4. Slowly roll your head five times to the left and five times to the right.

5. Bend backward from the waist as far as you safely can. Point your chin toward the ceiling and breath deeply. Perform this five times.

6. Roll your wrists and ankles slowly five times each.

7. Pull your knees up to your waist, one by one, 5 to 10 times each.

8. Visit the lavatory. Wash your hands and face, comb your hair, and brush your teeth.

9. If possible, converse or play a quick game of cards with travel partners, newfound friends on the plane, or flight personnel. If this is not possible, play solitaire or read a book or magazine.

7 WHEN IS THE BEST DEPARTURE TIME?

AS A GENERAL RULE, YOU WANT TO SCHEDULE YOUR flight so that you arrive during the active phase of the day (between 8am and 8pm) in your destination time zone. The closer to 8am you arrive the better. You should try to avoid arriving between midnight and dawn destination time, as you will have to force yourself to be active at an hour when you should be resting.

Unfortunately, most flights from the U.S. to Europe are overnighters. If you must take a red-eye flight, try to pick a time when you'll actually be able to sleep on the plane — an 8pm departure rather than a 5pm one, for instance.

Unless you're using special measures like the melatonin or the jet lag diet, it takes up to a day to adapt for every time zone over two you're traveling past.

WEST-TO-EAST DEPARTURE & ARRIVAL TIMES

When you're flying east, pick a flight that departs as early as possible. For short trips east, don't rise too early the morning of the flight. For medium-length trips east, don't take a flight that forces you to rise before 5:30am. For long trips east, plan to leave either as late as you can — though still before midnight — and arrive the next morning after 6am; or depart as early as possible after 6am and arrive very late the same day — though before midnight, destination time.

EAST-TO-WEST DEPARTURE & ARRIVAL TIMES

When you're flying west, choose a flight that leaves as late as possible. For short trips west, sleep at least as late as usual, later if you can. For medium-length trips, try to sleep as late as the expected rising time at your destination. Pick a flight that allows you to do this. For long trips west, depart at an hour that will allow you the longest possible rest period before your destination-time breakfast feast on board the plane. If you're able to sleep on a plane, depart as early as possible after 8am.

8

SKY HOUNDS: HOW TO MAXIMIZE YOUR FREQUENT-FLIER MILEAGE

There is no downside. Frequent-flier programs are a painless way to turn everything you do (especially flying) into free trips. You don't need to be a globe-trotting frequent flier to earn major miles. Pump gas, buy a head of lettuce, stay in a hotel, make long-distance calls, or use a credit card — all of these activities rack up the miles. Now more than ever, you can shop, dial, drive, and eat your way to a free trip.

The proliferation of airline-based alliances and partnerships over the past few years has made redeeming your miles more flexible than ever. You can use them for trips to Timbuktu, hotel stays, magazine subscriptions, or dozens of other travel and consumer goodies.

But as mileage programs have grown more flexible, they've become more complicated. Just as it's worth a few hours' study to pick the right mortgage loan or retirement plan, it's worth analyzing the serpentine convolutions of plan details. If you read the fine print, and understand how to work within the restrictions, you can strike mileage gold.

1 HOW TO PLAY THE MILEAGE GAME

JOINING FREQUENT-FLIER PLANS IS FREE, SO JOIN AS many as possible. As a frequent-flier member you'll get better customer service, more focused attention in the event that your luggage is lost or if you need to switch your seat, and a greater chance of securing a hotel voucher if your flight is canceled and you're stranded overnight.

But loyalty to one program does pay off. If you fly one airline (or within one airline alliance) often, you'll accumulate free trips quickly. Elite status — usually earned by flying at least 25,000 miles per year — gives you further mileage bonuses, free upgrades to first or business class, and VIP benefits that range from priority boarding, seating, and baggage claim to discounts on club membership. (See "Achieving Elite Status," later in this chapter, for detailed info on various elite programs.)

Unfortunately, it's not as easy to use miles for free trips as it is to earn them. All major airlines restrict frequent-flier seats to just a few per flight, and those usually get snagged well in advance. (See table "How Easy Is It to Redeem Miles?," below, for frequent fliers' success rates at getting the

WHICH AIRLINE AWARDED THE MOST SEATS IN 2000?

AIRLINE	AWARD SEATS	% OF ALL PASSENGER MILES	% CHANGE*
American	2,800,000	9.2	+4%
Continental	1,476,847	7.6	+34%
United	1,970,000	7.2	−12%
Delta	2,600,000	7.0	+13%
Northwest	1,263,000	6.6	−2%
US Airways	1,200,000	6.0	+9%
Southwest	1,571,000	4.9	+4.9%
Alaska	281,000	4.8	+21%
America West	190,781	2.6	−12%

*Compared with 1999. Source: WebFlyer.com

HOW EASY IS IT TO REDEEM MILES?

AIRLINE	SUCCESS RATE
Southwest	96%
Continental	69%
United	64%
American	62%
Delta Air	58%
Northwest	56%
US Airways	50%
America West	44%
Alaska Airlines	40%

Source: WebFlyer, March 2002

* Success Rate measures the percentage of frequent-flier members who reported getting the exact reward they requested on the first try.

seats they want.) If you want to fly on or around major holidays, you'll find that on some airlines the free-flight awards with the lowest mileage requirements are subject to draconian "blackout dates" — you'll have to use tens of thousands of additional miles to get access to "unrestricted seats."

Frequent-flier programs offer a range of options and perks. And yet even the most frequent fliers seem to favor a single program by default, rather than by educated choice. Perhaps an airline's hub is near their hometown. Or another carrier offered a great sale on flights to Europe 2 years ago, and what's the point in switching accounts and losing miles? If you take time to shop around, however, you're sure to find a plan with features that match your needs.

Among the highlights:

- Southwest's plan offers the cheapest and easiest free tickets — one free round-trip for every eight round-trips you fly. But they have no airline partners, thus limiting the destinations you can fly to.

- Alaska Airlines' plan allows you to earn Alaska miles when flying on American, Continental, and Northwest

MAJOR AIRLINES' FREQUENT-FLIER SERVICE NUMBERS & WEBSITES

AIRLINE	PHONE NUMBER	WEBSITE
Alaska	☎ 800/654-5669	http://mileageplan.alaskaair.com/
America West	☎ 800/247-5691	www.americawest.com/flightfund/ff_home.htm
American	☎ 800/882-8880	www.aa.com/aadvantage
Continental	☎ 800/621-7467	http://onepass.continental.com
Delta	☎ 800/323-2323	www.delta.com/skymiles/
Northwest	☎ 800/447-3757	www.nwa.com/freqfly/
Southwest	☎ 800/248-4377	www.southwest.com/rapid_rewards/
United	☎ 800/421-2655	www.mileageplus.com
US Airways	☎ 800/428-4322 or 336/661-8390*	www.usairways.com/dividendmiles/

* US Airways has no toll-free number designated exclusively for frequent-flier-related questions. General reservationists will be able to field most of your questions, but they may refer you to the toll number for complicated issues.

flights, so it's great if you live in the West and fly those three airlines.

- Continental, Northwest, and America West offer unlimited upgrades at their lowest elite level, so they're especially good for the extra-tall or long-haul frequent flier.

- American, Northwest, and United have particularly good global partner networks, if you often fly abroad.

- American and United allow the easiest way of earning miles: through shopping, dining, and buying a car or home.

- Delta's credit card racks up free trips the quickest of all the majors, delivering 2 miles per dollar spent on many household goods.

- United has the only frequent-flier program geared for college students, with a 10,000-mile bonus at graduation.

✐ THE ART OF MILEAGE RUNNING

There are flagpole-sitters, trainspotters . . . and mileage runners. These frequent-flier fanatics take unnecessarily long routings to rack up frequent-flier miles or maintain elite flier status. A mileage runner flying from Boston to Atlanta, for example, may choose an airline routing through Minneapolis or Chicago, thus doubling miles for his money.

For the devoted, this can pay off big. When LatinPass, a group of Latin American airlines, announced a million-mile bonus for its most frequent fliers, dozens of Americans hopped on planes and zipped around South America. For about $4,000 worth of tickets, these globetrotters reaped miles that could be redeemed for more than $75,000 in travel.

2 FREQUENT-FLIER PROFILES OF THE MAJOR DOMESTIC AIRLINES

FREQUENT-FLIER PROGRAMS ARE IN CONSTANT FLUX, so check airline websites for the latest details. There are some things most programs have in common, though.

Most airlines have two classes of frequent-flier trips. The cheaper awards, which we've shown below, cost fewer miles but may be subject to blackout dates and strict capacity controls. Higher-class awards cost roughly double the miles for the same coach seat, but will get you on any flight, no restrictions.

Blackout dates vary depending on where you're flying. We've listed below blackout dates for trips within the U.S., but you'll have to check your member guide for rules for international flights.

On most airlines, flights under 500 miles earn a minimum of 500 frequent-flier miles.

WebFlyer, the online arm of the frequent-flier magazine *InsideFlyer,* run by mileage guru Randy Petersen, rates mileage programs each year. (Programs are rated on a 1 to 10 scale, with 10 being the best program.) They also hand out awards — see "And the Winner Is . . .," later in this chapter. We've included their ratings below.

ALASKA AIRLINES MILEAGE PLAN (☎ 800/654-5669)
http://mileageplan.alaskaair.com

BASIC FF ACCOUNTS

WebFlyer rating: 8.1

Miles earned: Mile per mile; 500-mile minimum.

Mile longevity: Miles do not expire as long as there is activity in the past 36 months.

Minimum number of miles needed for a domestic round-trip: 20,000

Minimum number of miles needed for a U.S.–Europe round-trip: 40,000 to 50,000. *Note:* Alaska does not fly to Europe, but its partner airlines do — so the minimum mileage requirements vary by partner airline.

When can you confirm a seat? Up to 330 days in advance of departure.

Domestic blackout dates for 2002 (will change each yr.): January 1; November 27, 30; December 1, 2, 20 to 22, 27 to 29.

Do first or business class tickets earn more miles than economy tickets? Travelers flying first class receive a 50% bonus.

Can you maintain a new account without accruing miles? Yes, for 9 months.

Is literature available? The program guide is available on the website.

What are the penalties for canceling a ticket purchased with frequent-flier miles? Members are charged $50 to change the name on an unused award, extend unexpired certificates, or redeposit miles for an unused award. There is no fee for a simple date change on an award.

Can you buy miles? Yes, $25 per 1,000 miles. The limit for how many miles you can purchase depends on which award level you're trying to reach.

Partners: American Airlines, British Airways, Continental Airlines, Hawaiian, Horizon Air, KLM, LanChile, Northwest Airlines, Qantas; also hotels, car rental, Amtrak, restaurants.

Can you accrue miles on partner airlines? Yes.

Can you use miles on partner airlines? Yes.

I live east of the Rockies. Should I ignore all of this? Not necessarily. If you fly American, Continental, and Northwest, but not enough to earn rewards on any single one of them, look into joining the Alaska plan, which allows you to combine miles flown on all three airlines for rewards.

Elite Qualifications & Rewards

All MVP members receive priority boarding, first-class check-in privileges, a priority reservations line, and priority seating. Members are entitled to purchase first-class upgrades for only 5,000 miles on Alaska Airlines.

MVP: Members must fly 15,000 miles per calendar year on Alaska or Horizon Air, or 25,000 miles (or 30 flight segments) on a combination of Alaska, American, Horizon, LanChile, KLM, and Northwest. Members earn a 50% bonus; two one-way upgrades per 10,000 miles; and additional bonuses for each 10,000 miles from 35,000 to 75,000 (see "Upgrading Policies of the Major Domestic Airlines" for more details).

MVP Gold: Members must fly 45,000 miles per calendar year (or 60 flight segments) on a combination of Alaska, American, Horizon, KLM, LanChile, and Northwest. Members earn a 100% bonus for miles accrued, free airport lounge access, one first-class upgrade per 5,000 miles and a 25,000 mile bonus for reaching 100,000 miles on Alaska and its elite-qualifying partners in one calendar year.

AMERICA WEST FLIGHTFUND (☎ 800/247-5691)
www.americawest.com/flightfund/ff_home.htm

Basic FF Accounts

WebFlyer rating: 7.9

Miles earned: Mile per mile on both domestic and international flights; 500-mile minimum.

Mile longevity: Miles will not expire if you accrue miles every 3 years.

Minimum number of miles needed for a domestic round-trip: 20,000

Miles needed for a round-trip from the U.S. to Europe: 50,000. (You'll be flying on Continental or Northwest.)

When can you confirm a seat? Up to 320 days in advance.

Domestic blackout dates for 2002 (will change each yr.): January 2, 5, 6; March 24, 29; April 7; November 16 to 18 (flights to Las Vegas only), 22 (all flights), 24 (flights from Las Vegas only), 27 (all flights); December 1, 2, 20 to 22, 27 to 29.

Do first or business class tickets earn more miles than economy tickets? First-class travelers receive a 50% mileage bonus.

Can you maintain a new account without accruing miles? Yes.

Is literature available? A complete membership guide is available on the website and mailed to new members.

Sayonara to Blackout Dates

At press time, American, Northwest, Delta, and Midwest Express had completely eliminated blackout dates for 2002. While this frees up opportunities to use miles for holiday travel, capacity controls remain strict (meaning you'll still be fighting for the same small number of seats). Try to redeem your miles as far in advance as you possible can. (For details on Midwest Express, see chapter 9, "Cheap Fares.")

What are the penalties for canceling a ticket purchased with frequent-flier miles? The cost is $75 to redeposit miles in your account, or to change the city pair from the original reservation. However, you can change the date on the ticket with no penalty.

Can you buy miles? Yes; miles cost 2.5¢ each for up to 15,000 miles.

Partners: British Airways, Northwest, Virgin Atlantic; also hotel, car rental, MCI, long-distance, dining, Earthlink Internet access, online shopping.

Can you accrue miles on partner airlines? Yes.

Can you use miles on partner airlines? Yes.

How many miles do you get for a Slurpee at the Circle K? Two. With an America West credit card, you get 2 miles per dollar at the Circle K.

ELITE QUALIFICATIONS & REWARDS

All elite members receive priority boarding and standby, first-class check-in, a priority reservations line, and preferred seating. Members also receive $75 off club membership.

Silver: Members must fly 25,000 miles per calendar year (or 30 flight segments) and receive a 50% bonus for miles accrued. Upgrades are unlimited, complimentary, and on a space-available basis (see "Upgrading Policies of the Major Domestic Airlines" for more details).

Gold: Members must fly 50,000 miles per calendar year (or 60 flight segments) and receive a 100% bonus for miles accrued. Unlimited complimentary, space-available upgrades and companion upgrades are available (see "Upgrading Policies of the Major Domestic Airlines" for details).

Platinum: Members must fly 75,000 miles per calendar year (or 90 flight segments) and receive a 125% bonus for miles accrued. Unlimited complimentary, space-available upgrades and companion upgrades are available (see "Upgrading Policies of the Major Domestic Airlines" for details). Platinum members also get to bless one friend with Silver

Elite membership, plus one friend per 25,000 miles or 30 segments flown over the Platinum minimum.

AMERICAN AADVANTAGE PROGRAM
(☎ **800/882-8880**) www.aa.com/aadvantage

BASIC FF ACCOUNTS

WebFlyer rating: 8.6

Miles earned: Mile per mile; 500-mile minimum.

Mile longevity: Miles will not expire if you accrue miles every 3 years.

Minimum number of miles needed for a domestic round-trip: 25,000

Minimum number of miles needed for a U.S.–Europe round-trip: 35,000

When can you confirm a seat? Up to 330 days in advance. Book 21 days before departure to avoid a $50 fee.

Domestic blackout dates for 2002 (will change each yr.): No blackout dates for 2002.

Do first or business class tickets earn more miles than economy tickets? Business-class travelers receive a 25% mileage bonus. First-class travelers get a 50% bonus.

Can you maintain a new account without accruing miles? Yes.

Is literature available? Members receive detailed literature after joining. Some information is available on the website.

What are the penalties for canceling a ticket purchased with frequent-flier miles? You may use the ticket at a later day within a year. It costs $50 to reinstate miles. It costs $100 to change the routing.

Can you buy miles? Yes, up to 15,000 miles. Prices start at 2.75¢ per mile, dropping with larger purchases.

Partners: Aer Lingus, Air Pacific, Air Tahiti Nui, Alaska Airlines, American Eagle, Asiana Airlines, British Airways, Cathay Pacific, Crossair, EL AL, Finnair, Grupo Taca, Hawaiian Airlines, Iberia Airlines, Japan Airlines, LanChile

Where to Find Up-to-Date Information Online

For the latest information on special frequent-flier offers or changes in airline policy, log on to the individual airline's website or try the very helpful WebFlyer (**www.webflyer.com**). The online arm of *Inside Flyer* magazine, WebFlyer is a clearing-house for frequent-traveler information concerning flight, hotel, and car-rental programs. In addition to a continually updated list of last-minute deals and bonus award opportunities, webflyer.com is constructed so that you can establish new frequent-flier accounts and access existing accounts from within the site.

Airlines, LOT, Qantas Airways, SWISS, TAM, Turkish Airlines; also dining, MCI, AOL, and online shopping.
How many miles do you get for feeding hungry children?
A $50 donation to UNICEF nets you 500 miles.

ELITE QUALIFICATIONS & REWARDS

All elite members receive priority boarding, a priority reservations line, and priority seating. Members do not receive priority baggage, guaranteed reservations on sold-out flights, or free club membership.

Gold Elite: Members must fly 25,000 miles or 30 flight segments per calendar year and receive four one-way North American upgrades every 10,000 miles (see "Upgrading Policies of the Major Domestic Airlines" for details).

Platinum Elite: Members must fly 50,000 miles or 60 flight segments per calendar year and receive four one-way North American upgrades every 10,000 miles (see "Upgrading Policies of the Major Domestic Airlines" for details).

Executive Platinum: Members must fly 100,000 miles per calendar year and receive a 100% bonus for miles accrued, eight one-way system-wide upgrades, plus four one-way upgrades for every 10,000 miles (see "Upgrading Policies of the Major Domestic Airlines" for details).

CONTINENTAL ONEPASS PROGRAM
(☎ **800/621-7467**) http://onepass.continental.com

BASIC FF ACCOUNTS

WebFlyer rating: 8.7

Miles earned: Mile per mile traveled; 500-mile minimum.

Mile longevity: Miles never expire, even when account is inactive.

Minimum number of miles needed for a domestic round-trip: 20,000

Minimum number of miles needed for a U.S.–Europe round-trip: 40,000

When can you confirm an award seat? 320 days in advance.

Domestic blackout dates for 2002 (will change each yr.): January 1; February 15, 24; April 7; June 28; July 7; November 27; December 1, 2, 20, 21, 27 to 29.

Do first or business class tickets earn more miles than economy tickets? Both receive a 50% mileage bonus.

Can you have an account without miles? Yes.

Is literature available? Members receive literature after joining; complete information is available on the program website.

What are the penalties for canceling a ticket purchased with frequent-flier miles? There's no penalty to change tickets, but it costs $35 to redeposit miles in your account.

Can you buy miles? Yes, for $25 per 1,000. You can purchase up to 20% of an award's value.

Partners: Aces, Air France, Alaska Airlines, American Eagle, British Midland, Continental Connection, Copa Airlines, Emirates, EVA Air, Frontier Airlines, Hawaiian Airlines, Horizon Air, Midway Airlines, Northwest Airlines, Qantas; also dining, car, hotel, and shopping partners.

Can you accrue miles on partner airlines? Yes.

Can you use miles on partner airlines? Yes.

How many miles are there in a box of chocolates? A $30 purchase from Godiva nets 300 miles.

Elite Qualifications & Rewards

All elite members receive priority boarding, use of the priority reservations telephone line, priority baggage, priority seating, and guaranteed reservations on sold-out flights. Members do not receive free club membership.

Silver Elite: Members must fly 25,000 miles or 30 segments per calendar year. Silver elites earn a 50% bonus and unlimited complimentary, space-available upgrades (see "Upgrading Policies of the Major Domestic Airlines" for details).

Gold Elite: Members must fly 50,000 miles or 60 segments per calendar year. Gold elites earn a 100% bonus; unlimited complimentary, space-available upgrades; and standby companion upgrades (see "Upgrading Policies of the Major Domestic Airlines" for details).

Platinum Elite: Members must fly 75,000 miles or 90 segments per calendar year. Platinum elites earn a 150% bonus unlimited complimentary, space-available upgrades and standby companion upgrades (see "Upgrading Policies of the Major Domestic Airlines" for details).

DELTA SKYMILES PROGRAM (☎ 800/323-2323)
www.delta.com/skymiles/

Basic FF Accounts

WebFlyer rating: 8.3
Miles earned: Mile per mile; 500-mile minimum.
Mile longevity: Miles will not expire if account is activated at least once every 3 years.
Minimum number of miles needed for a domestic round-trip: 25,000
Minimum number of miles needed for a U.S.–Europe round-trip: 50,000
When can you confirm a seat? 331 days before departure.
Domestic blackout dates for 2002 (will change each yr.): No blackout dates for 2002.

✐ WHAT IF YOUR AIRLINE GOES UNDER?

If one airline purchases another, your miles on the purchased airline are usually safe. Members of the TWA Aviators program were able to transfer their miles to American's AAdvantage program on November 30, 2001, after American absorbed TWA. They even kept their elite-flier levels intact. Fliers on Eastern and the original Pan Am saw their miles become Continental and Delta points when those airlines were purchased.

Miles on bankrupt airlines, or miles on airlines that end scheduled service, simply vanish. When Sun Country suspended scheduled flights on December 8, 2001, thousands of "Smiles Miles" went on indefinite hiatus. When the original Midway Airlines went belly-up in 1991, 700,000 frequent fliers lost all of their miles.

If you're holding miles on an airline in shaky financial health, redeem them as soon as possible – ideally, for tickets on partner airlines with better economic prospects. Or invest in Award-Guard (☎ **800/487-8893;** www.privilegeflyer.com), which "insures" miles from 12 airlines. If insured airlines go belly-up, AwardGuard will let members use their miles for trips on other airlines as if the bankrupt airline still existed. The brainchild of one-man frequent-flier industry Randy Petersen, AwardGuard costs $119 for a 1-year subscription.

Do first or business class tickets earn more miles than economy tickets? Business-class travelers receive 25% bonus mileage; first-class travelers receive 50% bonus mileage.

Can you maintain a new account without accruing miles? Yes, for 12 months.

Is literature available? Complete information is available on the website. Members receive detailed literature 1 month after date of first activity on the account.

What are the penalties for canceling a ticket purchased with frequent-flier miles? Members may reinstate the miles for $40, or change the destination city for $50. They can change the date, within 1 year, for free.

Can you buy miles? Yes. Miles cost $25 per 1,000, up to 5,000. Buy them when you make your award reservation.

Partners: AeroMexico, Air France, Air Jamaica, Alitalia, China Southern, Czech Airlines, Korean Air, Malaysia Airlines, SAA, Singapore Airlines, United Airlines; also hotels, car rental, dining, Nextel wireless phones, and shopping partners.

Can you accrue miles on partner airlines? On United, yes. For non-U.S. airlines, only on more expensive tickets.

Can you use miles on partner airlines? Yes.

Can you use miles on *Arthur Frommer's Budget Travel Magazine?* Yes. Delta partners with MilePoint.com to offer magazine subscriptions and online shopping for miles. A year's worth of *AFBTM* costs 600 miles.

ELITE QUALIFICATIONS & REWARDS

All elite members receive priority boarding, use of the priority reservations telephone line, priority baggage, and priority seating. Only Platinum members receive guaranteed reservations on sold-out flights (24 hr. before departure). Only Platinum Medallions receive free club membership. Silver and Gold Medallions receive discounts on club membership.

Silver Medallion: Members must fly 25,000 miles, 30 segments, or 5 transoceanic segments per calendar year. Silver elites receive a 25% bonus for miles accrued, two North American upgrades after reaching 40,000 miles, four 800-mile segment upgrades plus four more every 10,000 miles after achieving elite status (see "Upgrading Policies of the Major Domestic Airlines" for details).

Gold Medallion: Members must fly 50,000 miles, 60 segments, or 10 transoceanic segments per calendar year. Members receive a 100% bonus for miles accrued; two North American upgrades plus two every 20,000 miles over 40,000; four 800-mile segment upgrades and eight more every 10,000 miles after achieving elite status (see "Upgrading Policies of the Major Domestic Airlines" for details).

Platinum Medallion: Members must fly 100,000 miles, 100 segments, or 20 transoceanic segments per calendar year. Members receive a 100% bonus for miles accrued and unlimited complimentary upgrades (see "Upgrading Policies of the Major Domestic Airlines" for details).

NORTHWEST WORLDPERKS PROGRAM
(☎ 800/447-3757) www.nwa.com/freqfly/

BASIC FF ACCOUNTS

WebFlyer rating: 8.8

Miles earned: Mile per mile; 500-mile minimum.

Mile longevity: Miles never expire as long as there's been activity in the past 3 years.

Minimum number of miles needed for a domestic round-trip: 20,000

Minimum number of miles needed for a U.S.–Europe round-trip: 40,000

When can you confirm a seat? Up to 11½ months in advance.

Domestic blackout dates for 2002 (will change each yr.): No blackout dates for 2002.

Do first or business class tickets earn more miles than economy tickets? First- and business-class travelers receive 150% mileage.

Can you maintain a new account without accruing miles? Yes.

Is literature available? The full member's guide is available on the website.

What are the penalties for canceling a ticket purchased with frequent-flier miles? Members may reinstate miles for $50.

Can you buy miles? No.

Partners: Air China, Alaska, Alitalia, America West, Braathens, Cebu Pacific, Continental, Garuda Indonesia, Hawaiian, Japan Air Systems, Jet Airways, Kenya Airways, KLM, Malaysia Airlines, Midwest Express, Pacific Island Aviation, Swisswings, Transavia; also dining, lodging, car rental, Sprint phone service.

Can you accrue miles on partner airlines? Yes, on Alaska, Hawaiian, Braathens, KLM, Continental, Alitalia, Cebu, Jet, JAS, Kenya, Malaysia, Pacific Island, Swisswings, Transavia, and Midway; sometimes on other airlines.

Can you use miles on partner airlines? Yes.

How many miles do you earn for flying a B-2 bomber? 700, if it's a remote-controlled Stealth bomber from www.eToys.com. WorldPerks members get 2 miles per dollar spent at the online toy shop.

ELITE QUALIFICATIONS & REWARDS

All elite members receive priority boarding and priority seating. Gold and Platinum elites receive use of the priority reservations telephone line. Full-fare Gold elites and full-fare or business-class Platinum elites receive guaranteed reservations on sold-out flights. Members do not receive priority baggage, but they do receive special bag tags. Elite members do not receive free club membership.

Silver Elite: Members must fly 25,000 miles per calendar year (excluding bonus miles). Silver elites receive a 50% bonus for miles accrued and unlimited domestic upgrades (see "Upgrading Policies of the Major Domestic Airlines" for details).

Gold Elite: Members must fly 50,000 miles per calendar year and receive a 100% bonus for miles accrued. Gold members receive unlimited domestic and companion upgrades (see "Upgrading Policies of the Major Domestic Airlines" for details).

Platinum Elite: Members must fly 75,000 miles per calendar year and receive a 125% bonus for miles accrued and unlimited domestic and companion upgrades (see "Upgrading Policies of the Major Domestic Airlines" for details).

SOUTHWEST AIRLINES RAPID REWARDS
(☎ 800/248-4377) www.southwest.com/rapid_rewards/

BASIC FF ACCOUNTS

WebFlyer rating: 7.9

Miles earned: Southwest counts "credits," not miles. Each one-way flight is considered one credit.

Mile/Credit longevity: Each individual credit is valid 12 months from the date of travel.

Number of credits needed for a domestic round-trip: After 16 flight credits (or 8 round-trips) within a 12-month period, travelers are awarded a free ticket.

Number of credits needed for a U.S.–Europe round-trip: Southwest does not fly to international destinations, and has no partner airlines.

When can you confirm a seat? No boarding passes are issued on Southwest flights, so it's first-come, first-served on the day of the flight.

Domestic blackout dates for 2002 (will change each yr.): January 1; May 24, 27; July 7; November 26 to 27; December 1 to 2, 20 to 21, 24, 27 to 29.

Do first or business class tickets earn more miles than economy tickets? Southwest only has one cabin class, but there is the opportunity to earn "double credits" if you book your ticket online.

Can you maintain a new account without accruing miles? Yes, but credits will expire 12 months from the date of travel.

Is literature available? Some information is available on the website. Once you achieve Freedom Reward status (meaning once you earn 16 credits), detailed membership packets are mailed to you.

What are the penalties for canceling a ticket earned with flight credits? No penalties; free ticket is valid for 1 year from date of issue.

Can you buy miles? No. But airfares can be very cheap, making credits easy to earn. Same-day, Saturday round-trips between Islip and Providence, Phoenix and Las Vegas, or Houston and Austin, for example, can all net you two credits for under $100.

Partners: No airline partners, but like other airlines, Southwest has partnerships with hotels, car rental companies, and credit cards.

Can you accrue miles on partner airlines? N/A.

Can you use miles on partner airlines? N/A.

How else is Southwest's program unlike the others we've listed? Tickets are fully transferable (this has created a major black market on eBay). There are no capacity controls — if there's a seat available when you call, you can have it. Each award ticket comes with an in-flight drink coupon, so you can toast your good fortune on your free flight.

ELITE QUALIFICATIONS & REWARDS

A Freedom Reward Member (someone who has already reached the 16-credit level) who accumulates 100 flight credits within 12 consecutive months becomes a **Companion Reward Member** and is eligible for a Companion Pass, which entitles one friend to fly free with you for 1 year. You are limited to one Companion Pass at any time, and the designated Companion can be changed three times within the 12-month period. Companion Reward Membership must be re-earned every 12 months.

UNITED AIRLINES MILEAGE PLUS (☎ 800/421-4655)
www.mileageplus.com

BASIC FF ACCOUNTS

WebFlyer rating: 8.5
Miles earned: Mile per mile; 500-mile minimum.

Mile longevity: Miles will not expire if you accrue miles every 3 years.

Minimum number of miles needed for a domestic round-trip: 25,000

Minimum number of miles needed for a U.S.–Europe round-trip: 35,000

When can you confirm a seat? Any time.

Domestic blackout dates for 2002 (will change each yr.): March 15, 17, 22, 24; November 27; December 1, 2, 19 to 21.

Do first or business class tickets earn more miles than economy tickets? Business-class travelers receive a 25% fare bonus.

Can you maintain a new account without accruing miles? Yes, for 12 months.

Is literature available? The complete member's guide is available on the website.

What are the penalties for canceling a ticket purchased with frequent-flier miles? If canceled more than 14 days from travel, no fee. Within 14 days, members may reinstate miles for $75.

Can you buy miles? Yes. Buy up to 15,000 miles for 2.5¢ per mile, plus tax, at www.ualmiles.com.

Partners: Aeromar, Air Canada, Air New Zealand, Aloha Airlines, Austrian Airlines, bmi British Midland, BWIA West Indies Airways, Cayman Airways, Delta, Emirates, LAPA, Lufthansa, Mexicana, All Nippon Airways, SAS, Saudi Arabian Airlines, Singapore Airlines, Spanair, Thai Airways International, VARIG; also shopping, Nextel phones, MSN Internet access, hotels, and car rental partners.

Can you accrue miles on partner airlines? Yes.

Can you use miles on partner airlines? Sometimes, though the agreements are constantly in flux; call the airline or check the website for the most up-to-date rules.

Are miles worth a hill of beans? That's for you to decide. But a hill of beans is worth miles. Mileage Plus members who shop at five supermarket chains get 125 miles per $250 they spend on groceries.

Elite Qualifications & Rewards

All elite members receive priority boarding, use of the priority reservations telephone line, priority standby, priority waiting list, and Economy Plus seating with extra legroom in coach. Members do not receive priority baggage or guaranteed reservations on sold-out flights.

Premier: Members must fly 25,000 miles or 30 segments per calendar year. Premiers receive a 25% bonus for miles accrued and four 500-mile upgrades every 10,000 miles after reaching elite status (see "Upgrading Policies of the Major Domestic Airlines" for details).

Executive Premier: Members must fly 50,000 miles or 60 segments per calendar year and receive a 100% bonus for miles accrued, free access to airport lounges, and four 500-mile upgrades every 10,000 miles after reaching elite status (see "Upgrading Policies of the Major Domestic Airlines" for details).

Premier 1K: Members must fly 100,000 miles or 100 segments per calendar year and receive a 100% bonus for miles accrued, free access to airport lounges, and four 500-mile upgrades every 10,000 miles after reaching elite status (see "Upgrading Policies of the Major Domestic Airlines" for details).

US AIRWAYS DIVIDEND MILES (☎ 800/428-4322 or 336/661-8390) www.usairways.com/dividendmiles/

Basic FF Accounts

WebFlyer rating: 7.8
Miles earned: Mile per mile with a minimum of 500 miles.
Mile longevity: Miles will not expire if you make at least one flight every 3 years.
Minimum number of miles needed for a domestic round-trip: 20,000

Minimum number of miles needed for a U.S.–Europe round-trip: 40,000

When can you confirm a seat? Up to 331 days in advance.

Domestic blackout dates for 2002 (will change each yr.): January 2; November 26 to 27; December 1 to 2, 20 to 21, 28 to 29.

Do first or business class tickets earn more miles than economy tickets? First-class travelers receive 50% bonus for miles accrued.

Can you maintain a new account without accruing miles? Yes, for up to 3 years.

Is literature available? Literature is available at the airport and on the program website; members do not receive literature by mail.

What are the penalties for canceling a ticket purchased with frequent-flier miles? Members may reinstate miles for $40 or change the destination city for $50.

Can you buy miles? Yes, with no limit for 3¢ per mile.

Partners: Alitalia (partnership to end Jan 1, 2003), LatinPass, Northwest, Qantas, also hotel, car rental, dining, shopping.

Can you accrue miles on partner airlines? Yes.

Can you use miles on partner airlines? Yes.

Excuse me, are those your miles calling? Yes, if you use a Nextel mobile phone. Nextel offers 5,000 Dividend Miles for each handset purchased.

Elite Qualifications & Rewards

All elite members receive priority boarding, use of the priority reservations telephone line, priority baggage, and priority seating. Members do not receive guaranteed reservations on sold-out flights or free club membership.

Silver: Members must fly 25,000 miles or 30 segments per calendar year. Members receive a 50% bonus for miles accrued; four complimentary, 800-mile, one-way upgrades; plus six more for every 10,000 miles flown (see "Upgrading Policies of the Major Domestic Airlines" for details).

Gold: Members must fly 50,000 miles or 60 segments per calendar year. Members receive a 100% bonus for miles accrued; eight complimentary, 800-mile, one-way upgrades per 10,000 miles flown; plus 10 more per 20,000 miles flown (see "Upgrading Policies of the Major Domestic Airlines" for details).

Chairman's Preferred: Members must fly 100,000 miles or 100 segments per calendar year. Members receive a 100% bonus for miles accrued and unlimited upgrades (see "Upgrading Policies of the Major Domestic Airlines" for details).

3 How to Manage Your Miles

ONCE YOU'VE CHOSEN A PROGRAM AND STARTED accruing miles, a few general rules will help you maximize your miles.

WHEN TO REDEEM

- For domestic travel, it's best to **redeem mileage for long flights** rather than short hops. You'll use the same number of frequent-flier miles for each. Unless the published fare for a short hop is exorbitant — as it is on certain routes monopolized by a single airline — you're better off saving your miles for a longer trip.

- On **flights to Europe, redeem your miles during summer months,** when standard fares to Europe are much higher. In the winter, it's best to grab a cheap fare (and bank *those* miles) and wait for a better bargain.

- **Book as far in advance as possible.** The few frequent-flier seats on each plane are first-come, first-served.

- **Book a trip as soon as you have the necessary miles.** Partnerships may shift and mileage requirements may rise. A ticket in hand is your best insurance against changes.

- **Don't use miles for first-class tickets.** If you must
  fly in business- or first-class, see if you can buy an
  economy-class ticket and use (fewer) miles to upgrade
  when possible (see "Upgrading Policies of the Major
  Domestic Airlines," for details). You'll get twice as
  much from your miles this way.

GET THE CREDIT

- **Keep your frequent-flier member card handy
  in your wallet** and provide it to travel and ticket
  agents every time you make a reservation or purchase
  a ticket with that airline. This will help ensure that
  your account is credited properly. (If you don't have
  your card, airline agents will look it up for you at
  the airport, but they won't be happy to if the check-
  in line is long. In this event, you're better off asking
  for help at a shorter line, even if it's for a different
  flight.)

- If you have a PalmPilot or handheld organizer, **write
  down all of your membership numbers** in the organizer as a back-up in case you forget your card.

- Get in the habit of **asking when you check in
  whether your mileage for that flight was credited** to
  your account, particularly if you made changes to your
  initial reservation.

- If you forget to credit a flight, a hotel stay, or a car
  rental, **hold on to your receipts** so you can request
  the mileage once you return home.

STAY INFORMED

- **Keep close track of the mileage you earn.** Don't lose
  precious miles because of an airline's computer error,

🅒 AND THE WINNER IS . . .

Every year ***InsideFlyer*** magazine sponsors the "Freddies," awarded for excellence in frequent traveler programs. Awards are voted on by those who know the programs best – frequent travelers themselves.

"Freddie" is Freddie Laker, a British mogul whose transatlantic SkyTrain service in the 1970s pioneered low-fare, no-frills travel. He's been cited as an inspiration to both Southwest's Herb Kelleher and Virgin's Richard Branson.

13TH ANNUAL FREDDIE AWARD WINNERS

- **Program of the Year, Domestic:** Continental OnePass

- **Program of the Year, International:** SAS EuroBonus

- **Best Award, Domestic:** Continental OnePass
  (Reduced awards from the U.S. to Latin America)

- **Best Award, International:** SAS EuroBonus
  (Intercontinental Bonus-"2 for 1" Award)

- **Best Bonus Promotion, Domestic:** Southwest Rapid Rewards (earning double credit for booking online)

- **Best Bonus Promotion, International:** SAS EuroBonus (Intercontinental Bonus-"+40,000" Award)

- **Best Frequent-flier Website:** Continental OnePass

- **Best Elite-Level Program:** Continental OnePass

- **Best Award Redemption:** Southwest Rapid Rewards

- **Best Customer Service:** Midwest Express Frequent Flier

- **Best Affinity Credit Card:** Diners Club Club Rewards

which happens all too often. Save your ticket receipts and boarding passes at least until you receive your next mileage statement and can verify that the airline properly credited your account. In case they didn't, you may need to provide documentation to correct the error. If you like to travel with e-tickets, buy them with a credit card or you'll have no other way to document the purchase.

- **Check your statement carefully** as soon as it arrives and report discrepancies immediately.

- **Look over your frequent-flier newsletter** when it arrives to see if policies have changed regarding award rates; blackout dates; deadlines for using available miles with other airlines; or earning opportunities with car-rental companies or consumer products and services like mile-earning credit cards, utilities, and so on.

- **Book online whenever possible.** Many airlines now offer bonus miles for passengers who book e-tickets on their websites. Check each site for details.

- New services such as **e-mail alerts and online check-in** often offer mileage bonuses. Log on to airline web-sites to see what the latest promotions are.

- Some airlines will **double or triple mileage for new routes.** Make a habit of asking if your carrier has started any new itineraries each time you make a reservation.

- Consider a **mileage-consolidation service** such as MileageManager.com to keep track of several different frequent-flier accounts.

4   THE POLITICS OF UPGRADING

AIRLINES HAVE CRACKED DOWN ON FREE UPGRADES in recent years, doling them out only to elite frequent fliers. But given the right gate agent, the right airport, and the right flight, it is occasionally possible for ordinary travelers to taste the sweetness of first or business class.

THE PARTY LINE

At press time, no major carrier allows basic frequent fliers to upgrade for free. Basic frequent fliers must purchase upgrades with cash or frequent-flier miles. (On average, the cost of a round-trip upgrade on a discount coach ticket is 20,000 points — 5,000 points shy of the cost of a round-trip ticket for domestic travel.) It's much harder to upgrade on a discount economy ticket than on a full coach fare.

America West, Continental, and Northwest are the only major airlines that allow elite frequent fliers unlimited complimentary upgrades.

Delta and US Airways give only their top fliers (who reach 100,000 miles or more) this privilege. On American and United, even the highest elite travelers earn only a fixed number of upgrades per miles traveled, though they get a boatload of certificates for flying 100,000 miles.

On all the airlines, superior elite ranking does entitle travelers to confirm award seats farther in advance. So a pecking order is established: travelers who fly 100,000 or 50,000 or even 25,000 miles per year have first dibs on the small number of upgrades available to frequent fliers, which doesn't leave much for the average leisure traveler or light business flier.

A WINNING ARGUMENT: HOW TO TALK YOURSELF UP

Many first- and business-class seats are assigned at the airport. Ticket and gate agents have wide latitude to assign seats, and use it frequently to reward passengers who they think may be most deserving. Talking your way into an upgrade requires finesse and luck. A few tips:

- **If you look like you mean business,** you're much more likely to receive an upgrade at the airport, even if you're just confirming an upgrade you earned as a frequent flier. Dress well.

- **Be *really* nice.** If the gate agents like you or remember you positively, you may score the seat.

- **Be *really* opportunistic.** If it's your birthday, honeymoon, or anniversary, or if you've been flying for days and feel bedraggled and confused, mention it offhandedly to gate agents. But don't demand, don't nag, and don't look like you're gunning for an upgrade.

- If you or your flying companion has a first-class or business-class ticket, **ask if you can sit together.** Do this at the gate, never the ticket counter.

- If you **arrive at the airport very early** with only carry-on baggage and ask at the gate (never at the ticket counter) to get on the standby list for an earlier flight to your destination, good karma might bounce your way and you may end up in first class.

- If you **volunteer to be bumped** from an oversold flight or if your flight is canceled, ask for a round-trip upgrade as part of your compensation. (For more on the ins and outs of bumping, see chapter 2, "Ticketing Pitfalls.")

- As a last resort, it's still worth **asking your travel agent for an upgrade** if you're a very frequent customer. According to Ed Perkins, consumer advocate for the American Society of Travel Agents, some travel agents are able to reward their own loyal customers with upgrades — even when the airline's reservationist says seats are unavailable. Unfortunately, there isn't a published list of agencies with both the access to this information and the willingness to do this — primarily because the airlines would quash the practice if they knew who was involved.

ACHIEVING ELITE STATUS

As mentioned earlier, the only way to guarantee yourself free upgrades these days is to reach elite status on the right airline.

Elite status is a tricky thing to achieve, as it's based on "elite-qualifying miles" which usually exclude certain partners (especially non-airline partners), and count only actual miles flown (not class-of-service or online-booking bonuses). On partner airlines, discount tickets may not count as elite-qualifying miles. Discount tickets on American Airlines only count half their miles as elite-qualifying. Generally, no miles booked through consolidators are elite-qualifying. And elite status must be re-earned every year.

Every airline's elite program has several tiers, defined by the number of miles flown within one calendar year. Two round-trips to Europe and one domestic round-trip flight should bring you to the first tier, which requires 25,000 miles. The second tier requires 50,000 miles. The third tier requires 100,000 miles (with the exception of America West, Continental, and Northwest, which require only 75,000 miles). Alaska's program is an exception, with only two elite tiers at 15,000 and 45,000 miles.

Elite status can also be achieved by flying many short flights, even if they total to fewer than 25,000 miles (except on Northwest). By that method, first-tier status is gained with 30 one-way flight segments, second-tier with 60, and third-tier with 100 (on Continental the third tier is 90; the top level of American's program can't be earned with segments only).

Elite frequent fliers receive a host of perks. First, the rich get richer: Travelers who have reached the first tier receive a 25% to 50% mileage bonus for every flight they take. For instance, if you travel 800 miles one-way, you receive 800 frequent-flier miles plus an additional 200- to 400-mile bonus. Second-tier elites receive a 50% to 100% bonus for miles flown. Third-tier elites receive a 100% to 150% bonus. In other words, as a third-tier elite that same 800-mile one-way flight earns 1,600 to 2,000 frequent-flier miles!

Of course, those bonuses aren't "elite-qualifying miles," so your 800-mile coach ticket only gets you 800 miles closer to renewing your elite status.

Elite status also entitles you to **free upgrades** and **companion upgrades** — either unlimited or a set amount of segment upgrades, depending on the airline and the level of elite status you've reached (see "Upgrading Policies of the Major Domestic Airlines," below). The highest elite travelers are allowed to confirm their upgrades either when they make their reservation, or 72 to 100 hours in advance, well before the lower elite levels. Each level is allowed to confirm at least 24 hours before the level beneath it. This may seem to be a minor privilege, but it's crucial because airlines make fewer seats available for reward travel. Even if all of the free class-upgrade seats are snapped up by Gold and Platinum members, basic elite fliers still get to upgrade to the front of the coach cabin, which makes for more comfort — especially on United, where seats in the Economy Plus section up front have more legroom than seats behind them.

Elite members receive a range of additional benefits which may include priority boarding, priority seating, a designated elite reservations line, guaranteed reservations on sold-out flights, priority baggage, and discounted or free membership to airport lounge clubs.

As always, Southwest's program is unique among large airlines. The low-fare carrier doesn't have an elite level per se, but fliers who clock 100 segments in a year receive a pass that allows one companion to fly free with them for a year.

5 Upgrading Policies of the Major Domestic Airlines

UNLESS OTHERWISE NOTED, ONE-WAY MILEAGE-BASED upgrades below are for flights in the continental U.S., Alaska, and Canada. Upgrades to other destinations cost more miles, and are charged by geographic zone — meaning upgrades to Europe are usually double the mile price of U.S. upgrades.

ALASKA

- **Non-elite:** Non-elite Mileage Plan members can purchase one-way first-class upgrades for 10,000 miles.

- **MVP members** can purchase one-way first-class upgrades for 5,000 miles. Members receive automatic first-class upgrade certificates for any "Y" class fare for every 10,000 actual air miles flown. They may use two certificates to achieve an upgrade from some lower fares. Complimentary upgrades can be confirmed any time before departure. MVP Gold members receive automatic first-class upgrades for every 5,000 air miles traveled.

AMERICA WEST

- **Non-elite:** Non-elite FlightFund members can purchase one-way upgrades on America West and Continental flights within North America for 5,000 miles on a full coach fare, or 10,000 miles on any other paid fare. These upgrades may be confirmed at any time.

    If you're not a member of FlightFund, you can purchase an upgrade for $50 per 500 miles. Cash upgrades may only be purchased between 4 hours and 30 minutes before departure.

- **Elite members** receive unlimited, one-way, space-available upgrades on America West and select Continental flights. Silver members can confirm upgrades on the day of departure. Gold members can confirm upgrades 2 days prior to departure. Platinum members may confirm any time after ticketing on a full-fare ticket, 3 days prior to departure for other paid tickets, and 2 hours prior to departure for companion upgrades. All upgrades at all levels on Continental are confirmed 2 hours before departure.

AMERICAN

- **Non-elite:** One-way upgrades are 5,000 miles on full-fare tickets and 15,000 miles on many discount tickets. Upgrade coupons are $55 per upgrade for one to seven 500-mile segments; $50 per upgrade for eight or more 500-mile segments. Confirmation available 24 hours before departure.

- **Elite members** receive four complimentary one-way upgrades, every 10,000 miles. Gold members can confirm upgrades 24 hours before departure; Platinum may confirm 72 hours before departure; Executive Platinum may confirm 100 hours before departure. All elites may use upgrades for companions traveling on the same flight.

  Elite members can purchase 500-mile upgrades for $45 each for one to seven upgrades, $31.25 each for eight or more. They can also get eight upgrades for 35,000 miles and 16 upgrades for 50,000 miles.

CONTINENTAL

- **Non-elite:** OnePass members may purchase domestic one-way upgrades on Continental, Northwest, Frontier, and America West flights for 5,000 miles on full-fare tickets and 10,000 miles on discount tickets. Some full-fare coach tickets get free upgrades upon request. Always request them.

- **Elite:** All Continental elite members receive unlimited, complimentary, space-available upgrades and companion upgrades.

  Silver elites may confirm their own upgrades 1 day before departure on full fares, day of departure on discounted fares. Companion upgrades may be confirmed 2 hours before departure.

  Gold elites may confirm their own upgrades anytime after ticketing on full fares, 48 hours before departure on discounted fares. Companion upgrades may be confirmed 2 hours before departure.

Platinum elites may confirm their own upgrades anytime after ticketing on full fares, 72 hours before departure on discounted fares. Companion upgrades may be confirmed 2 hours before departure.

DELTA

- **Non-elite** members may purchase a round-trip upgrade on a full coach fare for 10,000 miles; on some, but not all discounted coach fares, a round-trip upgrade costs 20,000 miles. The absolute cheapest fares aren't upgradeable. Confirmation is available at the airport 3 hours before departure.

- **Elite: Silver Medallion** members receive four, 800-mile segment upgrades plus four every 10,000 miles after achieving elite status. Silver elites may confirm upgrades 24 hours in advance on all but the lowest discount fare (L and U fares), which can't be upgraded.

    Gold Medallion members receive four, 800-mile segment upgrades plus eight every 10,000 miles after achieving elite status and two North American upgrades plus two every 20,000 miles over 40,000. Gold elites may confirm upgrades 72 hours before departure on all but the lowest discount fare (L and U fares), which can't be upgraded.

    Platinum Medallion members receive unlimited complimentary upgrades, which may be confirmed at any time, plus six one-way upgrades which may be used for companions anywhere on Delta's system, as long as they're traveling on tickets of the more expensive fare classes (Y, B, and M).

NORTHWEST

- **Non-elite:** On a domestic full-fare or BizFlex ticket, if a passenger checks in at an E-Ticket kiosk or online, upgrades are available upon check-in for $25 (flights of less than 750 miles), $35 (flights up to 2,100 miles), or $50 (all flights).

If you don't use a kiosk, full-fare tickets cost $25 to $150 to upgrade depending on distance. (A trip of 2,000 miles, for example, would cost $100 to upgrade.)

Full-fare coach tickets on selected routes get free upgrades upon request.

WorldPerks members may also buy one-way domestic upgrades for 5,000 miles on a full-fare ticket; 10,000 miles on some discount tickets. Confirmation is available at the time of reservation. Such upgrades are valid on both Northwest and Continental flights

- **Elite: Silver Elite** members receive unlimited domestic upgrades. Confirmation is available 48 hours before departure on full fares; day of departure on discounted fares.

  Gold Elite members receive unlimited domestic and companion upgrades. On full fares, confirmation is available when the flight is booked; on discount fares, 48 hours before departure.

  Platinum Elites receive unlimited domestic and companion upgrades. Confirmation is available at the time of booking on full fares; 72 hours before departure on discounted fares.

  Alaska Elite: Alaska MVP and MVP Gold members can be upgraded to first class on Northwest flights in North America if they are traveling on the most expensive fare classes. Confirmation 24 hours before departure.

SOUTHWEST AIRLINES

Southwest has only one class of service, so upgrades are not available. (But if you're really nice, you may get the flight crew to act even more cheerful than usual.)

UNITED

- **Non-elite:** Non-elite members may purchase upgrades at an airport or a city ticket office, on their day of departure. Four 500-mile upgrades for use on full-fare tickets cost $200; eight 500-mile upgrades for use on full-fare tickets cost $400.

   For fliers using mileage to upgrade, one-way upgrades from full-fare coach tickets to the next class of service are 5,000 miles; from some discount fares they're 10,000 miles. The cheapest coach fares aren't upgradeable.

- **Elite:** All elite levels get four 500-mile upgrades every 10,000 miles after reaching elite status. Confirmation for Premier and Executive Premier members is available 72 hours before departure on full fares, 24 hours before departure on discounted fares. For Premier IK members, confirmation is available 100 hours before departure on full fares, 24 hours before departure on discounted fares.

US AIRWAYS

- **Non-elite:** Upgrades for full-fare tickets cost $50; some full-fare coach tickets, called "GoFirst," can be upgraded for free if you ask at time of reservation. Non-GoFirst upgrades can be purchased and confirmed at time of reservation.

   For fliers using mileage to upgrade, round-trip upgrades cost 10,000 miles with full-fare tickets and 20,000 with discount tickets. They are confirmed at time of reservation.

- **Elite: Silver Preferred members** get four 800-mile, North American upgrades for every 10,000 miles flown plus six more for every 20,000 miles flown. They may confirm upgrades anytime for full-fare tickets, 24 hours in advance for discount tickets. No domestic flight requires more than three 800-mile certificates, no matter how long it is.

Gold Preferred members get eight 800-mile, North American upgrades for every 10,000 miles flown plus 10 more for every 20,000 miles flown. They may confirm upgrades anytime on full fares; 72 hours in advance on all other fares.

Chairman's Preferred members get unlimited system-wide and companion one-class upgrades. They may confirm upgrades anytime on full fares; 7 days in advance on all other fares.

6   ALLIANCES & MULTIPLE ACCOUNTS

AIRLINE PARTNERSHIPS AND ALLIANCES HAVE MADE frequent-flier miles much more powerful — and more confusing.

Partnerships are continually shifting. When the last edition of this book was published, US Airways and American had a deal — no longer. Alliances, on the other hand, are complex business mergers rather than mere frequent-flier partnerships, and are therefore more stable. As groupings of airlines, Oneworld, SkyTeam, and the Star Alliance seem to be here to stay. (See "Allied Forces," in chapter 2, "Ticketing Pitfalls.")

In almost every instance, frequent-flier partnerships work to your benefit. If you have an account with Continental, you can use your miles to fly on Northwest. If you have a ton of Alaska miles, you can use their partnership with Continental to fly to Europe. If you take one flight on an obscure foreign airline, you can use it to add thousands of miles to an existing domestic partner account. (You cannot, however, combine miles from several partner accounts to reach a single award level.)

Currently, all the major airlines except Southwest allow their miles to be used on at least some domestic and international partners, and allow fliers to accumulate miles by flying on those partners.

It's not quite as easy as it sounds, though. When you travel on a partner airline, you travel according to their rules — so you need to understand the blackout dates and seat limitations for two airlines, not just one.

Rules for earning miles on partner airlines can be truly Byzantine, as well. Usually you're pretty safe if you stick to an airline's global alliance — Oneworld, SkyTeam, the Star Alliance, or the Northwest/KLM/Continental combination. For other partnerships, you may only earn miles in certain fare classes or on certain tickets.

The most notorious gap in the partnership system is with the American Airlines–British Airways deal. American AAdvantage members earn miles on BA flights — **except** on the transatlantic flights that Americans are most likely to take. Why? Politics, mostly. American and BA spent late 2001 trying to form a profit-sharing alliance, a deal looked on with great suspicion by the U.S. Congress because it would give the new alliance a dominant position for flights from the U.S. to London's Heathrow airport.

The alliance plans were called off in February 2002, but the effect on the two airlines' frequent-flier programs remained at press time: the airlines don't want to give credit for flights to Heathrow, in case Congress thinks the airlines are thumbing their noses at the government.

Codeshares are simpler when it comes to earning and redeeming miles. If it says "United" on your ticket — even though the plane's logo says Lufthansa or All Nippon Airways (ANA) — you're flying under United's seat controls and blackout dates and earning United miles. But even though ANA and United are Star Alliance allies, discount flights purchased using ANA's code only earn 70% of their miles flown in the United program.

So call your frequent-flier program before booking an international ticket to be sure of the restrictions that apply to you. Here are some questions to ask when you book:

- **Does a portion of your flight involve a codeshare partner's aircraft?** If so, and if you have accounts with both airlines, be sure to find out which account will be credited with your mileage.

- **How many miles will you earn?** If the flight is a codeshare or on a partner airline, compare the reward to what you would earn if you used your regular frequent-flier carrier. The frequent-flier literature you receive after joining a program should tell you this, but the rules change so often that it's wise to double-check when you make the reservation.

- **What restrictions are there?** Is mileage credit available on the route, flight, fare, and date you plan to travel?

Finally, **check your mileage statements carefully** and make sure your account was credited properly, with the same terms you agreed to when you made your reservation.

MOVING MILES

Airline alliances don't let you move miles among airline accounts. There are, however, ways around this restriction.

Members of Hilton's free HHonors frequent-stay program (☎ **800/548-8690;** www.hhonors.com) can use the RewardExchange function to turn one airline's miles into Hilton points, and then back into another airline's miles. Partners are AeroCalifornia, American, Continental, Delta, Hawaiian, LanChile, LatinPass, Mexicana, Midwest Express, South African, TWA, United, and Virgin Atlantic.

But keep in mind you will lose miles in the conversion. If you're moving miles to American from another carrier, 5 "old" miles will become 2 "new" ones. For everyone else, the conversion ratio is 10 old miles to 3 new ones. If you transfer miles out of American to another airline, the conversion is an abysmal 20 AAdvantage miles to 3 new miles. Amazingly, Hilton allows this transaction, though the company does not encourage the practice.

Hilton's Mutual Fund feature allows another perk: You can combine Hilton points with your spouse and transmute them into miles. Of the major frequent-flier programs, only British Airways permits this without Hilton getting involved.

KEEPING TRACK OF MILES

If you can't keep the regulations straight for your many frequent-flier accounts, hire MileageManager (www.mileagemanager.com) as your accountant. The Web-based automated service lets you monitor balances, activity, and elite status for 22 airline programs, seven hotel programs, American Express Membership Rewards, and Diners Club Club Rewards.

Even better, MileageManager keeps you informed through e-mail alerts regarding bonus-mile promotions and other changes to your programs. The service is run by Randy

ONLINE BOOKING BONUSES

Most airlines offer bonus miles for tickets booked through their websites. Here's a snapshot of some of the rewards on airline websites at press time:

AIRLINE	BONUS FOR ONE R/T FLIGHT	OTHER WEB BONUSES (CUMULATIVE WITH ONLINE BOOKING BONUS)
Alaska	5,000	1,500 for sign-up and online account management sign-up
American	1,000	3,000 for first-time booking
America West	3,000	2,500 for first-time booking
Continental	1,000	1,000 for e-ticketing
Delta	1,000	N/A
Northwest	1,000	1,500 for first-time booking
Southwest	1 credit	2 credits on sign-up
United	1,000	N/A
US Airways	2,000	1,000 for using an e-ticket kiosk

Follow the One-Penny Rule

Restaurants, car dealerships, and online stores all try to seduce patrons by offering frequent-flier miles with purchase. When do the bonuses outweigh slightly higher prices? Frequent-flier guru Randy Petersen says to think of miles as worth a penny apiece. Getting a 1,000-mile bonus with purchase, then, would only be worth a $10 increase in the price of an item.

Petersen, one of the world's frequent-flying authorities, and costs $14.95 per year.

7 Buy to Fly: Using Credit Cards to Earn Miles

MANY CREDIT CARD COMPANIES, CAR-RENTAL AGENCIES, utilities, and other vendors also offer frequent-flier miles with a particular airline for every dollar you spend. *Consumer Reports Travel Letter* recommends that you compare the price of goods that offer miles with similar merchandise from other vendors, to see if you're really getting a deal (see "Follow the One-Penny Rule," above).

MILE-EARNING CREDIT CARDS

Charge cards, credit cards, and a few debit cards provide frequent-flier bonuses merely for shopping and paying your bills. They're no-brainers for accumulating thousands of miles.

Charge cards are the safest of the bunch, as you pay off your bill in full each month. Credit cards let you carry a balance, on which you must pay interest. Debit cards should *never* be used to purchase travel — they take money straight out of your checking account, and offer no protection or dispute mechanism in case a travel supplier does you wrong.

Diners Club and **American Express** charge cards can be used to earn miles on many different airlines. Diners

Club has the most airline partners, including all the major players. Cardholders get a thousand-mile bonus each month they use the card for their first year, and access to 70 first-class airport lounges. But relatively few merchants accept Diners Club cards, and the card costs $80 per year.

American Express has been known for decades for their traveler services, including a top-rank travel agency and worldwide offices that hold members' mail. With the optional Membership Rewards program, Amex members get points that become miles on Continental, US Airways, Delta, Southwest, and several foreign carriers. Membership Rewards points can also be used for store gift certificates, hotel stays, magazine subscriptions, and car rentals. The program costs $40 per year on top of the normal American Express annual fee of $55 (the fee is higher for gold and platinum cards).

Of the airline cards, Delta's special American Express credit card offers an especially tasty deal — 2 miles per dollar for most household purchases. Southwest's offers the quickest domestic round-trips, with one free ticket per $16,000 charged.

All airline credit cards have annual fees, but there's a way around that. **Amtrak's Guest Rewards Visa (☎ 800/780-5561;** www.amtrakguestrewards.com) has no annual fee and accumulates one point per dollar spent. Five thousand points equals 5,000 miles on United, Continental, or Midwest Express. But you get only 500 points for your first purchase, a much smaller bonus than airline cards offer.

The **Starwood Preferred Guest American Express Credit Card (☎ 800/297-1000;** www.americanexpress.com) has no fee for the first year, with a $30 fee in following years — still lower than airline cards. Its points can be converted one-for-one into miles with Alaska, America West, Continental, Delta, Northwest, United, and US Airways. When you hit 20,000 miles, they tack on an extra 5,000 as a thank-you. But there's no sign-up bonus at all, unless you stay at Starwood hotels and resorts.

MILEAGE-EARNING CREDIT CARD ROUNDUP

Student-Only Cards

AMERICAN EXPRESS BLUE FOR STUDENTS
(☎ 800/600-2583) www.americanexpress.com
Type of Card: Credit card, can pay over time
Annual Fee: None
Credit Line: $8,000
Miles Earned: 14 round-trip, discount travel certificates on Continental Airlines

AMERICAN EXPRESS CARD FOR STUDENTS
(☎ 877/237-2069) www.americanexpress.com
Type of Card: Charge card, must pay in full each month
Annual Fee: $55
Spending Limit: None
Miles Earned: 14 round-trip, discount travel certificates on Continental Airlines
Other Bonuses: Eligible for American Express Membership Rewards (see "Airline-Independent Cards," below)

UNITED COLLEGEPLUS VISA (☎ 888/211-3095)
www.collegeplus.com
Credit Limit: $5,000
Type of Card: Credit card, can pay over time
Annual Fee: None
Miles Earned: 1 mile per $2 spent

Airline-Independent Cards

Several companies, such as NextCard, FirstStar, WebMiles, and First Union offer credit cards that earn travel rewards. But only two of them are as flexible or earn tickets as quickly as the airline credit cards. Diners Club and American Express both allow you to transfer points directly into your regular frequent-flier account.

AMERICAN EXPRESS MEMBERSHIP REWARDS
(☎ 800/843-2273) www.americanexpress.com
Type of Card: Charge card, must pay in full each month
Annual Fee: $40 for holders of existing American Express cards

Miles for Students

Many credit card companies run special travel programs for students; call your credit card company for more information. If your lack of a credit history prevents you from getting a "grown-up" credit card, United Airlines and American Express offer three good options. (See above.)

United's CollegePlus program gives 2,500 frequent-flier miles to students making their first and third round-trips on United, plus a whopping 10,000 at graduation. Students also earn 5,000 miles per 50 hours' worth of community service with seven charities, including Habitat for Humanity and the Make-a-Wish Foundation. Best, CollegePlus is free. Sign up at www.collegeplus.com.

Miles Earned: One "point" per dollar spent; 1,000 points equals 1,000 miles at Delta, US Airways, Hawaiian, Virgin Atlantic, Korean Air, AeroMexico, LatinPass, Mexicana, ANA; 1,250 points equals one Southwest credit; 1,050 points equals 15 El Al Matmid points; hotel and car rental partners as well.

DINERS CLUB (☎ 888/923-4637) www.dinersclubus.com
Type of Card: Charge card, must pay in full each month
Spending Limit: None
Annual Fee: $80
Joining Bonus: Earn up to 12,000 miles for joining (1,000 miles per month for first year, provided you charge one purchase each month).
Miles Earned: Earn 1 mile for every dollar spent; partnered with all major airlines plus Aloha, AirTran, ATA, Frontier, Hawaiian, Midway, Midwest Express.
Other Extras: Access to more than 70 airport lounges (see "Lounging Around," in chapter 2).

Airline-Specific Cards

All cards earn 1 mile per dollar spent on all purchases, unless otherwise noted. Most cards offer occasional special incentives to award miles for balance transfers as well.

All non-metallic cards (meaning cards that don't have "gold," "silver" or "platinum" in their names) have mileage caps unless otherwise noted, usually 50,000 to 60,000 miles per year; it's unlikely normal shoppers will run up against these caps. (If you're spending more than $60,000 on a credit card annually, you should get a platinum card anyway.)

Metallic cards have higher credit limits, unless otherwise noted.

ALASKA AIRLINES VISA (☎ 800/274-5060)
www.bankofamerica.com/creditcards/
Type of Card: Credit card, can pay over time
Annual Fee: $45
Joining Bonus: 3,000 miles
Other Cards: Gold card: $45 annual fee. Platinum card: $75 annual fee; 5,000 bonus miles upon sign-up and 2,000 extra bonus miles per year; 2 miles per dollar spent on Alaska and Horizon tickets; one $50 companion ticket voucher per year; two one-way first class upgrades per year; two airport lounge passes per year.

ALOHA AIRREWARDS VISA AND MASTERCARD
(☎ 800/342-2778) www.fhb.com/pb_alohacard.htm
Type of Card: Credit card, can pay over time
Annual Fee: $25
Miles Earned: 1.5 Aloha Pass miles per dollar spent
Gold Card: $55 membership fee; 1,000 extra bonus miles per Aloha flight

AMERICAN AIRLINES CITIBANK AADVANTAGE VISA AND MASTERCARDS (☎ 800/359-4444)
www.citibank.com
Type of Card: Credit card, can pay over time
Annual Fee: $50

Joining Bonus: 3,000 miles earned after first purchase
Other Cards: Gold card: 5,000 bonus miles upon joining; $85 fee. Platinum card: 7,500 bonus miles upon joining, $125 fee.

AMERICA WEST FLIGHTFUND VISA
(☎ **800/274-5060**) www.bankofamerica.com/creditcards/
Type of Card: Credit card, can pay over time
Annual Fee: $45
Joining Bonus: 2,500 miles upon approval
Platinum Card: $75 annual fee; 5,000 bonus miles upon approval; 1,000 extra bonus miles per year; no mileage cap; 2 miles per dollar spent on America West tickets; two free one-time passes for two people each to airport lounges.

CONTINENTAL AIRLINES VISA AND
MASTERCARD FROM CHASE (☎ **800/245-9850**)
www.chasecardsonline.com
Type of Card: Credit card, can pay over time
Annual Fee: $45
Joining Bonus: 4,000 miles
Other Cards: World MasterCard and Visa Signature Card: 2 miles per dollar for tickets booked directly through Continental; free domestic companion ticket, no sign-up bonus, $65 annual fee. Platinum Card: $65 annual fee; 6,000 miles upon sign-up.

DELTA/AMERICAN EXPRESS SKYMILES CARD
(☎ **877/376-1237**) www.americanexpress.com
Type of Card: Charge card, must pay in full each month
Annual Fee: $55; free if you have another fee-paying American Express card
Joining Bonus: 5,000 miles
Miles Earned: One mile per dollar spent, but earn 2 miles per dollar spent on Delta tickets; at supermarkets, gas stations, home improvement stores, drugstores, and the U.S. Postal Service; and when you use the card to pay your wireless phone bill.

Other Cards: Options card: no annual fee; 1,000 bonus miles on first purchase; .5 miles per dollar spent; 1 mile per dollar on Delta purchases. Gold card: $85 annual fee, $30 for existing AmEx cardholders; 10,000 bonus miles for joining; 100,000-mile annual limit on non-Delta purchases. Platinum card: $135 annual fee; 15,000 bonus miles for joining; no annual mileage limit.

HAWAIIAN AIRLINES HAWAIIAN MILES CARD
(☎ 800/729-6106) www.hawaiianair.com/hawaiianmiles/memberservices/mc.asp
Type of Card: Credit card
Annual Fee: $24
Joining Bonus: 5,000 miles
Other Extras: Three people can combine purchases into one frequent-flier account.
Platinum Card: $50 annual fee; 10,000-mile sign-up bonus

MIDWEST EXPRESS MASTERCARD
(☎ 800/388-4044) http://elan.midwestexpress.com/
Type of Card: Credit card, can pay over time
Annual Fee: $45
Joining Bonus: 1,000 miles earned with first purchase
Gold Card: $70 annual fee; 2,500 bonus miles upon joining; double miles on Midwest Express tickets.

NORTHWEST WORLDPERKS VISA CARD
(☎ 800/360-2900) www.usbank.com/worldperks49/
Type of Card: Credit card, can pay over time
Annual Fee: $55
Joining Bonus: 3,000 bonus miles with first purchase
Other Extras: No mileage cap, but all miles earned after 50,000 per year are earned at half speed
Gold Card: $90 annual fee; all miles earned after 60,000 per year are earned at half speed.

SOUTHWEST AIRLINES RAPID REWARDS VISA
(☎ 800/792-8472) www.firstusa.com/xcards4/ccards/southwest_airlines/
Type of Card: Credit card, can pay over time

Annual Fee: $39
Joining Bonus: 4 bonus credits upon sign-up
Miles Earned: One Southwest credit per $1,000 charged
Platinum Card: $59 annual fee

UNITED MILEAGE PLUS SIGNATURE VISA
(☎ 888/819-3529) www.firstusa.com
Type of Card: Credit card, can pay over time
Annual Fee: $60
Joining Bonus: 5,000 bonus miles for joining
Other Extras: Free one-way upgrade certificate; free $25 discount certificate

US AIRWAYS DIVIDEND MILES VISA
(☎ 800/274-5060) www.bankofamerica.com/creditcards/
Type of Card: Credit card, can pay over time
Annual Fee: $50
Joining Bonus: 3,000 bonus miles upon approval
Other Cards: Gold card: $70 annual fee; 4,000 miles upon approval. Platinum card: $90 annual fee; 7,000 bonus miles upon sign-up; 2 miles per dollar earned on US Airways tickets; $99 companion certificate; one-time airport lounge pass; 10,000 extra miles if you spend $25,000 per year.

STRETCHING A SHORT TRIP

Even if you only take short or occasional trips, partnerships can make you a mileage master — though they don't help you qualify for elite status. Here's a weekend shopping trip on American Airlines:

ACTIVITY	MILES EARNED
Actual mileage for Philadelphia–Chicago trip	1,340 miles
$200 ticket bought with AA Visa card	200 miles
Bonus for first-time online booking	4,000 miles
Bonus for Chicago-based promotion	1,000 miles
Two-night stay at Hilton in Chicago	1,000 miles
$100 spent on Hertz rental car	100 miles
$50 dinner at participating restaurant	500 miles
$400 spent with AA Visa card	400 miles
$10 spent on MCI calling card for calls home	50 miles
TOTAL MILES EARNED	**8,590 miles**

8 Earn Miles on the Road

ALL THE MAJOR CAR-RENTAL COMPANIES AND HOTEL chains offer frequent-flier mileage if you provide your frequent-flier number when booking and when you arrive at the check-in counter.

For car rentals, awards are generally handed out per rental, per dollar spent, or per days traveled, rather than per miles traveled. A few companies require you to rent a vehicle for 2 days or longer, and sometimes credit is available only when the rental is in conjunction with a flight.

In a rare instance where leisure travelers are favored over business travelers, corporate, government, or other contract rates as a general rule yield almost half as many award miles as personal rentals.

Hotel chains generally award a fixed number of miles per night, no matter how much you pay (as long as you didn't book the hotel through Priceline or a similar service), though a few (notably Marriott and Holiday Inn) award miles per dollar spent. You'll have to choose between dumping your stay into your hotel frequent-stay account or your airline's mileage account unless you're staying at a Hilton, in which case you can "double-dip" and get points for both accounts.

MAJOR HOTEL CHAINS & THEIR U.S. FREQUENT-FLIER PARTNERS

Hotel Company	Airline Partners
Best Western	Alaska, America West, American, Delta, Northwest, US Airways
Choice Hotels (Comfort, Quality, Clarion, Sleep Inn, Mainstay, EconoLodge, Rodeway)	American, US Airways

Hilton (Hilton, Conrad, Embassy Suites, Hampton, Homewood Suites, Scandic, Camino Real)	Alaska, America West, American, Continental, Delta, Hawaiian, Midwest Express, Northwest, Southwest, United, US Airways
Hyatt	Alaska, American, America West, Continental, Delta, Northwest, United, US Airways
Marriott (Marriott, Courtyard, Renaissance, Residence Inn, Fairfield Inn, TownePlace Suites, Spring Hill Suites)	Alaska, American, Continental, Delta, Northwest, Southwest, United, US Airways
Ramada	American, Continental
Six Continents (Inter-Continental, Crowne Plaza, Holiday Inn, Staybridge)	Alaska, America West, American, Continental, Delta, Northwest, United, US Airways
Starwood (Four Points, Sheraton, St. Regis, Westin, W)	Alaska, America West, American, Continental, Delta, Northwest, United, US Airways

CAR-RENTAL COMPANIES & THEIR U.S. FREQUENT-FLIER PARTNERS

Carrier	*Car-Rental Partners*
Alamo	Alaska, Aloha, America West, American, Continental, Delta, Frontier, Hawaiian, Northwest, Southwest, Spirit, United, US Airways

Avis	Alaska, Aloha, American, America West, Delta, Hawaiian, Midwest Express, Northwest, United, US Airways
Budget	Alaska, American, Northwest, Southwest, Thai, United
Dollar	Alaska, Aloha, America West, American, Continental, Delta, Hawaiian, Northwest, Southwest, United, US Airways
Hertz	Alaska, Aloha, American, British Airways, Continental, Delta, Frontier, Hawaiian, Midwest Express, National, Northwest, Southwest, United, US Airways
National	Alaska, America West, American, ATA, Continental, Delta, Frontier, Midwest Express, Northwest, Spirit, United, US Airways
Thrifty	Alaska, America West, American, Continental, Delta, Northwest, United, US Airways

9 DIALING & SURFING FOR MILES

LONG-DISTANCE PLANS THAT EARN MILES

THE FOLLOWING IS A LIST OF THE FREQUENT-FLIER benefits offered by the major long-distance companies. Some fliers have reported being able to get mileage on their existing long-distance plan as if they're new customers. Call your phone company, explain that you're considering switching companies for the miles, and see if they can serve up their new-subscriber mileage bonus to make you stay.

Of all the long-distance carriers, **MCI WorldCom** (☎ 800/513-4090; www.mci.com) has the most extensive program. MCI offers frequent-flier miles for members of their "seven cent anytime" plan (there's a $3.95 monthly fee). Partners are American, America West, China Airlines, Delta, Hawaiian, Korean Air, Southwest, United, and US Airways. Members earn 5 miles for every dollar spent on MCI and a 3,000-mile bonus for joining. (Southwest fliers get three Rapid Rewards credits for joining, plus one credit per $150 spent with MCI.) Frequent fliers also receive a discount on Internet service.

Sprint (☎ 800/877-4040; www.sprint.com) offers mileage on Alaska, Northwest, Midwest Express, and Virgin Atlantic. New members get 5,000 bonus miles (4,000 miles on Midwest Express) for staying with the company for 6 months, plus 5 miles for each dollar they spend on various Sprint long-distance plans.

AT&T (☎ 800/222-0300; www.attconsumer.com) delivers 5,000 Continental OnePass miles for new customers who stay for 5 months, 1,000 Continental miles for signing up for online billing, and 5 miles for each dollar spent.

INTERNET & WIRELESS PLANS THAT EARN MILES

If you're willing to change your e-mail address, you can get frequent-flier bonuses with **Internet service providers.** Earthlink offers 5,000 Delta SkyMiles on sign-up; Northwest fliers get 5,000 miles plus 5 miles per dollar spent. MSN gives United fliers 1,000 miles on sign-up, plus 500 miles per month. New AT&T WorldNet subscribers (http://download. att.net/continental/) get 2,000 Continental OnePass miles.

Wireless phone companies are also big bonus partners. New Nextel customers get 5,000 Delta, United, or US Airways miles. Continental has partnered with VoiceStream with a 4,000-mile bonus for new subscribers.

With all of these offers, you won't get them unless you ask — so ask.

10 SHOPPING FOR MILES

BUYING STUFF

HEY, YOU'RE GOING TO SPEND THE MONEY ANYWAY – why not get the miles? The American, Continental, US Airways, Northwest, and United frequent-flier programs have deals with online retailers so people who buy through a particular link earn miles. Check on your frequent-flier program's website. Bonuses range from 1 to 5 miles per dollar spent. Dozens of retailers participate; here are the affiliations of some stores you may be familiar with:

- **Ashford:** Northwest, Continental

- **Eddie Bauer:** US Airways, United, American

- **FTD.com:** Northwest

- **Godiva:** Continental

- **J. Crew:** Continental, US Airways

- **Lands' End:** American, US Airways

- **Magellan's:** US Airways

- **MarthaStewart.com:** US Airways

- **OfficeMax:** American

- **Spiegel:** American, United, US Airways

Shopping and playing online games on MileSource (www.milesource.com) can eventually earn $25 discount gift certificates on various airlines. (MileSource uses its own mileage currency, not airline miles.) They've got an especially excellent list of partners, including Barnes & Noble, The Gap, Staples, and Tower Records. If possible, it's still better to shop directly through your airline's program, as the miles you earn there are more flexible.

MileSpree.com (www.milespree.com) also promotes its own "currency." Twenty-five thousand MileSpree miles can be traded for one domestic ticket worth up to $350 on any airline, though you have to buy 30 days in advance through MileSpree's travel agent. The site offers 3,000 MileSpree miles for signing up and completing a profile, plus at least 5 miles per dollar for most shopping partners, so it's a pretty good deal. It also solves the problem of Priceline tickets not earning frequent-flier miles by giving 1 mile per dollar for purchases at Priceline.

BUYING A CAR

Really big purchases can earn the biggest mileage bonuses. American's AAdvantage Auto & Recreational Program (☎ **888/289-2359;** www.aabuy2fly.com/) awards 1 mile per $4 of your car's purchase price — but you have to buy from participating dealers. United offers 10,000 miles for buying a new vehicle (☎ **800/733-2062;** www.vehiclemiles.com/).

Alaska, American, Continental, Delta, Northwest, US Airways, and United all participate in another car buyers' program called DealerMiles (www.dealermiles.com). It's clunky — miles take up to 10 weeks to be added to your account, and as there are no fixed awards, the miles become another bargaining chip between you and the dealer. DealerMiles CEO Jim Burness said awards range from 1,000 to 40,000 miles for a new car purchase, with the average award around 5,000 miles.

BUYING A HOUSE

Most major programs also give huge mileage bonuses for taking out a mortgage or for buying or selling a home through a real estate partner. Northwest, for example, will pony up 50,000 miles for a $200,000 home sold through GMAC or Better Homes and Gardens Real Estate. United offers 1 mile per $10 on mortgages through North American Mortgage Company.

On major investments like these, mileage bonuses will rarely outweigh better deals found elsewhere, but they're worth keeping in mind.

11 DINING FOR MILES

ALASKA, AMERICA WEST, AMERICAN, CONTINENTAL, Northwest, Delta, and United all offer 10 frequent-flier miles per dollar spent while eating at more than 7,000 restaurants nationwide. All share one list of restaurants as partners of iDine (www.idine.com), a subsidiary of dining rewards company Transmedia. Alaska Airlines has a second program, DineAir (www.dineair.com), with extra restaurants west of the Rockies that reward fliers at a rate of 3 miles per dollar.

Some of these restaurants may be near you; you'll probably have more options if you live in a major city. iDine lists 37 restaurants in Chicago's hot River North district, 33 in Indianapolis's Broad Ripple neighborhood, and 12 in central Beverly Hills, for example. Sign up for these programs on the airlines' websites.

If you prefer to cook for yourself, you can use your Safeway, Von's, Pak n' Save, Genuardi's, Pavilions, or Dominick's supermarket club card and garner 125 United Airlines miles for each $250 spent.

9

CHEAP FARES: EASY WAYS TO CUT THE COST OF AIR TRAVEL

After a rash of sales immediately following September 11, 2001, the major airlines have bounced back to their high fares and confusing ways.

The same coach seat on the same plane may cost $250 or $1,000, depending on who buys it, when they buy it, and from whom. Buying through a travel agent, the airline's website, or during one of the airlines' unpredictable sales can make the difference between getting a cheap seat and paying a king's ransom.

But the past few years have seen the growth of consumer-friendly discount travel websites and low-cost airlines such as JetBlue, AirTran, and Southwest (which we list as one of the majors, but is strictly no-frills).

Those sites and airlines sometimes ask you to give up amenities like (in Southwest's case) in-flight food and seat reservations, or (in Priceline's case) the exact times of your flights, but they're possibly the best way to fight ticket inflation.

In any case, the number-one rule for ticket buyers is: **research, research, research.** Read through the ideas we outline below, check out multiple travel agency websites, airline websites, and newspaper advertisements. Nearly every one will have different fares.

CAVEATS: READ THE FINE PRINT

The lowest-priced fares are often non-refundable or carry penalties for changing dates of travel. Be sure to investigate the hidden costs before you book. Fees vary widely, depending on both the airline you're flying and the type of ticket you're purchasing.

- **APEX (advanced purchase excursion) fares** are often rigged with stiff penalties if you need to change your reservation, and you may not be entitled to any refund whatsoever if you have to cancel — though you may be able to use your ticket at a later date for a fee of roughly $75 to $150. Typically, you will also have to purchase your ticket within 24 hours of making a reservation, stay over a Saturday night, and return home within 30 days. After the post-9/11 travel slump, airlines began to redefine the term "last minute". Consumers can now often book "last minute" fares weeks, even months in advance. Check each airline's website to see what deals are available.

- **International fares** may include myriad add-on costs, such as departure taxes, Customs fees, international taxes, and security surcharges. For some destinations, you may have to pay a departure tax in the local currency before you're permitted to leave.

- **Non-refundable tickets** may become worthless if you fail to make the flight you booked. At best, you may be allowed to fly standby if you arrive within 2 hours of your scheduled departure, but this is not guaranteed. If you fall ill or suffer a death in the immediate family and can furnish proof of the fact, you may be entitled to compensation, usually a travel voucher for another flight on the same airline. While it's always wise to show up at the airport well ahead of time, it's crucial if you are flying on a non-refundable ticket. (See the "Airlines' Boarding Gate Deadlines" table in chapter 2.)

1 HOW THE FARE GAME WORKS

THE MYSTERY OF AIRLINE FARES

Ever wonder why the same seat, on the same plane, can cost $250 or $1,225? Welcome to the weird world of **yield management.**

Airlines want to fill all their seats, at prices as high as possible. So they engage in a bit of prognostication, try to guess how many deep-pocketed business travelers they'll have on a flight, and offer the rest of their seats at fares just low enough to get leisure travelers to bite.

Things get more complicated from there. Panicked business travelers who need to fly at the last minute are willing to pay bucketloads — so that's another fare class. A price war with a competitor may necessitate the release of a few seats at rock-bottom fares — another fare class.

Eventually you've got a soup of fare levels comprehensible only to a computer, where the number of seats available in any given class shrinks and grows daily based on how demand is living up to predictions. One thing's clear, though — very few people do pay "full" fares.

Delta gives one example of a flight from New York to Orlando with 178 seats. At takeoff, 173 seats are filled — and passengers are paying 16 different fares. Of the 156 coach-class travelers, only five pay the full coach fare. In first class, the hypocrisy of "full fares" is even more glaring — only one of the 17 fliers is paying the full first-class fare, and 10 of the 17 are in first class on free upgrades.

(No, there's no way for you, the traveler, to find out how many seats are available at which fares. Airline reservation agents and travel agents can, but new fares appear and disappear continually.)

However, there are some reliable rules you can follow to get the lowest fares:

RULE #1: TIMING IS EVERYTHING

The most crucial factor in snaring a cheap fare is probably your timing. It's almost always cheaper to book 21 days, 14 days, or 7 days in advance. Booking 3 weeks in advance snares the greatest savings, up to 75% over walk-up prices.

If for some reason you can't commit to travel plans in advance, you may also be able to snag a bargain with "e-saver" tickets, sold on airline websites each Tuesday and Wednesday for trips the following weekend. And just before major holidays, airlines often declare fare sales that bring prices way down. But this trick is very risky, and you have a good chance of getting stuck with a fare up to five times the advance-purchase price.

Travel at off-peak times; fares are usually cheaper for flights before 7am and after 7pm. You'll also save money if you can afford to travel on a Tuesday, Wednesday, or Thursday, because most leisure travelers like to get away on weekends and therefore demand is greatest at that time. You'll save even more if you can agree to stay over a Saturday night. Business travelers usually want to fly during the week and return by the weekend, so you'll save money in coach if you stay through a Saturday.

All of these rules are especially true if you are traveling on a route that's popular with business travelers. Airlines cater to business travelers, because they fly so frequently and book tickets at the last minute, paying much higher prices for their seats. When a flight is carrying many business travelers, the airline doesn't need the business of economy passengers, so coach fares are much less likely to be discounted. Business travelers tend to fly just before 9am and just after 5pm, so coach seats are liable to be more expensive at these hours.

According to the same principles of supply and demand, traveling to a destination like Brazil will be more expensive from the United States in January, when it's winter here and summer there. Nantucket will be priciest in summer. New Orleans will cost the most during Mardi Gras.

RULE #2: SHOP ONLINE

For pure bargain hunters, the Internet has eclipsed travel agents. Internet research takes time but almost always pays off.

Internet travel agencies are the easiest way to compare several airlines' fares, but airlines often have better deals on their own websites. The past few years have also seen the rise of "opaque fare" services like Priceline, which deliver ultra-cheap tickets to travelers who aren't picky about what time of day they fly.

If you have Internet access, investigate the best going rates to your destination before you book a ticket. Booking online can also bring extra frequent-flier miles, lowering the cost of future tickets.

RULE #3: WATCH FOR LATE-BREAKING SALES

Keep your eyes peeled for promotional rates or special sales even after you purchase your ticket. Airlines periodically lower prices on their most popular routes, which may even make it worth your while to exchange your ticket — despite the $75 to $100 charge. (Southwest is the only airline without a change fee on non-refundable tickets.) Otherwise, all funny refundable tickets have a "fare guarantee," which lets you trade them in for a lower fare if you ask, for free. Check your newspaper for advertised discounts or call the airlines directly to stay on top of late-breaking discounts.

RULE #4: COMPETITION IS GOOD

If even one low-fare carrier, such as Southwest or JetBlue, operates on your route, fares will be much lower than if the route is dominated by major airlines. Of the 10 greatest fare drops on routes between 2000 and 2001, according to the Department of Transportation, four were caused by Southwest entering Albany, New York; two by Southwest entering Buffalo, New York; two by JetBlue coming to New York City; and two by AirTran extending its Atlanta-based tentacles.

Low-fare carriers don't show up on many online or real-life travel agents' systems, so you have to reach out to their phone hot lines or websites to get these choice fares. Many are as comfortable and safe (or safer) than the major airlines. For more information on major domestic and international budget airlines, see "A Look at the Budget Airlines," later in this chapter.

Alternately, if your route is dominated by one airline, fares will generally be higher (unless that airline is Southwest). Flights into major airline hubs, such as Atlanta or Chicago's O'Hare airport, usually cost much more than other flights of comparable distances.

RULE #5: USE "SECRET" AIRPORTS

In major cities with multiple airports, make sure you ask about *all* the local airports. Smaller airports such as Midway in Chicago, Oakland near San Francisco, Ontario outside Los Angeles, and Islip outside New York often host smaller airlines and lower fares.

But be aware that some of these airports are distant from the city. Midway and Oakland are both small, convenient, and actually closer to their cities than the better-known O'Hare and San Francisco airports. But Ontario and Islip are each 50 miles (81km) outside their cities — a very long drive or train ride for a short holiday.

And just say "no" to inter-airport transfers. O'Hare, for instance, is on the other end of Chicago from Midway — not a trip you want to make if you're on a deadline to catch a flight.

RULE #6: AVOID BUSINESS ROUTES

Airlines make their money on business travelers. Paying from deep corporate pockets, these travelers are willing to spend big bucks for frequent flights on changeable tickets to business destinations.

If a route is popular with business travelers and hasn't been opened up by low-fare airlines, fares will be higher, as airlines try to squeeze every profit-making penny they can out of their most well-heeled clientele.

2   BOOKING ONLINE: SAVING ON THE INTERNET

THE INTERNET HAS FINALLY SUPPLANTED TRAVEL agents as the primary method of buying travel, at least among folks with online connections. According to research firm PhoCusWright, 41% of people who flew in the past year and used the Web in the past month usually booked flights online, as opposed to a mere 26% who used travel agencies.

The American Society of Travel Agents says their members sell nearly 75% of all airline tickets — but their number and PhoCusWright's aren't contradictory. First of all, only 62% of Americans have Internet access. Second, PhoCusWright only surveyed individuals buying tickets, and travel agents sell tickets to many businesses as well.

While Internet research can be tremendously rewarding, it isn't easy. You need time, patience, and persistence. If your idea of booking a trip is having one call do it all, go with an experienced travel agent who knows the ropes. Complex multi-city itineraries are also best handled by travel agents. And travel agents generally provide better post-purchase customer service than websites, especially for changing tickets. But if you find a little fun in tracking down the best deals on your own, read on.

Staying Secure

Far more people look online than book online, partly due to fear of putting their credit cards through on the Net. Secure encryption makes it almost impossible for a hacker to sniff out your credit card number as it passes through the ether. To be sure you're in secure mode when you book online, look for a little icon of a key (in Netscape) or a padlock (Internet Explorer) at the bottom of your Web browser.

STEP ONE: ONLINE TRAVEL AGENTS

The first rule of online booking is that no one source always has the best deals. Checking the three major online travel agencies is just the start of a good research expedition; airlines often offer extra frequent-flier miles or even lower fares on their own sites. And no online travel agency offers fares or tickets on Southwest, the cheapest airline in many markets.

That said, online travel agents are by far the best way to get the lay of the land when searching for airfares. Buying through a reputable online travel agent offers you some of the customer-service cushion you'd get with a real travel agent. The three major agencies all allow you to book flights, hotels, and cars online; offer toll-free access to a live agent; allow you to sign up for e-mail updates on fares and sales; and can send flight information and updates to your e-mail account, handheld computer, or mobile phone.

ORBITZ www.orbitz.com

Travel agents quaked in fear when Orbitz entered the business. Owned and operated by Northwest, Continental, United, US Airways, Delta, and American Airlines, Orbitz serves up Internet-only fares from the "big six" that other sites — and live travel agents — don't have access to. However, in December 2001 Orbitz began charging a $5 per ticket service fee.

Orbitz's grid-style presentation of fares also makes it much easier to compare all the available prices and routings at a glance than on the other sites.

But Orbitz is a poor source for fares on smaller airlines. The mega-site got slapped with a lawsuit by Southwest in May 2001; Southwest said Orbitz was inflating its fares and making it look bad. The lawsuit was dismissed when Orbitz stopped listing Southwest fares entirely.

And the site has a relatively thin selection of international fares — which they acknowledge, and plan to improve in 2002.

EXPEDIA www.expedia.com

Microsoft-owned Expedia offers some useful innovations with its generally excellent selection of fares.

"Fare Compare" lets users see the best deals found by other travelers recently, and lets them try to book the same itineraries. "Fare Calendar" lets you navigate a list of published fares by the dates they're available, for flexible travelers.

Expedia's acquisition of Travelscape gave them access to a large library of vacation packages; for those who like to combine hotels, flights, and car rentals, there's considerable convenience and some savings there.

By the time this book hits shelves, Expedia will have been sold to Barry Diller's USA Networks — but that shouldn't make any difference in its service or selection of flights.

TRAVELOCITY www.travelocity.com

Rounding out the top three is Travelocity, owned by American Airlines' parent company, AMR. But don't worry that Travelocity fares prefer American — the site is a fair broker, regularly delivering cheaper fares on other airlines.

Travelocity's most unique feature is the Dream Map, a map of the nation or the world showing all the destinations to which you can fly for a set price (say, $400). Clicking on one of the cities brings up a list of possible itineraries. The site's "Dream, Plan, Go" section lets you find destinations similar to those you know you like (a request from a couple who like New York turned up Boston, Paris, Venice, Chicago, and London).

Travelocity also tells you what kind of plane you'll be flying on before you buy, useful for the propeller-wary or those seeking the comforts of a Boeing 777.

Unlike Expedia and Orbitz, Travelocity requires a (free) registration to search more than a few times.

QIXO www.qixo.com

SIDESTEP www.sidestep.com

Both Qixo and SideStep are aggregators — companies that scan airline websites for specials. Qixo's fares seem to be average, but the SideStep site has some helpful bonus features. The site is actually a browser plug-in for Microsoft Internet Explorer that lets you compare their fares side-by-side with Expedia or Orbitz. It also tells users about the frequent-flier mileage bonuses that would be available by booking directly on the airlines' sites.

STEP TWO: AIRLINE WEBSITES

The cheapest way for an airline to sell a ticket is to offer an e-ticket through its own website, so carriers try to suck consumers in with frequent-flier bonuses and online-booking discounts of 10% or more off the ticket price you'd be able to get from a travel agent.

Airline websites are also the source of "e-saver" e-mails, special deals mailed out on Tuesdays or Wednesdays and usually offering radical discounts for travelers willing to fly the following weekend. Sometimes, though, they offer cheap tickets several weeks in advance. If you don't want to sign up for several e-mails, Smarter Living (www.smarterliving.com) does a good job of aggregating all the Web specials on one list, as does the Best Fares travel club (www.bestfares.com; click on "Internet-only" and look for "This Week's Weekend Internet Airfares").

Here are the sites for the major airlines:

- **Alaska Airlines:** www.alaskaair.com

- **America West:** www.americawest.com

- **American Airlines:** www.aa.com

- **Continental Airlines:** www.continental.com

- **Delta Airlines:** www.delta.com

- **Northwest Airlines:** www.nwa.com

- **Southwest Airlines:** www.southwest.com

- **United Airlines:** www.united.com

- **US Airways:** www.usairways.com

If you want to add small airlines to the mix, you've got to check their sites. As noted above, no online travel agent lists Southwest, and online agents seem to regularly overestimate prices on JetBlue. The addresses of smaller airlines are listed in "A Look at the Budget Airlines," at the end of this chapter.

STEP THREE: "OPAQUE" FARES

The absolute cheapest domestic fares are almost always through one of the "opaque fares" services — Priceline and

---

Insomniac Bonus Fares

The best time of day to book tickets is between midnight and 1 am in your travel agent or airline's time zone, when tickets that were put on hold, but never paid for, are released into the system. Airline fare sales and Web specials also generally start at midnight, so booking then gives you the widest selection of seats. Check airlines' websites for which day of the week (usually Tues or Wed) their Web specials come online.

What Does "Non-refundable" Really Mean?

When opaque fares sites say "non-refundable," they do make occasional exceptions – anything having to do with illness or death (of the traveler, a family member, or someone being visited) can usually get you a refund if you can get through the opaque services' endless voice-mail loops to a live operator.

Hotwire are the leaders, with Expedia, Travelocity, and One-Travel dabbling in this end of the industry.

When you take an opaque fare, you give up control of your flight times and your choice of airline (though you're guaranteed a full-service, large-scale carrier). You give up frequent-flier miles and lock yourself into a non-changeable, non-refundable ticket.

You *can* specify the days you travel, whether you're willing to take "off peak" flights (those that leave before 6am or after 10pm), and how many connections you can tolerate (with a minimum of one). You can choose to refuse prop planes, and pick the airports you'll fly into and out of.

When you pay for your ticket, you get the full details of your flight. And once you're en route, airlines must legally treat you like any other passenger. Policies on bumping, delays, and cancellations are the same for opaque tickets as for non-opaque ones. (Individual airline employees are sometimes misinformed about this, but stand your ground.)

Opaque fares aren't for those who can't stomach a 6am departure, who want to change their tickets, who demand nonstops, or who think they may need to contact customer service (both Priceline's and Hotwire's are notoriously bad. Priceline's was so bad in 2000 that they were booted out of the Connecticut Better Business Bureau for 3 months before promising to shape up). And you should never, ever use an opaque fare for a 2-day trip — you might swoop in at 10pm on Saturday and be forced to leave at 6am Sunday, 8 hours later!

Domestically, awkward routings like New York to Houston via Minneapolis are largely a thing of the past. Now that Priceline and Hotwire have nearly all the major airlines on board, they have a much broader inventory of convenient flights. Priceline guarantees that all domestic layovers will be less than 3 hours; Hotwire says that 90% of their layovers are 2 hours or less, but makes no guarantees.

The opaque fare sites are less useful for international flights. Priceline's the best of the bunch, often able to beat consolidators on trips to Europe. But routings like New York–Frankfurt–London are relatively common, and consolidators and courier services routinely beat Priceline on trips to Asia or the Southern Hemisphere.

Opaque Fares 101

Hotwire (www.hotwire.com) is a good place to start your opaque odyssey. They only let you check their fares once every 48 hours for a particular route, but you can register as many times as you like under fake names with free e-mail accounts to get around that. (Use the fake names to check fares first, and then buy the ticket with your real name and e-mail account.) Hotwire's fares will usually provide a comfortable savings over standard fares. During Christmas 2001, I used Hotwire and flew from New York City to Tucson, Arizona, on America West for $311 — the next-lowest fare I found through other channels was $450.

Beginners may also stumble upon Expedia's **Bargain Fares,** Travelocity's **Travelocity Fares,** and OneTravel's **White Label** fares while searching those sites. All have similar terms to Hotwire — tickets are non-refundable, non-changeable, can leave between 6am and 10pm, and can have one connection unless you specifically agree to more.

I Can Name That Fare in Five Bids

Dealing with **Priceline** (www.priceline.com) is more like playing poker in Vegas than like booking a "normal" air ticket. The super-discounter's coy premise is not so much "name your price" as it is "name *our* price." They have an inventory of tickets, and you have to *guess* how much they cost. If you "bid" above Priceline's minimum price, they will pocket the difference.

The rewards, though, can be great. Sheryl Mexic, who has seen thousands of Priceline bids as the head of the volunteer Priceline-assistance board BiddingForTravel.com, said Priceline beats the competition at least 80% of the time on domestic routes. Some tips:

1. **Research, research, research.** Check as many sites as you can before finding a price to beat. Priceline's Brian Ek suggests starting bids at up to 40% below last-minute airfares, up to 25% below advance-purchase airfares, and 10% to 20% below Hotwire's price. Of course, Hotwire has been known to beat Priceline from time to time, and some truly breathtaking discounts have been acquired on Priceline — such as the fellow who flew back and forth from L.A. to Las Vegas several times for $1 plus taxes and Priceline's $5.95 fee.

2. **Get help.** The volunteers at BiddingForTravel.com have been providing "bidding strategies" for more than 2 years now, and the FAQ on that site is a mandatory stop before starting a Priceline experience.

3. **Use bonus money.** Priceline usually gives its most frequent customers' bids a $25-a-ticket boost — you can access it at BiddingForTravel.com.

4. **Ignore blandishments.** Priceline will goose you by saying your bid is "much too low," that they have a "guaranteed counteroffer" for more than you want to pay, or that you'll have a better chance if you pay more for paper tickets. Mexic says to ignore all this and keep bidding.

5. **Maximize your bids.** Priceline only allows one bid
   per combination of dates, cities, and airports — if
   you bid too low, you're out of luck and can't try again
   for another 7 days. But there are ways to add airports
   and change cities to create new combinations, which
   scan the same list of flights, but look like different
   bids to Priceline. That way, you can start at a very
   low price and work your way up in $10 to $20
   increments until you hit Priceline's sweet spot.

Strategies for Maximizing Your Bid

Generally, the best way to maximize your bid is to add airports that have no service or limited service to your arrival
city; or change your designation departure city to a one
nearby that uses the same airports. If you choose an airport
with no service to your stated departure or arrival city,
the search engine automatically considers the newer price
(or "re-bid") for the same area airports you chose in your
first bid.

Let's use a trip from New York to Chicago as an
example — one I've flown several times with Priceline, for as
little as $85 round-trip plus tax. (I usually received US Air-
ways flights via Pittsburgh.)

Always start with all of the airports acceptable to you —
in my case, LaGuardia, JFK, Newark, Chicago O'Hare, and
Chicago Midway. That's bid #1.

If that bid fails, I could raise the price and add Chicago
Meigs, which I know receives no flights from New York.
(Try to schedule a flight to Meigs on Orbitz. It won't work.)
Bid #2.

If that fails, I could raise the price yet again and start an
entirely new bid, claiming to be traveling from the nearby
suburb of White Plains, New York, to Chicago. But that
means LaGuardia, JFK, and Newark are still available
as departure airports. (The White Plains airport is also

available, but you can leave it unchecked and out of the picture.) Two more bids, one with and one without Meigs.

Starting another new bid claiming to be leaving from suburban Islip, New York (yup, choose the same airports; this time, simply refuse flights from the Islip airport). This generates bids five and six.

For a list of Priceline's cities so you can construct a free rebidstrategy,seewww.priceline.com/travel/airlines/lang/en-us/CityCodes.asp. For help, ask the experts at www.BiddingForTravel.com.

OTHER USEFUL TRAVEL WEBSITES
FROMMERS.COM
www.frommers.com

We're a little biased, of course. This excellent travel-planning resource offers travel tips, reviews, monthly vacation give-aways, and online-booking capabilities. Among the special features are our popular **Message Boards,** where Frommer's

---

A Window into Opaque Fares

When you book on Priceline or Hotwire, you're guaranteed to get one of the airlines below — and not a charter plane or a smaller airline. Airlines listed with an H or a P are only partners of one of the services.

Domestic flights: Aloha (H), American, America West, Continental, Delta (P), Hawaiian, Northwest, United, US Airways.

International flights: Aer Lingus, AeroMexico, Air Canada, Air France, Air Jamaica (P), Air New Zealand, Alitalia, All Nippon Airways, Austrian Airlines (P), BWIA (H), Cathay Pacific (H), Copa (H), El Al (P), Finnair (H), Iberia, Icelandair, JAL (P), KLM (H), Korean Air (P), Lufthansa, Malaysia Airlines (P), Mexicana (H), Qantas (P), South African (H), SAS, TACA (H), Varig, Virgin Atlantic, Turkish Airlines (P), Singapore Airlines.

Ⓒ PRICELINE POWER

Priceline does make a difference. Some great deals cited by BiddingForTravel users during December 2001:

- Champaign, IL–Hartford, CT $133.25 on American Airlines ($255 on American's site, $156 on Hotwire)

- San Francisco–San Diego last minute during the Christmas holidays $108.95 on United ($411 on Orbitz, $202 on Hotwire)

- New York–Chicago $78.95 on Continental ($137 on Hotwire)

- Missoula, MT–Boston $193.45 on Delta ($325 on Delta's site, around $290 on Hotwire)

---

readers post queries and share advice (sometimes even Frommer's authors show up to answer questions); **Frommers.com Newsletter,** for the latest travel bargains and inside travel secrets; and Frommer's **Destinations Section,** where you'll get expert travel tips, hotel and dining recommendations, and advice on the sights to see for more than 2,500 destinations around the globe. When your research is done, the online reservation system (www.frommers.com/book_a_trip) takes you to Frommer's favorite sites for booking your vacation at affordable prices.

BESTFARES www.bestfares.com

This travel club, run by budget seeker Tom Parsons, combines travel advice and exclusive consolidator-style airfare bargains. The News Desk compiles hundreds of bargains, but it's a long list, not broken down by city or even country, so it's not easy trying to find what you're looking for. If you

 BUMPING FOR SAVINGS

If you've got a few hours to spare, why not make some money? If you don't mind killing time in the airport or nearby (I hear the beaches near New York's JFK airport are lovely in the summer), buy tickets at peak times when airlines are most likely to pay volunteers to stay off an overbooked flight.

The drop in air travel since September 11, 2001, has made it harder to get bumped than during the busy years of 1999 and 2000. But flights are most likely to be crowded during the weekends before and just after holidays, on Monday mornings, on Friday and Sunday evenings, and on weekdays between 7:30 and 9:30am and 5:30 and 7:30pm.

If you're interested in getting bumped, call your airline the day before and ask if your flight is oversold, and if there are similar itineraries with more available seats later that same day.

When you check in for a boarding pass, ask the ticket agent if the flight is oversold and whether they could confirm you on

---

have time to wade through it, you might find a good deal. Booking most of the bargain fares is available only to paid subscribers.

SMARTER LIVING www.smarterliving.com

Best known for its e-mail dispatch of weekend deals on 20 airlines, Smarter Living also serves up a potent blend of travel news and opinion columns.

WEBFLYER www.webflyer.com

WebFlyer is the ultimate online resource for frequent fliers and also has an excellent listing of last-minute air deals. Click on "DealWatch" for a roundup of weekend deals on flights, hotels, and rental cars from domestic and international suppliers.

another flight later that day if you go "DV" – airline slang for "denied voluntarily."

If you go DV on an average business morning, you'll probably be able to get on the next flight (even one from a different airline) and be at your destination in a few hours. Requesting a bump during a holiday, though, could saddle you with a long delay. I turned down a bump last Christmas because the only alternative flight the agents could find would have landed me at my destination 8 hours late, with a 5-hour layover in Boston.

What do you get? At least a $200 flight voucher if you're delayed up to 2 hours, or a $400 flight voucher for delays longer than that. Those are the minimums, and you may be able to bargain up; airlines get particularly desperate on major holidays. Passengers on international flights regularly see $800 vouchers. See "Voluntary Bumpings," in chapter 2, for tips on skillful bargaining, as well as how to avoid the hazards of bumping.

3 CONSOLIDATORS: THE PRICE CLUBS OF THE TRAVEL BIZ

CONSOLIDATORS, OR "BUCKET SHOPS," BUY TICKETS in bulk from airlines and resell them for cheaper than the airlines' usual discounted rates. They're especially useful if you're flying overseas or are booking at the last minute — and they're almost always the best way to get tickets to Third World destinations. They advertise in the Sunday travel sections of newspapers, set up storefronts in ethnic neighborhoods, or pop up in searches on websites such as google.com.

Unfortunately, the consolidator industry has attracted quite a few fly-by-night operators. Some just take your money; some sell counterfeit tickets. To avoid problems, make sure your consolidator is a member of the American Society of Travel Agents (☎ 703/739-2782) or the International Airlines Travel Agent Network (☎ 516/663-6000). You can search ASTA's website (www.astanet.com/travel/agentsearch.asp) and IATAN's as well (www.locateatravelagency.com) to see if the agent's a member in good standing.

If you're booking on your own, be sure to pay with a credit card. If the company goes under or you never receive your ticket, you can get your money back by filing a claim with your credit card company. Ask the consolidator for a record-locator number and then confirm your seat with the airline itself. (Be prepared to book your ticket with a different consolidator if the airline can't confirm your reservation.)

You may also want to specify the airline or airlines on which you'd like to fly. Be aware that some consolidators sell tickets on charter flights or on carriers with poor safety records. If you want to fly on a major carrier, say so when you make your reservation.

You should also know that most bucket shop tickets won't earn you frequent-flier miles. Usually, they're also non-refundable or rigged with stiff cancellation penalties, often $250 or more. Be sure to ask what the penalties are before you pay.

The following bucket shops have been around for a while, handle worldwide destinations, and have a reputation for reliability:

- **Council Travel** (☎ 800/226-8624; www.counciltravel.com) and **STA Travel** (☎ 800/781-4040; www.statravel.com) cater especially to young travelers, but their bargain-basement prices are available to people of all ages.

- **Travac Tours and Charters** aka **flights.com** (☎ 800/TRAV-800 or 212/563-3303; www.flights.com) offers top-quality fares and an excellent online search engine.

⟍ ONE-WAY & WEEKDAY STRATEGIES

Major airlines *really* want you to book round-trip tickets with a Saturday night stay to get discount fares. That's because short weekday and one-way trips are dominated by deep-pocketed business travelers.

One way to get around the Saturday night rule is to book on a smaller, budget airline – or even just on a route that a budget airline serves. Budget airlines generally charge by the leg, not by the round-trip, and don't penalize for lacking a Saturday stay. Major airlines then try to compete – once JetBlue came to the New York–New Orleans route, for instance, Delta slashed its one-way fare to half that of a round-trip.

"Throwaway" ticketing, using only the first half of a discount round-trip for a one-way ticket, is a perfectly legal practice frowned upon by the airlines, but they don't pursue offenders particularly zealously.

A risky way to reduce weekday round-trip fares is to book back-to-back tickets. Buy two cheap round-trip tickets on different airlines – one that leaves your point of origination and one that leaves your destination – and use only the first half of each. If you buy both tickets on the same airline, their computer system will probably detect it and you will be found out. And if you do this often, even on different airlines, they'll start inquiring as to why you only fly the first halves of your tickets. Airlines hate it when you do this (even though it's technically legal), and they'll void the tickets and penalize your frequent-flier account if they catch you.

You should also keep in mind that if airlines believe you exhibit a pattern of "erratic" ticket purchasing behavior, it may raise the suspicions of airport security personnel.

- **Air Tickets Direct** (☎ **800/778-3447;** www.airtickets direct.com) is based in Canada, leveraging the weak

Canadian dollar to provide low fares. They're an especially good choice for destinations with which the U.S. has shaky or nonexistent relations, such as Cuba.

- **FlyCheap** (☎ **800/FLY-CHEAP;** www.flycheap.com/) is now owned by one of Europe's largest package-tour operators, AirTours. That gives them access to an unusual library of charter flights to sunny destinations, though they sell tickets heading anywhere in the world.

- **TFI Tours International** (☎ **800/745-8000** or 212/736-1140; www.lowestairprice.com/) provides convenient charts on their website allowing you to see all of an airline's fares throughout the year.

- **New Frontiers USA** (☎ **800/366-6387** or 212/779-0600; www.newfrontiers.com) sells cut-rate tickets to all the major cities of Europe, but specializes in Paris.

4 WORKING WITH A TRAVEL AGENT

FOR TRIPS MORE COMPLICATED THAN THE SIMPLE airline flight, a good travel agent can be a solid ally and a critically important guide. The **American Society of Travel Agents (ASTA)** runs a toll-free referral line (☎ **800/965-2782;** www.astanet.com) to help you find a reliable operator in your area, and the **International Airlines Travel Agent Network** runs a website (www.locateatravelagency.com) with listings of reliable agents.

For domestic air-only journeys, travel agents may not be able to beat the prices and service you get on websites. Only 63% of travel agents were able to give the lowest-fare non-stop options on 12 domestic routes in a 2001 survey of 840 agencies by *Consumer Reports Travel Letter.* But for complex, multi-city trips, journeys to foreign lands, or package holidays, their smarts and experience can make a huge amount of difference.

You want to look for an agent who not only consistently finds cheap fares for you, but who will call you if a lower fare is announced — even if you've already made a reservation. If you're headed to a particular part of the world, find an agent who specializes in that area. You may want to trawl the main streets of local ethnic neighborhoods or ask at ethnic restaurants (as the owners do fly home occasionally). It's always wise to ask friends and family for recommendations, too, to help you find an agent with a proven track record. Loyalty and established relationships matter to travel agents, and they may treat a customer better if he or she has been recommended by a tried-and-true client.

Always get a second opinion when using a travel agent, though. Research available fares directly on airline websites or through an electronic travel agent (see "Booking Online: Saving on the Internet," earlier in this chapter) to be sure you're getting a bargain. Individual travel agencies often have preferred destinations and preferred airlines, and won't be able to find the best fares to parts of the world they don't have much experience with.

Also unfortunately, many agents now charge fees for their services — and in this case, the airlines are to blame. Agents used to earn a standard 10% commission on each ticket sale, but the airlines, after several reductions recently eliminated commission payments entirely.

In turn, agents have begun trying to recoup the money from consumers. Before the first commission cuts in 1995, only 20% of travel agencies charged fees; now 88% charge an average fee of $13.21, according to a May 2001 survey of American Society of Travel Agents operators. Fees can occasionally run as high as $200 for refunds and exchanges, visa and passport services, and trip planning. And the online travel agencies aren't immune; they're charging $10 fees to book tickets on many airlines, citing commission cuts.

Although travel agents no longer receive standard commissions from airlines for each ticket sale, they still often

Third-Country Tickets

New York to London via India? Well, sort of. The cheapest fares from the U.S. to Europe can often be snagged on long-haul foreign airlines that make a stop on the Continent before heading to their final destinations. Air India's flights to London are one famous example; Kuwait Airways and Air New Zealand also cover that New York–London route. Russia's Aeroflot flies from New York to Shannon, Ireland. These flights won't come up on most online travel agents, so ask a real-life travel agent or a consolidator if you're interested.

---

receive kickbacks, known in the business as "override commissions," from the carriers they work with most frequently. With this incentive to favor certain carriers, agents may be inclined to book you with the airline that offers them the greatest reward for your reservation, rather than the carrier that would offer you the cheapest flight. Although a federal guideline requires travel agents to reveal override deals to consumers, many of the 840 agents surveyed by *CRTL* refused to answer questions about their preferred-supplier agreements — so beware.

CRTL's survey found the most disturbing results on routes served by low-fare airlines such as Frontier and Southwest. In many cases, the newsletter reported, agencies will mention only major airline options, even when a small carrier offers lower prices.

5 CHECKING OUT CHARTER FLIGHTS

IF YOU'RE PLANNING TO TRAVEL DURING HIGH SEASON to a popular vacation destination like Europe, the Caribbean, Mexico, or Hawaii, charter flights can often provide bargains — though not without risks.

Charter flights are typically sold to tour operators as part of a package vacation, but independent travelers can purchase just the airfare portion through a travel agent, often at rates far below the fares available on scheduled flights. You may not have to stay at your destination through Saturday night or for fewer than 30 days in order to secure this rock-bottom fare. Depending on the charter, you may not have to purchase your ticket as far in advance as you would for another low fare either.

Charters make especially good bargains for leisure travelers who hate to ride in coach but can't afford a premium fare. In the summer, when rates to Europe are very high, you can pay as little as $1,300 from the U.S. East Coast and $1,800 from the West Coast for a first- or business-class seat that would typically cost you $2,400 to $6,750.

On the other hand, keep in mind that charter flights are sometimes scheduled on smaller budget carriers, which are often criticized for operating older planes under lower safety standards. Ask when you book what company and what kind of plane you'll actually be flying. Also, charter flights and tours also tend to be laden with restrictions. Choose a charter only if the fare is significantly cheaper or the schedule is significantly more convenient than what you'd find on a scheduled flight. Otherwise, the drawbacks easily outweigh the advantages.

Charter companies are much more prone to go belly up than an airline or even most travel agencies. If something does go wrong, your contract is with the tour operator or travel agent, not the airline, so you may have a harder time securing a refund. You will not earn frequent-flier credit for miles traveled. Flights tend to be crowded, scheduled at inconvenient times, delayed for hours, or canceled suddenly. (You, on the other hand, will not be able to cancel or reschedule without paying stiff penalties.) In addition, check-in usually takes much more time — up to 3 hours, even, on international flights.

Charter operators typically don't sell seats or advertise fares directly to the public, so ask a travel agent or consolidator about charter options. FlyCheap, for instance, sells many tickets on charter airlines.

WHAT YOU SHOULD KNOW
ABOUT CHARTER TICKETS

- **Be prepared for major changes in fare or itinerary.**
Your contract does not guarantee that a charter won't
raise the fare or change your itinerary. It does guarantee you a penalty-free refund if you can't accept the
terms of any "major changes." "Major changes"
include: a change in departure or return city (not
including a change in the order in which cities are
visited); a change in departure or return date, unless
the date change is the result of a flight delay under
48 hours; the substitution of a hotel that was not
named in your contract as an alternate hotel; a price
increase of more than 10% (though in the 10-day
period before departure, price increases of any kind are
prohibited). If a major change is issued after your trip
has begun, you can reject the change, pay for your
own alternative plans, and insist on a refund.

- **One-way fares.** Charters may be sold on a one-way
basis, but the Department of Transportation forbids
"open returns" on charter tickets. Be sure you have
a specific return date, city, and flight, so you're not
stranded.

- **Remember that charter flights operate independently
from scheduled airline flights.** If you need to fly to
your charter's departure city on a scheduled airline, and
that flight is delayed, you'll usually lose your charter
flight and the money you paid for it. Likewise, if your
charter flight returns late and causes you to miss a
scheduled airline flight home, you'll be responsible for
any expenses incurred. Be sure you allow yourself plenty
of time between flights to make connections safely.

- Remember, too, that **you can't check your baggage
from a scheduled flight to a charter.** Allow plenty of
time to retrieve and recheck your bags before flights —

especially if international flights are involved, because you'll have to clear Customs as well.

QUESTIONS TO ASK BEFORE YOU BOOK A CHARTER FLIGHT

Your charter agreement will usually be called an **"operator/ participant contract,"** which you should read very carefully before signing. The Department of Transportation requires that these documents spell out certain restrictions and consumer rights. Be sure you know where you stand on these key issues before you hand over a dime.

- **What steps does the charter take to protect your money?** By law the charter is required to have a surety agreement, like a bond. The charter should also hold your money in an escrow account until your flight departs. Be sure the bank or surety company is named in your contract. If the charter goes out of business before you depart, contact the bank or surety company for a refund.

- It's best **not to pay by check.** If you must, you should make your check out to either your travel agent or the bank or surety company named in your contract — not the charter operator itself. Be sure to write your destination and departure date on the face of the check.

- **What is the charter's cancellation policy?** If a charter flight doesn't fill up, the operator may be able to cancel it anywhere up to 10 days before departure. Be sure to pay by credit card when you book a flight, so you're guaranteed reimbursement under federal credit regulations. During the 10-day period before departure, a charter may cancel only because physical operation is for some reason impossible.

- As a general rule, **summer charters fill up more quickly** than others and are more likely to fly as scheduled.

- **What are the cancellation penalties?** Once you've signed a contract with a charter, you typically pay a penalty for canceling. The penalty rates grow higher as your departure date approaches. Most discount fares on regularly scheduled airlines are also non-refundable, but they do allow you to use your ticket at a later date with a fee, usually between $50 to $75; with a charter, however, once you cancel you forfeit your chance to fly on that fare. Some may allow a surrogate traveler to fly in your stead for a fee of $25.

- **How much is cancellation insurance and what does it cover?** You may be able to purchase insurance for a refund in case of a cancellation due to a death in the family or illness. Ask your travel agent or operator which health conditions the policy covers. Be aware that you may not be reimbursed for illness that results from a preexisting condition. Be sure to buy your policy from an independent provider, not the charter itself. (See "Travel Insurance Demystified," in chapter 6, "Life Preservers.")

- **If you are traveling with the charter tour and your luggage is lost, who is responsible?** While charter airlines will process claims for luggage that was lost or damaged while in their possession, both the airline and the charter operator may deny liability if it is not clear when the bag was lost. If you are traveling with the charter tour, for example, and you realize your bag is lost only after you reach your hotel, the airline may try to blame the tour operator.

- **How much delay time is the charter allowed?** Charter flights are very often delayed or rerouted. By law, however, the charter must allow you to cancel for a full refund if the flight is delayed for more than 48 hours.

WHOLE-PLANE CHARTERS

ONE SEAT NOT ENOUGH? HOW ABOUT CHARTERING A whole plane?

Whole-plane charters aren't just for heads of state and billionaires. If you have a large group flying, or are flying to a string of less-served destinations, renting a private plane can save you time and money over first-class or last-minute, full-fare commercial flights.

Consumer Reports Travel Letter gave two compelling examples in an analysis of charter flights — a group of eight people flying from one small city to another, who saved $440 per person over "regular" tickets; and a complex, multiple-stop Colorado ski vacation where the skiers saved $500 per person and 10 hours of flight time by bringing their own plane.

As charter operators charge by the hour, charters work best for relatively short flights. For short round-trips, the plane will stay on the ground at a cost of around $500 per day. For longer trips, prices are negotiable based on the availability of nearby aircraft and whether the charter operator can combine your trip home with ferrying other people to your vacation destination (this cuts ticket costs for you and operating costs for the chapter company).

There are security and convenience bonuses, too. Charters can fly out of small "executive" airports with no lines and no stress, airports that are close to major destinations and yet not likely to be terrorist targets. And unlike on a commercial flight, you'll be able to personally check every passenger and every bag on the plane.

Safety-wise, charter operators are put through strict scrutiny by the FAA. But you should still make sure the company maintains its own aircraft and its pilots have air transport pilot (ATP) licenses, *CRTL* advises.

Nothing is guaranteed on private planes — not even the existence of lavatories, and certainly not food. (Pets, however, are usually welcome.) Some planes have telephones and VCRs; others do not. Most have seats much more comfortable than domestic commercial airlines' seats. Some small planes restrict the amount of luggage you can bring. Double-check about any amenity you might possibly want.

You're also on less secure financial footing with a charter operator than you are with a commercial airline. Ask about the charter operator's cancellation and change policies, what happens if the charter operator cancels the flight, and what happens if your flight is delayed because of weather or other concerns. Always buy with a credit card.

Most private aircraft carry between 5 and 16 people, and renting a smaller, propeller-driven plane can cost as little as $300 per hour, plus taxes, fees, and aircraft parking charges. Jets are more expensive, up to $5,000 per hour.

Major whole-plane charter operators analyzed by *CRTL* include **Jet Express** (☎ **888/806-8833;** www.jetexpress. com), **Tag Aviation** (☎ **800/311-1930;** www.tagaviation. com), and **American Jet International** (☎ **888/435-9254;** www.iflyaji.com). The online Air Charter Guide (www.air charterguide.com) has a search engine which allows you to request quotes from several charter companies at once.

6 TRAVELING AS A COURIER

INCREASED AIRPORT SECURITY HASN'T ENDED THE need for businesses to deliver high-priority packages to overseas destinations. By signing up as a courier, you give up your checked-luggage allowance for an important business parcel in exchange for a very cheap, or even free, ticket to an exotic foreign land.

Yes, this is on the level. Reputable courier companies are insured and carry only real business packages — you won't be stuck with anything illicit or immoral.

Courier tickets usually require you to travel alone, to book at least 30 days in advance or (more often) at the very last minute, and to pack very light — you usually only get that one carry-on, though there are exceptions. (Some trips from New York to Hong Kong lasting more than 2 weeks, for instance, let you check one of your own bags.)

Courier flights leave from a few U.S. gateways, primarily New York, San Francisco, Los Angeles, and Miami, with occasional flights from other major cities like Boston, Orlando, and Chicago. Though flights to Europe are about the same price as consolidator fares and many flights to South America have been canceled in the wake of September 11, 2001, prices to Pacific destinations can be breathtaking — last-minute specials from New York to Hong Kong of $300 or even $150 round-trip are common.

Courier firms fade in and out of business on a regular basis, so joining one of the three air courier associations is a smart idea. All have been in operation for more than 5 years and act as clearinghouses for several different courier companies. They also sell consolidator tickets and discounted travel insurance and make sure that you'll be able to get home if (for instance) a courier company spontaneously goes under in the middle of your trip.

Traveling courier isn't just a one-time option, it's a lifestyle. Many courier companies offer even lower fares to fliers who they know and trust, and the courier associations' membership-based structures reward those who fly often.

Courier Travel (☎ **303/570-0282;** www.couriertravel. org/), in operation for 7 years, is a great place to start. Browsers can search lists of courier fares without paying the $40 lifetime membership fee, and the website's flight lists seem to be the most up to date of the three organizations.

The **Air Couriers Association** (☎ **800/282-1202;** www.aircourier.org) recently listed free trips from Boston to Seoul, Miami to London, and Greensboro to Hong Kong. They charge $49 per year for membership.

The **International Association of Air Travel Couriers** (☎ **352/475-1584;** www.courier.org) is the oldest of the bunch, founded in 1989. They throw in a glossy, bi-monthly magazine with their $45 annual fee.

7 SPECIAL DISCOUNTS FOR PEOPLE WITH SPECIAL NEEDS

"Status fares" provide discounted airline tickets based on who you are rather than how you're flying. Seniors, children, students, active military, employees of certain corporations, and bereaved persons all qualify for these discounts.

SENIOR PRIVILEGES

In general, seniors are entitled to a standard 10% discount on fares from most U.S. and international airlines. Several carriers also operate special programs for seniors that allow for more significant savings. The travel site **Smarter Living** (www.smarterliving.com/senior/airfare/) monitors senior discounts on dozens of airlines. Here are a few:

Senior Coupons

Coupons can add predictability to the usual shell game of finding cheap airfares; savvy Internet surfers or sale watchers can find cheaper fares on some flights, but coupons can be used (almost) any week of the year and on any domestic route. A 14-day advance purchase is usually required, and blackout dates apply, usually around major holidays.

Of the major airlines, America West, American, Continental, Delta, Northwest, United, and US Airways offer books of four or eight one-way coupons good for flights in North America to travelers age 62 or older.

Prices for coupon books range from $596 for four one-way tickets on America West and Continental to $676 on Delta, Northwest, and US Airways. This makes round-trips $300 to $340 per person — great if you're flying from Boston to Tucson, but a lousy deal if you're hopping from San Francisco to Los Angeles. Flights to Alaska, Hawaii, Canada, and Mexico generally require four coupons, making round-trips $596 to $676. US Airways is unusually flexible — they only require two coupons to fly round-trip anywhere in North America, and one coupon can cover a round-trip within Florida.

Coupons aren't transferable, but most airlines allow seniors to tote along up to two grandchildren ages 2 to 11 at the adult coupon price. Inquire when buying your coupons.

Airline Discounts

Members of **United's Silver Wings Plus travel club** (☎ **800/720-1765;** www.silverwingsplus.com) more than make back their $75 2-year memberships with three $25 discount coupons on United and a $100 coupon for an international trip on Lufthansa. A $225 life membership garners more certificates and 2,500 frequent-flier miles. Silver Wings members can buy discount airline tickets priced by geographic zones; domestic round-trip tickets cost from $124 round-trip for short hops between nearby states to $376 for cross-country jaunts. International tickets start at $525 to Europe and $600 to Asia, once again priced by geographic zone. Those prices are only for flights Monday through Thursday, bought 14 days in advance with a Saturday night stay; Friday and Saturday flights tack on $20 each way. Yes, you can probably do better with consolidators. Silver Wings members also get a newsletter full of travel deals, various Mileage Plus bonuses, and access to last-minute "On Call" package vacations. If you're a frequent flier, the membership might be worth it just for the coupons.

Continental Airlines Freedom Flight Club (☎ **800/441-1135**), for travelers over 62, is simpler. Members receive a 15% to 20% discount on all fares, including first class, at all times. For Monday through Thursday and Saturday departures, you'll receive 20% off the ticket price; for travel on Friday and Saturday, the discount drops to 15%. You can even qualify for discounts over the holidays, as no blackout periods apply; no minimum stays are required, unless the standard fare warrants such a restriction. Itineraries are not restricted by zones, and you don't have to stay over on a Saturday night.

Membership costs $75 per year for domestic travel in all 50 states. Membership for international travel is $125 per year, but make sure Continental flies to your chosen destinations.

US Airways offers special fares to members of AARP, the organization for people over 50 (☎ **800/424-3410**). These fares are quite good, such as $98 round-trips on the Boston–New York–Washington shuttle and $298 cross-country flights. Inquire at ☎ **866/886-2277.**

Delta also has special fares on that Northeast shuttle route; seniors can buy four-packs of one-way tickets for $245 (New York–Boston), $248 (New York–Washington), or $369 (Washington, DC–Boston). Travel must be outside business rush hours (before 10am, and 2:01–6:59pm, weekdays). Call ☎ **800/221-1212** and request the Delta Shuttle Flight Pack.

For Europe-hoppers, **bmi British Midland** (☎ **800/788-0555;** www.flybmi.com/forfun/discoverea.asp) offers a 25% senior discount on its Discover Europe Airpass, making one-way flights under 500 miles (805km) $82 and longer flights $119. **Virgin Atlantic** offers a higher-than-usual 20% senior discount on transatlantic flights during October for one AARP member and a companion to London; call ☎ **800/862-8621.**

Other Ways for Seniors to Save

There are several other ways for seniors to find cheap flights. Because most seniors do not have to report to work on a daily basis, they make perfect candidates for courier flights, where you can receive deep discounts — and sometimes even free fares — by allowing a courier operator to use your luggage allowance. (See "Traveling as a Courier," above.) One minor drawback: You'll need to pack economically to fit your belongings into one carry-on. Flights also often come up only at the last minute. But your schedule is likely to be more flexible than that of younger travelers.

By the same reasoning, seniors are much better able to take advantage of the last-minute sales that airlines offer to fill up unsold seats. By all means, sign up for E-saver programs with your favorite airlines for vastly reduced fares, even on international flights, for travel the following weekend. (See "Booking Online: Saving on the Internet," above.) Also be sure to check the newspaper for late-breaking flight discounts.

Finally, if you've got all day and love to get away, make a habit of volunteering your seat on overbooked flights. Chances are you'll only have to wait a few more hours for the next flight out, and you'll receive free tickets for future travel to other destinations. (See "Voluntary Bumpings" in chapter 2, "Ticketing Pitfalls"; and "Bumping for Savings," earlier in this chapter.)

You can also take advantage of the myriad organizations, publications, and tour operators that cater to seniors. Though most won't entitle you to discounted airfares per se, many do purchase airline tickets in bulk — usually at relatively low rates — as part of package-travel programs for older travelers.

Grand Circle Travel is one of the hundreds of travel agencies specializing in package vacations for seniors, 347 Congress St., Suite 3A, Boston, MA 02210 (☎ **800/ 221-2610** or 617/350-7500; www.gct.com). While you can save on airfare through many of these packages, be aware that they are often of the tour-bus variety, with free trips thrown in for those who can organize a group of 10 or more. If you prefer more independent travel, you should probably consult a regular travel agent. **SAGA International Holidays,** 222 Berkeley St., Boston, MA 02116 (☎ **800/ 343-0273;** www.sagaholidays.com), offers inclusive tours and cruises for those 50 and older, with discounted airfare rates. SAGA also sponsors the more substantial **Road Scholar Tours** (☎ **800/621-2151**), which are fun-loving but have an educational bent.

If you want fare discounts for something more than the average vacation or guided tour, try **Elderhostel,** 75 Federal St., Boston, MA 02110-1941 (☎ 877/426-8056; www. elderhostel.org), or the University of New Hampshire's **Interhostel** (☎ 800/733-9753), both variations on the same theme: educational travel for seniors. On these escorted tours, the days are packed with seminars, lectures, and field trips, and the sightseeing is all led by academic experts. Elderhostel arranges study programs for people 55 and over (and a spouse or companion of any age) in the United States and in 77 countries around the world, including Asia, Africa, and the South Pacific. Most courses last about 3 weeks and many include airfare, accommodations in student dormitories or modest inns, meals, and tuition. Write or call for a free catalog, which lists upcoming courses and destinations. **Interhostel** takes travelers 50 and over (with companions over 40), and offers 2- and 3-week trips, mostly international. The courses in both these programs are ungraded, involve no homework, and often focus on the liberal arts. They're not luxury vacations, but they're fun and fulfilling.

Publications for Traveling Seniors

Two recently published books provide good general advice and contacts for the savvy senior traveler. ***Unbelievably Good Deals and Great Adventures That You Absolutely Can't Get Unless You're Over 50*** (McGraw Hill) has been revised regularly for a decade, and ***Travel Unlimited: Uncommon Adventures for the Mature Traveler*** (Avalon) focuses on off-the-beaten-path trips like Alaskan eco-tours and African safaris. Also check out your newsstand for the quarterly magazine ***Travel 50 & Beyond*** (www. travel50andbeyond.com).

Another helpful publication is ***101 Tips for Mature Travelers,*** available from **Grand Circle Travel,** 347 Congress St., Suite 3A, Boston, MA 02210 (☎ 800/221-2610 or 617/350-7500; fax 617/346-6700; www.gct.com).

STUDENT DISCOUNTS

While students don't qualify for nearly as many price breaks as seniors, a few airlines, travel agencies, and associations make it easier for young people to see the world on a shoe-string budget. The travel site **Smarter Living** (www.smarter living.com/student/) monitors deals for students. Here are some of the best:

Special Fares

Delta and **US Airways** offer discounted youth fares on their shuttle services between Boston, Washington, and New York City. US Airways requires that passengers be between the ages of 12 and 24 and not travel during rush hours (before 10am, and 2:01–6:59pm weekdays). US Airways charges $78 round-trip to or from New York if you book online; packs of four one-way tickets between Boston and Washington are $343. Delta's $98 round-trip fare applies to passengers ages 2 to 22, except during rush hours, and a Friday night stay is required. Book by calling the airlines or through Council Travel.

AirTran's X-Fares program lets travelers from 18 to 22 stand by on any AirTran flight for $52 per segment, plus around $5 in fees. No checked baggage is allowed. For details, call ☎ **888/493-2737.**

Several credit cards for college students, such as **American Express Blue For Students,** come with discount airfare coupons as part of their sign-up package. The membership program **Student Advantage** (www.studentadvantage.com) provides discounts on US Airways fares and a shower of US Airways Dividend Miles bonuses.

Student Travel Agencies

Many airlines, especially international airlines, offer student fares that are only available through a travel agent. The best resource for students is the **Council on International Educational Exchange,** or CIEE. Their travel branch,

Council Travel Service (CTS) (☎ **800/226-8624;** www. counciltravel.com), is the biggest student travel agency operation in the world. They can also set you up with an ID card that will entitle you to other travel discounts. Ask them for a list of CTS offices in major cities so you can keep the discounts flowing (and aid lines open) as you travel.

From CIEE you can obtain the student traveler's best friend, the $22 **International Student Identity Card** (ISIC). This card gets you cut rates at museums, tourist attractions, railway lines, airlines, and almost anywhere else a student tourist might go. It also provides you with basic health and life insurance and a 24-hour help line. If you're no longer a student but are still under 26 years of age, you can get a "GO 25" card from the same outfit, which will entitle you to insurance and some discounts, but not student admission prices in museums.

In Canada, **Travel CUTS,** with offices in nearly every major city in the country (☎ **866/246-9762** or 416/ 614-2887; www.travelcuts.com), offers similar services. **USIT Campus** (☎ **0870/240-1010;** www.usitcampus. co.uk/), with 52 branches around the U.K., is Britain's leading specialist in student and youth travel.

CHILDREN'S FARES

Although a child younger than 2 years old can ride for free on a parent's lap on domestic flights, your infant will be much safer booked in a separate, discounted seat and secured in an FAA-endorsed restraining device. All major domestic airlines except Southwest now offer 50% off the parent's fare for infant seats (for children 2 years of age or younger, except on Continental, which gives children under 3 infant discounts or allows them to ride free on a parent's lap), to make it more affordable for you to reserve a separate adjacent seat and a restraining device for your baby. (Southwest does offer infant fares, but at variable discount rates.)

If a seat adjacent to yours is available, the child can also sit there free of charge. When you check in, ask if the flight is crowded. If it isn't, explain your situation to the agent and ask if you can reserve two seats — or simply move to two empty adjacent seats once the plane is boarded. You might want to shop around before you buy your ticket and deliberately book a flight that's not very busy. Ask the reservationist which flights tend to be most full and avoid those.

On international journeys, children may not ride free on parents' laps. On flights overseas, a lap fare usually costs 10% of the parent's ticket (for each carrier's specific policy, see "Minor Policies of Major Carriers" in chapter 6, "Life Preservers"). Children who fall below the airline's age limit (which ranges from ages 11–15 years) can purchase international fares at 50% to 75% of the lowest coach fare in certain markets. Some of the foreign carriers make even greater allowances for children.

Northwest provides unusual "adoption fares" for parents heading abroad to pick up adopted children — 50% to 65% off undiscounted fares, with great flexibility on the tickets. See www.nwa.com/features/adopt.shtml or call ☎ 800/322-4162.

If a child is traveling alone: Individual airline policies differ, but for the most part children ages 5 to 11 pay the regular adult fare. Kids from 5 to 7 can generally travel alone as unaccompanied minors only on flights without a change of planes; children 8 and older can usually travel on any flight. An unaccompanied minor gets an escort from the airlines — a flight attendant who seats the child, watches over her during the flight, and escorts her to the appropriate connecting gate or to the adult who will pick her up. Fees for the service vary widely, from $30 to upwards of $90, depending on the airline, and whether the flight is domestic or international. For each airline's specific policy, see "Minor Policies of Major Carriers," in chapter 6.

MILITARY FARES

Active-duty military can get discounts of up to 50% off regular fares with their green identification cards. Special rates are also available to military dependents and personnel within 7 days of discharge (bring your papers). Alert your travel agent to your military status.

CORPORATE BULK FARES

The deals that large companies make to get discount business fares can often trickle down to their employees. Employees of Disney and its subsidiaries, for instance, get 40% off the lowest available fares on United when they book through their corporate travel desk. If you work for a large company, inquire whether your corporate travel desk handles personal travel.

BEREAVEMENT FARES

Airlines try to ease the pain of death and illness by offering discounted, last-minute tickets to travelers who can produce a doctor's note or the name and number of a funeral home. These tickets are fully refundable and changeable, unlike most discount tickets. But they're rarely the cheapest you can find. Hotwire, Priceline, and discount airlines can usually beat major airlines' bereavement fares — though remember that those tickets come with sharp restrictions on refunds and exchanges.

8 One-Stop Shopping: Purchasing a Package Tour

PACKAGE TOURS ARE NOT THE SAME THING AS escorted tours — where you're led around on a bus through activity-packed days spent with strangers. They are simply a way to buy airfare and accommodations at the same time and they can save you a lot of money without costing you your freedom. In many cases, a package that includes airfare, hotel, and transportation to and from the airport will cost you less than just the hotel alone would have, had you booked it yourself. That's because packages are sold in bulk to tour operators — who resell them to the public at a cost that drastically undercuts standard rates.

Packages, however, vary widely. Some offer a better class of hotels than others. Some offer the same hotels for lower prices. Some offer flights on scheduled airlines, while others book charters. In some packages, your choice of accommodations and travel days may be limited. Some packages let you choose between escorted vacations and independent vacations; others will allow you to add on just a few excursions or escorted day trips (also at lower prices than you could locate on your own) without booking an entirely escorted tour. Each destination usually has one or two packagers that are cheaper than the rest because they buy in even greater bulk. If you spend the time to shop around, you will save in the long run. Call the foreign government or state tourist office where you're planning to travel and request a list of tour organizers.

FINDING A PACKAGE DEAL

The best place to start your search is the travel section of your local Sunday newspaper. Also check the ads in the back of national travel magazines like *Arthur Frommer's Budget Travel Magazine, Travel & Leisure, National Geographic Traveler,* and *Condé Nast Traveler.*

Liberty Travel (☎ **888/271-1584** for the location of an agent near you; www.libertytravel.com) is one of the biggest packagers in the northeast; they usually boast a full-page ad in the Sunday papers. And even if Liberty doesn't have an office in your area, you can still book vacation packages on its website.

American Express Vacations (☎ **800/346-3607;** http://travel.americanexpress.com/travel/) is another option. **Site59.com** (www.site59.com), an American Express partner, deals in extreme last-minute trips — no more than 14 days away — and they'll even sell you a package departing 3 hours from the time of purchase (that is, if you can get to the airport in time!).

SAVING ON A ROUND-THE-WORLD FARE

If you're looking for a true global odyssey, buy your ticket from a consolidator that specializes in round-the-world travel. They'll usually be able to beat the airlines' prices, and won't shackle you to the cities served by one global alliance. Two reliable round-the-world travel agencies are **Airtreks** (☎ 800/350-0612; www.airtreks.com) and **Air Brokers International** (☎ 800/883-3273;** www.airbrokers.com/), which offer hundreds of exciting round-the-world itineraries. You can also custom-design your own round-the-world route on their sites. Among their sample fares:

- $1,295: New York, London, Delhi, Bangkok, Hong Kong, New York (Airtreks)

- $1,795: Chicago, London, Athens, Bangkok, on your own over land to Singapore, Bali, Hong Kong, Chicago (Air Brokers)

- $1,895: San Francisco, Tahiti, Auckland, Sydney, Bali, Singapore, on your own to Bangkok, Hong Kong, San Francisco (Airtreks)

- $2,349: Los Angeles, Hong Kong, Bangkok, Kuala Lumpur, Cape Town, on your own to Johannesburg, Harare, Nairobi, Rome, on your own to London, Los Angeles (Air Brokers)

- $2,967: New York, Rome, Tel Aviv, Bombay, Bangkok, Rangoon, Sydney, Auckland, Tahiti, Los Angeles, New York (Airtreks)

Among the major online travel agencies, **Expedia** (www.expedia.com) has the strongest selection of packages, thanks to its purchase of packager Travelscape; **Orbitz** (http://packages.orbitz.com) is another good choice. **MyTravel** (☎ **800/246-6387;** www.mytravelco.com/vacations/) is now owned by AirTours, a European giant among package tour companies, and this bodes well for MyTravel's selection of packages. Look to them especially for sunny destinations.

Another place to look is at the airlines' own package-tour divisions. Pick the airline that has the most flights to your hometown or destination. **America West Vacations** (☎ 800/356-6611; www.americawestvacations.com/) specializes in packages to Las Vegas, Arizona, and Mexico. Other options include **American Airlines FlyAway Vacations** (☎ 800/321-2121; www.aa.com), **Delta Vacations** (☎ 800/654-6559; www.deltavacations.com), **United Vacations** (☎ 888/854-3899; www.unitedvacations.com), and **US Airways Vacations** (☎ 800/455-0123; www.usairways.com). Even smaller airlines, such as Las Vegas-based **National** (☎ 888/527-8687; www.nationalairlines.com) have gotten into the packaging game.

The biggest hotel chains, casinos, and resorts also offer package deals. If you already know where you want to stay, call the resort itself and ask if they offer land/air packages.

9 A LOOK AT THE BUDGET AIRLINES

SAFER THAN YOU THINK (SEE "SAFE LITTLE AIRLINES," below) and cheaper than the majors, budget carriers help even passengers who don't fly on them — because the entry of a budget airline into an airport lowers fares even on bigger carriers there.

(For the purposes of this section, Southwest counts as a budget airline, though it's the biggest of them all. When Southwest enters a city, as it did in Albany, New York, in 2001, fares drop like stones. The average one-way fare from Albany to Baltimore plummeted from $241 in 2000 to $63 in 2001, thanks to Southwest.)

The reaction of the major airlines to competition introduced by budget carriers has been, in the words of one federal judge, "brutal." When a budget carrier comes to an airport, the majors typically flood the airport with even cheaper, unprofitable service — just long enough to drive the little guy out of business. Then the big airline jacks fares right back up.

Unfortunately for air travelers, that same federal judge gave large airlines a green light to continue this predatory practice by throwing out a case against American Airlines in May 2001. American had managed to drive Vanguard, Sun Jet, *and* Western Pacific airlines out of its Dallas/ Fort Worth hub, and the Clinton Justice Department brought a suit in 1999 to stop the flood-and-smother practice American Airlines had used. The Justice Department is appealing the case.

An appeal can't come too soon for JetBlue, which is now facing similar predatory tactics from American on two New York–California routes. The most successful low-fare airline (other than Southwest) in recent years, JetBlue arrived on the scene with two big aces up its sleeve. The 1999 start-up found a powerful supporter in Senator Charles Schumer (D-NY), who helped the airline obtain an entire terminal at New York's JFK Airport. Secondly, its service (with seat-back TVs in coach and flight attendants wearing Hugo Boss designer duds) has won accolades from travelers who are frustrated by the continual comfort cutbacks of major airlines.

WHAT THE BUDGETS CAN DO FOR YOU

Budget airlines are good for the last-minute traveler who missed a 14- or 21-day cheap fare deadline or who can't afford to stay over a Saturday night. Many are no-frills, but some offer service exceeding the major U.S. airlines in quality. And the majors — by cramming in more seats (all except American, that is) and cutting back on food service in recent years — have made these little upstarts look better.

Safe Little Airlines

Of the airlines listed here, the following have had no fatal crashes since 1970: ATA, Frontier, Vanguard, JetBlue, Midway, National, Pan Am, WestJet, Icelandair, LTU, and Ryanair. (Source: airsafe. com)

Smaller airlines also may be your only choice if you're trying to fly one-way. Nearly all offer one-way fares for half the round-trip price — unlike major airlines, who may charge more for a single leg than for a round-trip. And budget airlines are more accommodating of long or short stays than their more established competition.

What you'll get on a budget carrier varies widely. The basic budget airline offers no food, one class of service (coach only), no frequent-flier program, and somewhat cramped seating. But many airlines are breaking out of this formula. Budget airlines' frequent-flier programs often deliver free round-trips at much lower mileage than large airlines', and Midwest Express and JetBlue have gotten raves for their comfort and service. In the list below, we've noted which carriers give you more than you might expect.

One problem most budget airlines can't overcome is their lack of extra planes and pilots in case something goes wrong. If a United plane has a mechanical problem, the mega-airline can usually whisk in another jet from a nearby city (or even just a nearby gate). The smaller-scale budget airlines don't have that luxury.

A smaller airline may mean a longer delay if problems occur, but in most cases you won't be completely stuck. All domestic airlines listed below except Pan Am and Spirit have interlining agreements that can send you home on another carrier's plane. For the two non-interline carriers, if your plane breaks down you may have to wait for a jet to zip in from another destination — which could take hours — or be bused to another airport the carrier serves.

A CLOSER LOOK

AIRTRAN (☎ 800/AIRTRAN) www.airtran.com/

Base: Atlanta.

Bonus: Affordable business class service.

Destinations: Akron/Canton, OH; Baltimore; Blooming-ton, IL; Boston; Buffalo, NY; Chicago (Midway); Dallas/Fort Worth; Dayton, OH; Flint, MI; Fort Laud-erdale; Fort Myers, FL; Grand Bahama; Greensboro, NC; Gulfport/Biloxi, MS; Houston (Hobby); Jacksonville, FL; Memphis, TN; Miami; Minneapolis; Moline, IL; Myrtle Beach, SC; New Orleans; New York (La Guardia); Newark, NJ; Newport News, VA; Orlando; Pensacola, FL; Phila-delphia; Pittsburgh; Raleigh/Durham, NC; Savannah, GA; Tallahassee, FL; Tampa, FL; Toledo; Washington, DC (Dulles).

Sample fares: Boston to Atlanta $187; Buffalo to Atlanta $120.

AMERICAN TRANS AIR (☎ 800/I-FLY-ATA)

www.ata.com/

Bases: Chicago, Indianapolis.

Facts: The oldest and one of the most basic of today's smaller carriers, founded in 1981.

Destinations: Aruba; Boston; Cancún; Dallas; Dayton, OH; Denver; Des Moines; Fort Lauderdale; Fort Meyers, FL; Grand Cayman; Grand Rapids, MI; Honolulu; Las Vegas; Los Angeles; Madison, WI; Maui; Miami; Milwau-kee, WI; Minneapolis; New York City (LaGuardia); Newark, NJ; Orlando; Philadelphia; Phoenix; San Francisco; San Juan, PR; Sarasota, FL; Seattle; South Bend, IN; Springfield, IL; St. Petersburg, FL; Washington, DC (Dulles).

Sample fares: New York to Seattle $283.50; Chicago to Miami $233.

FRONTIER AIRLINES (☎ 800/432-1FLY)

www.flyfrontier.com/

Base: Denver.

Facts: Offers frequent-flier program; Continental and Vir-gin Atlantic are partners.

Destinations: Albuquerque; Atlanta; Austin, TX; Baltimore; Boston; Chicago (Midway); Dallas/Fort Worth; El Paso, TX; Fort Lauderdale; Houston; Kansas City; Las Vegas; Los Angeles; Minneapolis/St. Paul; New Orleans; New York City (LaGuardia); Omaha; Orlando; Phoenix; Portland, OR; Reno, NV; Sacramento, CA; Salt Lake City; San Diego; San Francisco; San Jose; Seattle; Washington, DC (National); also many very small Western cities via partnerships.

Sample fares: Omaha to Denver $272; Kansas City to Albuquerque $115.

GREAT PLAINS AIRLINES (☎ 866-929-8646)

www.gpair.com/

Base: Tulsa, OK

Facts: All-jet service with leather seats and business-class legroom; frequent-flyer program; Krispy Kreme donuts and Subway sandwiches served onboard.

Destinations: Albuquerque, NM; Austin, TX; Colorado Springs, CO; Durango, CO (via codeshare); Nashville, TN; New Orleans, LA; Oklahoma City, OK; Taos, NM (via codeshare)

Sample fares: Nashville to Oklahoma City, $218; Albuquerque to Tulsa, $220.

JETBLUE (☎ 800/JET-BLUE) www.jetblue.com/

Base: New York (JFK).

Facts: Seat-back satellite TVs, all-leather seats, and new planes.

Destinations: Buffalo, NY; Burlington, VT; Denver; Fort Myers, FL; Fort Lauderdale; Long Beach, CA; New Orleans; Oakland, CA; Ontario, CA; Orlando; Rochester, NY; Salt Lake City; San Juan, PR; Seattle; Syracuse, NY; Tampa; Washington, DC (Dulles); West Palm Beach, FL.

Sample fares: Buffalo to New York City $100; New York City to Oakland $300.

MIDWAY AIRLINES (☎ 800/44-MIDWAY)

www.midwayair.com/

Base: Raleigh-Durham, NC.

Facts: Offers frequent-flier program; went bankrupt in 2001 and restarted service after receiving a $10 million federal handout.

Destinations: Boston; Fort Lauderdale; Newark, NJ; New York City (LaGuardia); Orlando; Tampa, FL; Washington (National).

Sample fares: Boston to Raleigh-Durham $107; Orlando to Raleigh-Durham $107.

MIDWEST EXPRESS (☎ 800/452-2022)

www.midwestexpress.com/

Bases: Milwaukee, WI; Kansas City, MO.

Facts: Award-winning cabin and food service; regularly wins Zagat awards for in-cabin food; frequent-flier program.

Destinations: Appleton, WI; Atlanta; Boston; Dallas/Fort Worth; Denver; Des Moines; Fort Lauderdale, FL; Fort Myers, FL; Hartford, CT; Las Vegas; Los Angeles; Madison, WI; New Orleans; New York City (LaGuardia); Newark, NJ; Omaha; Orlando; Philadelphia; Phoenix; San Antonio, TX; San Francisco; Tampa, FL; Washington, DC (Dulles and National); many other locations via partnerships.

Sample fares: Philadelphia to Milwaukee $203; Dallas to Milwaukee $203.

NATIONAL AIRLINES (☎ 888/757-JETS)

www.nationalairlines.com/

Base: Las Vegas.

Facts: Frequent-flier program; bankrolled by Vegas casino owners Harrah's.

Destinations: Chicago (Midway and O'Hare); Dallas/Fort Worth; Los Angeles; Miami; New York City (JFK); Newark, NJ; Philadelphia; San Francisco; Seattle; Washington, DC (National).

Sample fares: New York to Las Vegas $250; Dallas to Las Vegas $260.

PAN AMERICAN AIRWAYS (☎ 800/FLY-PANAM)

www.flypanam.com/

Base: Not a hub system.

Facts: No relation to historic, now-defunct Pan Am airline.

Destinations: Allentown, PA; Atlantic City, NJ; Baltimore; Bangor, ME; Freeport, Bahamas; Gary, IN (Chicago); Martha's Vineyard, MA; Naples, FL; Portsmouth, NH; San Juan, PR; Sanford, FL; St. Petersburg, FL; White Plains, NY; Worcester, MA; expanding throughout 2002.

Sample fares: Gary to St. Petersburg $249.50; Bangor to Baltimore $198.

SPIRIT AIRLINES (☎ 800/772-7117) www.spiritair.com/

Base: Detroit, but not really a hub system; mostly flights between the north and Florida.

Destinations: Atlantic City, NJ; Chicago (O'Hare); Denver, CO; Detroit, MI; Fort Lauderdale; Fort Myers, FL; Los Angeles; Myrtle Beach, SC; New York (LaGuardia); Oakland, CA; Orlando; San Juan, PR; Tampa, FL; West Palm Beach, FL.

Sample fares: Detroit to Los Angeles $251.50; Atlantic City to Fort Lauderdale $194.

VANGUARD AIRLINES (☎ 800/VANGUAR)

www.flyvanguard.com/

Base: Kansas City.

Facts: Offers business class service.

Destinations: Atlanta; Austin, TX; Buffalo, NY; Chicago; Colorado Springs; Dallas/Fort Worth; Denver; Fort Lauderdale; Las Vegas; Los Angeles; New Orleans; New York City (LaGuardia); Pittsburgh; San Francisco.

Sample fares: Kansas City to Dallas $170; Austin to Pittsburgh $242.

INTERNATIONAL BUDGET CARRIERS

Budget carriers have sprung up across Europe and Canada in recent years, as well. Here's a sample of the foreign airlines most useful to American travelers:

In addition to the carriers listed below, other reliable European budget carriers include EasyJet (www.easyjet.com), Go (www.go-fly.com), and Buzz (www.buzzaway.com), all based in London; and Virgin Express (www.virgin-express.com), a division of Richard Branson's Virgin Atlantic, based in Belgium.

ICELANDAIR (☎ 800/223-5500) www.icelandair.com/
Facts: Business class service with excellent food; frequent-flier program; free stopovers up to 3 days in Reykjavik.
Routes: Boston, New York (JFK), Baltimore, Minneapolis, and Orlando to Europe via Reykjavik, Iceland.
Sample fares: Boston to London $258; Minneapolis to Paris $444.

LTU (☎ 866/266-5588) www.ltu-airways.com/
Facts: First class and food service offered.
Routes: Miami, Fort Myers, Orlando, and Los Angeles to Germany and Switzerland.
Sample fares: Miami to Dusseldorf $399; Los Angeles to Dusseldorf $768 (spring/fall only).

RYANAIR (No phone in North America) www.ryanair.com/
Facts: Ryanair usually runs some form of absurd sale where many of their flights are $10 or less.
Routes: Many European destinations from hubs at Dublin, London (Stansted), Glasgow, Brussels, and Frankfurt (Hahn).
Sample fares: London to Pisa £69 (US$114); Dublin to London 36€ (US$41).

WESTJET (☎ 877/952-4638) www.westjet.ca/
Routes: Serves major cities in Canada from Ontario on west, plus Moncton, N.B.; no international routes.
Sample fares: Hamilton to Calgary C$385; Vancouver to Winnipeg C$314.

10

THE SQUEAKY WHEEL: HOW TO COMPLAIN EFFECTIVELY

In the last quarter of 2001, airlines cut flights, slashed food service, and grabbed multibillion-dollar handouts from the government. But Americans seem willing to give the airline industry the benefit of the doubt. They shouldn't.

Of course, 1999 and 2000 were particularly bad years, as unprecedented numbers of delays and cancellations pushed consumer complaints to record levels. The rate of complaints against major airlines more than doubled from 1998 to 1999, and inched even higher in 2000. Gripes had slipped by August 2001, but were still at 2.1 times the 1998 level.

A University of Michigan survey, meanwhile, found that fliers during the first 3 months of 2001 found their experience with airlines to be about as enjoyable as filing their taxes (see table "Satisfaction Ratings of Major Airlines, in Context," below).

At press time, no reliable measure of consumer complaints post–September 11, 2001, existed because mail to

SATISFACTION RATINGS OF MAJOR AIRLINES, IN CONTEXT

COMPANY	SATISFACTION RATING, Q1/2001
U.S. Postal Service	70
Southwest	70
Continental	67
Cable & satellite TV companies	64
Internal Revenue Service	62
American	62
Delta	61
US Airways	60
United	59
Northwest	56

Source: University of Michigan American Consumer Satisfaction Index. Figures for the IRS are for individual filers in all of 2001. The ACSI measures consumer satisfaction on a scale of 0 (absolutely no satisfaction) to 100 (highest possible satisfaction).

the Department of Transportation was disrupted by the anthrax scares of late 2001. The missives that got through allow comparisons between airlines, but not comparisons to past months.

Of the complaints that the DOT actually received in November 2001, most concerned problems in obtaining refunds post–September 11, 2001 — a departure from the usual complaints about delays, missed connections, baggage problems, and poor customer service. America West and United were the worst of the bunch, with reliable Southwest receiving the fewest complaints per 100,000 passengers.

Now that the airlines are flying on your tax dollars, you have more of a right than ever to speak up if something goes wrong. And financially shaky airlines have more incentive than ever to listen to their customers. So, what's the best way to get payback for an airline-related problem?

COMPLAINT RANKINGS OF MAJOR AIRLINES

COMPLAINTS PER 100,000 TRAVELERS

Airline	Nov 2001	Aug 2001	All of 2000	All of 1999
Southwest	0.18	0.44	0.47	0.4
Alaska	0.68	1.4	2.04	1.64
US Airways	0.72	2.31	2.59	3.13
Delta	0.76	2.25	2.01	1.81
Northwest	0.77	2.36	2.61	2.92
TWA	0.83	1.63	3.47	3.44
American	0.91	2.44	3.54	3.49
Continental	1.12	2.21	2.84	2.62
United	1.61	3.89	5.3	2.65
America West	1.63	3.85	7.5	3.72

Source: U.S. Department of Transportation. November 2001 totals were affected by mail delivery problems and cannot be compared to past figures.

1 COMPLAINING 101: HOW TO SQUEAK & GET THE GREASE

THE MINUTE YOU FEEL YOU'VE BEEN WRONGED OR deprived of your hard-earned money's worth, **calm yourself.** Instead of blowing up, breathe in deeply, clear your head, and channel your ire into documenting the situation as exhaustively as possible. Note times, take down names of individuals involved, and request the names and numbers of fellow passengers who may have experienced the same difficulty. If you approach members of the airline staff for immediate assistance and they deny you, get their names. Politely make it clear that you plan to write a letter of complaint when you get home. Hoard more details than you could possibly use in your letter. This way, when you make your case or sit down to write your letter, the facts will speak more loudly, and far more productively, than your anger.

1. **Know your rights.** If an airline has violated its own contract of carriage, you have a much stronger case

✆ RACIAL PROFILING: A POST-9-11 PROBLEM

The terrorist attacks of 2001 have made pilots *and* passengers nervous, and unfortunately, some are taking their fears out on darker-skinned Americans and legal aliens. Here's some advice on what to do if you are asked to leave the plane, or if you feel you're being harassed because of your ethnicity.

1. **Don't be paranoid.** People of all ethnicities are picked for random personal and baggage searches. If you're just being called in for a search, comply with a smile.

2. If a passenger or crew member refuses to fly with you on board, **stay calm.** Don't give the flight crew a legitimate reason to remove you from the plane.

3. **Explain that it's illegal and ask for details.** Urban legends notwithstanding, a pilot can't legally order someone off a flight just because he feels like it. It's against the law for anyone to demand that someone be removed from a flight because of race, ethnicity, gender, age, national

---

than if they've just done something impolite. Citing a rule number is especially impressive. Travel website **OneTravel** (www.onetravel.com) has an excellent explanation of each major carrier's contracts — click on "Know Your Rights" on the left side of their home page.

2. If your complaint regards something you can document with visuals and you have a camera, by all means **snap some photographs on the spot.**

3. **Try to resolve your dispute before you leave the airport.** The airlines usually keep someone on duty to resolve certain problems on the spot. These employees

origin, or religion. Legally, the flight crew must provide an explanation for why you're being removed. If the flight crew says you appear "suspicious" or they feel "uncomfortable," they must describe specifically what activity has made them uncomfortable. Make good notes and get the names of all staff involved; you may need them for your lawyer.

4. **File a complaint.** Contact the United States Department of Transportation, Aviation Consumer Protection Division, 400 7th St. SW, Room 4107, Washington, DC 20590 (☎ **202/366-2220** or 202/755-7687).

5. **Contact an advocate.** The American-Arab Anti-Discrimination Committee has recorded more than 30 suspected instances of racial profiling and can explain your legal options, even if you're not an Arab-American. Call them at ☎ **202/244-3196,** or send e-mail to legal@adc.org.

can usually write checks for small claims or pay denied boarding compensation. If your bags are delayed, you can probably get cash right away to buy some clothes. If you are stranded, you may be able to secure a hotel voucher and have the airline research hotels that offer distressed passenger discounts. You may receive compensation on the spot for damaged luggage as well.

First try to speak with the airline's shift supervisor or with an employee at the carrier's special services counter, which is usually located in the gate area. If you're still not satisfied, call the airline's central customer relations number (see "Consumer Contacts for the Major Domestic Airlines," later in this chapter) and ask where to locate the individual with the highest authority employed by the carrier at your particular airport.

4. **Don't exaggerate the wrongdoing.** The folks in consumer affairs have read many letters like yours and in the process have developed keen "BS" detectors. You don't want to undermine your otherwise valid argument by going overboard. Make sure minor gripes don't obscure the chief grievance you're addressing. Sit on the letter for a day after you've written it and screen for strident sarcasm or unfettered venom. You want to win their sympathy, not inspire them to chuck your letter into the loony bin or the circular file. Let the facts ring out your call for justice.

5. **Clearly state what you expect** as recompense. Again, don't shoot for the stars. Make sure your expectations are reasonable, and your letter will be taken more seriously.

6. Before you write a letter, **call the airline.** Get the e-mail address for letters of complaint and see if you can register your complaint by phone. Double-check the name of the director of consumer affairs or customer relations.

7. **Send an e-mail.** Many airlines nowadays respond to e-mailed complaints much more quickly than to paper letters. If you don't have the right e-mail address, go to PlanetFeedback.com (www.planet feedback.com) and click on "Travel" on the left side of their home page for an e-mail form that will be sent directly to the airline. Give the airline a few days to respond before moving on to a paper letter. Ignore form letter responses.

8. **Use your clout.** When writing a letter or sending an e-mail, mention your frequent-flier status (if any) or how much money you typically spend on that airline a year (if it's a significant amount). Write a brief, typed, professional letter. Since airlines hate to lose business travelers, you may want to register your grievance on your company's letterhead.

9. At the very least, **be sure your letter covers the basics.** Describe the problem and when, where, and how it occurred. Mention if you lost money as a result. What have you done about the problem so far? How would you like to see the issue resolved? In other words, what do you think you deserve as recompense and from whom?

10. **Save receipts** for any out-of-pocket expenses you incur as a result of the problem. Include copies with your letter.

11. **Send a copy of your letter and supporting documents to the following agencies:** Department of Transportation, Aviation Consumer Protection Division, 400 7th St. SW, Room 4107, Washington, DC 20590 (☎ **202/366-2220** or 202/755-7687); and the Aviation Consumer Action Project, P.O. Box 19029, 589 14th St. NW, Suite 1265, Washington, DC 20036 (☎ **202/638-4000;** www.acap1971.org/acap. html). These agencies function as ombudsmen. While they can't represent you in court or force an airline to compensate you, they can provide leverage and additional information to help you make your case.

It's also a good idea to file your complaint with your local member of Congress (☎ **202/225-3121**) and a few travel magazines. Be sure to tell the airline you're doing so. Many travel magazines print readers' letters, and the airlines hate bad publicity. *Condé Nast Traveler,* for instance, has a very effective ombudsman column. The ombudsman staff will investigate your claim and, if appropriate, try to use its clout to intervene on your behalf (*Condé Nast Traveler*, Ombudsman, 4 Times Square, New York, NY 10036; fax 212/286-2190).

2 HERE COMES THE JUDGE: GOING TO COURT

AS A LAST RESORT, YOU MAY WANT TO FILE YOUR case with a small-claims court. Almost all states and localities operate these as a cheap, prompt, and effective means for taxpayers to recover small sums of money without having to hire a lawyer and incur astronomical legal expenses. Be sure the airline knows you plan to follow this course of action. The very threat may prompt the carrier to negotiate to your satisfaction.

If you can demonstrate that an airline owes you money or has harmed you financially, you will have the chance to present your case in person to an impartial judge. Court procedures are usually very simple, informal, and inexpensive. If the judge rules in your favor, he or she can subpoena the carrier and demand remuneration.

IF AT FIRST YOU DON'T SUCCEED . . .

Persist in your efforts if you don't hear from the airline right away. In June 1999, airlines that belong to the Air Transport Association (ATA) agreed to draft new customer service policies according to the minimum required by ATA guidelines, which require member airlines to respond to all written complaints within 60 days. To find out which airlines are members of the ATA, consult www.airlines.org and click on "ATA Members."

Unfortunately, the Aviation Consumer Action Project says that those 60-day responses are often no more than "We're working on your problem," and actual dispute resolutions can still take much longer.

ACAP also says that often an airline will write a magnanimous letter of apology but then offer you less compensation than you requested. If the carrier offers you a ticket rather than cash, it might be wise to accept this payment in the form of services, as it may be worth more than the airline will pay you in cash.

You may also want plead your case to a local television station if you don't receive the desired response from the airline. Many stations' news operations have a full-time consumer advocate, air travel gripes make for lively news segments, and airlines hate to be embarrassed in public.

WHEN SHOULD YOU SUE?

Small claims court is not an appropriate venue for every case. The sum of money you seek must be less than the limit established by state or local law. The airline you are suing must do business in the court's jurisdiction. You must have carefully reviewed your contract of carriage with the airline, determined that the airline in fact acted in violation of the agreement, and given the carrier the opportunity and sufficient time to right the wrongdoing. Be sure that you have communicated your grievance clearly to the appropriate consumer affairs personnel at the airline; saved records of any letters or calls you received in response or made yourself to follow up on your complaint; and allowed the carrier at least a month to respond. On the other hand, don't wait too long to respond or your case may grow too old to stand up in court.

If it seems, after careful consideration, that a judge can help you settle your dispute, check your local telephone directory for the small-claims court number under the city, county, or state listings. A local consumer affairs office, bar association, or attorney general's office should also be able to help you locate the number for the court nearest you. Call or visit the clerk of court's office to confirm that your complaint falls within the court's jurisdiction.

Even if you decide to present your own case, it may be useful to consult with a lawyer briefly beforehand. A local legal aid or legal-services office may provide brief counsel for free, or for a small fee. If you have never appeared in small-claims court, it's wise to attend a session and familiarize yourself with the proceedings before your own court date. Proceedings are open to the public.

YOU'VE GOT A GOOD CASE ON YOUR HANDS

According to the Department of Transportation, consumers received compensation from a small-claims court judge in the following situations. While this doesn't guarantee remuneration, it does suggest that it's worth taking your case one step further if the airline fails to remedy your grievance.

- An airline cancels your connecting flight and arranges to transport you to your destination by van. The van is uncomfortable and takes 4 hours to cover the distance of a 1-hour flight. The airline denies your request that they pay the difference in price between ground and air transportation.

- You purchase a first-class ticket from a consolidator, also known as a "bucket shop." In the mail, however, you receive a coach ticket. The consolidator refuses to refund the difference in fares.

- Your flight is canceled, an alternate flight is not scheduled until the following day, and you're far from home. The airline refuses to reimburse you for a hotel room.

- A carrier loses your luggage. You can prove that the contents were worth far more than the airline compensated you for their mistake.

HOW TO FILE

From state to state, small-claims court procedures vary. While you should certainly call your local court clerk for particulars, a few guidelines should be universally helpful.

- Typically, you will have to **make your complaint either in person or by mail.** In some states, you will have to fill out a standard form to complete this step.

- **Word your grievance clearly.** Name the party you are suing, explain why you are suing, and name the amount you expect to receive. You will be the "plaintiff," and the offending airline will be the "defendant." If your complaint involves a particular employee or employees of the airline, name both the individual(s) and the airline itself as the defendant. Likewise, if the carrier offended another person traveling with you, name that person along with yourself as a second plaintiff.

- When you name your defendant, you must **use the carrier's legal name.** AirTran's legal name, for instance, is AirTran Airways. You must also name the carrier's address within the court's jurisdiction. For this information, call the local Better Business Bureau or the state bureau of consumer protection, listed in the blue pages of the telephone directory, under consumer problems in the human services section.

- You may also have to **pay a small filing fee** to make your claim. These, too, vary from state to state. If you win your case, some jurisdictions may refund this sum in the amount of your final award.

After you submit your claim, the court will schedule a hearing date and summon the carrier to send a representative to appear in court that day. The airline does have the right to request a different date. Scheduled court dates are often delayed by the court itself. Once the court confirms a date, you will also be obligated to make a personal appearance that day. You may not handle this stage of the process by mail, and no one may appear in court in your stead unless you have already named that person as a plaintiff in your claim. If the airline does not show up once the court date is confirmed, you will most likely win your case by default.

BUILDING YOUR CASE

The court proceedings are usually very simple. A few guidelines will help you make your case optimally effective.

- Arrive at the court on time.

- Bring copies of any documentation that may help you to substantiate your case, such as correspondence with the airline, your ticket and contract of carriage, bills, canceled checks, baggage stubs, written estimates of damages, or photographs of damaged property or goods.

- Prepare a written list of key points you'd like to make from your written statement and rehearse them several times before you relay your story to the judge. Present them politely and briefly.

- Prepare a few key questions for the airlines regarding their actions in your grievance. The judge may ask you to question the airline official directly.

PAYBACK: WHAT HAPPENS IF YOU WIN

If the judge decides in your favor, he or she will issue an order stating that you have won your case and that the airline or operator owes you money. The judge may allow the defendant to pay you in installments. If you do not receive your money by the date agreed upon, inform the court clerk. The court will not act as a collection agency on your behalf, but can advise you on how to collect.

If the judge decides against your case, you can appeal to a higher court. Ask the court clerk how to proceed. Be aware, however, that you'll probably need a lawyer to appeal.

You may also want to consider suing in a higher court with the help of an lawyer if: your claim involves a large sum of money; you know in advance the defendant is hiring a lawyer; you fail to collect the money owed you; or you receive notification that you are being sued.

3 Consumer Contacts for the Major Domestic Airlines

THE INFORMATION BELOW WAS CORRECT AT PRESS time; as mentioned earlier, it's wise to check with the airline before sending a letter to make sure the names and addresses haven't changed.

Alaska Airlines
P.O. Box 68900
Seattle, WA 98168
Attention: Raymond Prentice
☎ **206/870-6062,** option 7

America West
Ms. Jennifer Tongé
Manager, Customer Relations
4000 East Sky Harbor Blvd.
Phoenix, AZ 85034
☎ **800/363-2542** or 480/693-6719

American Airlines
Mr. Greg Clark
Managing Director
Consumer Relations
P.O. Box 619612 M/D 2400
DFW Airport, TX 75261-9612
☎ **817/967-2000,** option 5

Continental Airlines
Ms. Judy Dyar
Director, Customer Care
P.O. Box 4607
Houston, TX 77210
☎ **800/932-2732**

Delta Airlines
Ms. Valerie Henry
Director, Customer Care
P.O. Box 20980
Atlanta, GA 30320-2980
☎ **404/715-1450**

Northwest Airlines
Lynn Pahl
Director, Customer and Sales Support
Mail Stop C6590
P.O. Box 11875
St. Paul, MN 55111-3034
☎ **612/726-2046**

Southwest Airlines
Mr. Jim Ruppel
Director, Customer Relations
P.O. Box 36611, Love Field
Dallas, TX 75235-1611
☎ **214/792-4223**

United Airlines
Ms. Diane Bergan
Director, Customer Relations
P.O. Box 66100
Chicago, IL 60666
☎ **877/228-1327** or 847/700-6796

US Airways
Ms. Deborah Thompson
Director, Consumer Affairs
P.O. Box 1501
Winston-Salem, NC 27102
☎ **336/661-0061**

4 ADDITIONAL COMPLAINT & INFORMATION RESOURCES

CONSUMER COMPLAINTS

U.S. Department of Transportation (DOT)
Office of Consumer Affairs
400 7th St. SW
Washington, DC 20590
☎ **202/366-2220**
www.dot.gov

CONSUMER COMPLAINTS & SAFETY ISSUES

Aviation Consumer Action Project
Box 19029
Washington, DC 20036
☎ **202/638-4000**

CONSUMER RATINGS INFORMATION

Consumer Reports Travel Letter
Consumer's Union of United States
101 Truman Ave.
Yonkers, NY 10703-1057
☎ **800/234-1970** or 914/378-2300

LEGAL ACTION

Travel Law, by Thomas A. Dickerson
Law Journals Seminar Press
345 Park Ave. S
New York, NY 10010
☎ **212/779-9200**
Cost: $149

SAFETY RATINGS & COMPLAINTS

Federal Aviation Administration (FAA)
800 Independence Ave. SW
Washington, DC 20591
☎ **800/322-7873**
www.faa.gov

Consumer Hot Line: ☎ **800/322-7873**
Air Safety Hot Line: ☎ **800/255-1111**
Passenger Screening Hot Line: ☎ **866/289-9673**
Public Affairs (or for people calling the FAA from outside the U.S.): ☎ **202/267-8521**

Air Traveler's Association
☎ **800/577-5101** or 202/686-2870
www.1800airsafe.com

ACCIDENT RATES

National Transportation Safety Board (NTSB)
☎ **202/314-6551**
www.ntsb.gov

EMERGENCIES ABROAD

Department of State Overseas Citizens Services Office
☎ **202/647-5225**
http://travel.state.gov

AIRLINE PERFORMANCE RATINGS

DOT Bureau of Transportation Statistics
☎ **202/366-3282**

PLANE & ESTIMATED ARRIVAL TIME LOCATOR

Trip.com
http://www.trip.com/trs/trip/flighttracker/
flight_tracker_home.xsl

FlyteComm
http://www.flytecomm.com/cgi-bin/trackflight

AIRLINE SCHEDULES

Official Airline Guide
☎ **800/342-5624** or 630/574-6000
www.oag.com (for offices and telephone numbers outside the U.S.)

AIRLINE SEAT MAPS

About.com
http://airtravel.about.com/library/seats/blseatindex.htm

FLYING WITH DISABILITIES

U.S. Department of Transportation (DOT)
Office of Consumer Affairs
400 7th St. SW
Washington, DC 20590
☎ **202/366-2220**

Society for Accessible Travel and Hospitality (SATH)
347 Fifth Ave., Suite 610
New York, NY 10016
☎ **212/447-7284**
www.sath.org

COMPLAINTS ABOUT THE TREATMENT OF PETS

U.S. Department of Agriculture
Animal and Plant Health Inspection Service
Animal Care
4700 River Rd., Unit 84
Riverdale, MD 20737
☎ **301/734-4981**
www.aphis.usda.gov/ac

INDEX

FROMMER'S® MEMORABLE WALKS

Chicago	New York	San Francisco
London	Paris	

FROMMER'S® GREAT OUTDOOR GUIDES

Arizona & New Mexico	Northern California	Vermont & New Hampshire
New England	Southern New England	

SUZY GERSHMAN'S BORN TO SHOP GUIDES

Born to Shop: France	Born to Shop: Italy	Born to Shop: New York
Born to Shop: Hong Kong, Shanghai & Beijing	Born to Shop: London	Born to Shop: Paris

FROMMER'S® IRREVERENT GUIDES

Amsterdam	Los Angeles	San Francisco
Boston	Manhattan	Seattle & Portland
Chicago	New Orleans	Vancouver
Las Vegas	Paris	Walt Disney World
London	Rome	Washington, D.C.

FROMMER'S® BEST-LOVED DRIVING TOURS

Britain	Germany	Northern Italy
California	Ireland	Scotland
Florida	Italy	Spain
France	New England	Tuscany & Umbria

HANGING OUT™ GUIDES

Hanging Out in England	Hanging Out in France	Hanging Out in Italy
Hanging Out in Europe	Hanging Out in Ireland	Hanging Out in Spain

THE UNOFFICIAL GUIDES®

Bed & Breakfasts and Country Inns in:	Southwest & South Central Plains	Mid-Atlantic with Kids
California	U.S.A.	Mini Las Vegas
Great Lakes States	Beyond Disney	Mini-Mickey
Mid-Atlantic	Branson, Missouri	New England and New York with Kids
New England	California with Kids	New Orleans
Northwest	Chicago	New York City
Rockies	Cruises	Paris
Southeast	Disneyland	San Francisco
Southwest	Florida with Kids	Skiing in the West
Best RV & Tent Campgrounds in:	Golf Vacations in the Eastern U.S.	Southeast with Kids
California & the West	Great Smoky & Blue Ridge Region	Walt Disney World
Florida & the Southeast	Inside Disney	Walt Disney World for Grown-ups
Great Lakes States	Hawaii	Walt Disney World with Kids
Mid-Atlantic	Las Vegas	Washington, D.C.
Northeast	London	World's Best Diving Vacations
Northwest & Central Plains		

SPECIAL-INTEREST TITLES

Frommer's Adventure Guide to Australia & New Zealand
Frommer's Adventure Guide to Central America
Frommer's Adventure Guide to India & Pakistan
Frommer's Adventure Guide to South America
Frommer's Adventure Guide to Southeast Asia
Frommer's Adventure Guide to Southern Africa
Frommer's Britain's Best Bed & Breakfasts and Country Inns
Frommer's Caribbean Hideaways
Frommer's Exploring America by RV
Frommer's Fly Safe, Fly Smart
Frommer's France's Best Bed & Breakfasts and Country Inns
Frommer's Gay & Lesbian Europe

Frommer's Italy's Best Bed & Breakfasts and Country Inns
Frommer's New York City with Kids
Frommer's Ottawa with Kids
Frommer's Road Atlas Britain
Frommer's Road Atlas Europe
Frommer's Road Atlas France
Frommer's Toronto with Kids
Frommer's Vancouver with Kids
Frommer's Washington, D.C., with Kids
Israel Past & Present
The New York Times' Guide to Unforgettable Weekends
Places Rated Almanac
Retirement Places Rated